The Late Great

johnny ace

and the Transition from

R&B to Rock 'n' Roll

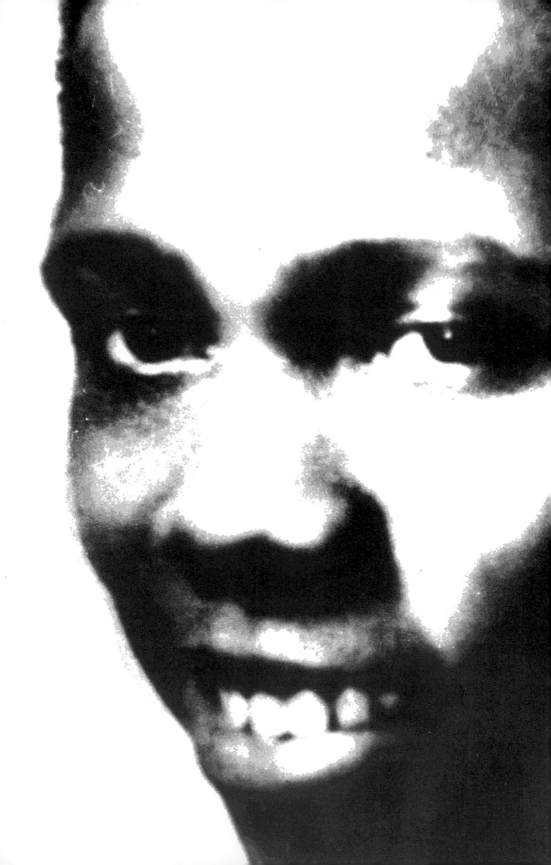

The Late Great

johnny ace

and the Transition from

R&B to Rock 'n' Roll

James M. Salem

University of Illinois Press

Urbana and Chicago

Publication of this book was
supported by a grant from the
University of Alabama.

Library of Congress
Cataloging-in-Publication Data
Salem, James M.
The late, great Johnny Ace and the
transition from R&B to rock 'n' roll /
James M. Salem.
p.   cm. — (Music in American life)
Discography: p.
Includes bibliographical references (p.   )
and index.
ISBN 0-252-02444-3 (cloth)
1. Ace, Johnny. 2. Singers — United States —
Biography. 3. Rhythm and blues music —
History and criticism. I. Title.
II. Series.
ML420.A16S25   1999
782.421643'092 — ddc21   98-25477
[B]   CIP
                             MN

Contents

Illustrations follow pages 22, 66, and 140

Acknowledgments

Twelve years ago I recovered the "lost" official Harris County, Texas, *Inquest Proceedings* of Johnny Ace's death that had been stored in a Houston warehouse for decades and began seriously researching his life and career. During that time I have been helped by many students, scholars, musicians, collectors, editors, fans, librarians, archivists, administrators, secretaries, disk jockeys, and people associated with Johnny Ace personally. I am indebted to them all.

At the beginning of my inquiry Colin Escott offered valuable advice, as did Robert Pruter of *Goldmine*, Pat Baird of BMI, and Galen Gart of Big Nickel Publications. Between musicologist Barry Hansen, collector Victor Pearlin, and sound recordings archivist Bill Schurk of Bowling Green State University, I was able to locate all of Ace's recorded sides and tribute songs, some of them quite rare.

I was also helped and encouraged by Susan Kaplan, licensing manager, BPI Communications, Inc.; Kathy Collins, budget director, Rice University; Laura Crain, archivist, Indiana University; Professor Louis Cantor, the author of *Wheelin' On Beale*; and various experts whose knowledge I sought about guns (Larry Moody), the postwar U.S. Navy (Rodney Badger), the Mitchell Hotel (Ernestine Mitchell), Willie Mae "Big Mama" Thornton (Mattie Fields), and the official investigation of the death of Johnny Ace (Drayton M. "Doc" Fults). In addition, special thanks are due Jean Holford of Houston, Texas.

In the research process I received invaluable assistance from several graduate students in the Department of American Studies at the University of Alabama, but I specifically need to thank Jerry Davis for his careful tracking of Johnny Ace in the pages of *Billboard*, and Dabney Poston Love for her assistance in synthesizing the histories of Memphis and Houston. Margaret Vines, Brenda Ipina, Beth Goode, and Janice Stewart all provided office and secretarial support.

I experienced enormous momentum halfway through the project from two sources. On the cultural side, Jack Salzman, editor of *Prospects: An Annual of American Cultural Studies*, published my article "Johnny Ace: A Case Study in the Diffusion and Transformation of Minority Culture." On the music side, Wayne Shirley of the Library of Congress helped me find an appropriate academic model for writing about rhythm and blues and rock 'n' roll and then accepted for publication "Death and the Rhythm-and-Bluesman: The Life and Recordings of Johnny Ace," the first such article to appear in *American Music*, the prestigious scholarly journal he edited.

All of my colleagues in American studies supported my efforts and helped to protect my writing time, but I must thank Rich Megraw, who read and helped tighten the first draft of the manuscript, and Reid Badger, who provided valuable recommendations for a subsequent revision. I am also grateful to Craig Morrison and Kip Lornell, my readers at the University of Illinois Press, to my manuscript editor, Louis Simon, for his careful reading and superb suggestions, and to my son, Jon Salem, who suggested more interesting chapter titles than I had originally provided. Thanks also to BPI Communications, Inc., for permission to quote "Talent Corner" (*Billboard*, 29 January 1955, 34. © 1955 BPI Commuications, Inc. Used with permission from *Billboard*.)

I am indebted to Jim Yarbrough, Dean of Arts and Sciences at the University of Alabama, who challenged me to write this book in the first place and then generously supported it, and Dave Klemmack, assistant dean, who helped me arrange research time so that I could actually do it. I am thankful along the way to have had Dr. Richard VanDerBeets of West Coast Literary Associates believe in this book first and Judith McCulloh of the University of Illinois Press believe in it next.

Most of all, however, I need to thank the people who knew Johnny Ace personally and who willingly shared their knowledge and memories with me, especially St. Clair Alexander, Johnny's younger brother; David James Mattis, who founded Duke Records; Bill Holford, who engineered most of the Ace sides; Johnny Otis, who produced them; Milton Hopkins, who played guitar in Ace's road band; Clarence "Gatemouth" Brown, the legendary performer signed to a companion label, who struggled with Ace's self-destructive tendencies; and Ernest Withers, who took the early photographs and whose knowledge of postwar Memphis makes him truly the "Dean of Beale Street."

Finally, there are the women who were responsible for this book: Jean Alexander, the gracious wife of Johnny Ace and mother of his children; Norma Alexander Williams, the sister so close in age that many people thought her Johnny's twin and the unofficial family historian; Evelyn

Johnson, the closest thing to a personal manager that Johnny ever had and head of the agency that booked his personal appearances; and Donna Salem, my wife and partner, whose presence, demeanor, and thoughtful questions yielded information from the women in Johnny Ace's life that I would never have known otherwise.

The Late Great

johnny
ace

and the Transition from

R&B to Rock 'n' Roll

Johnny Ace was a really splendid,
gentle, kind young man, and he should
never have been put in the position
that he was.
—David James Mattis

Introduction

Johnny Ace is remembered today, if at all, as the mellow crooner of the 1955 hit "Pledging My Love" ("Forever my darling, our love will be true . . ."). But he was much more than this. Ace was an influential transitional figure between rhythm and blues and rock 'n' roll, the first solo black male R&B star in the postwar era to attract a white audience with material outside the novelty song tradition. He may have even started the trend that celebrated youthful rebelliousness and romantic self-destruction, but he certainly did not die at age twenty-four playing Russian roulette with Little Esther in a motel room in El Dorado, Arkansas.

I heard this version of his death from a woman who paid $2.50 in 1953 ("a hard amount to get in those days") to see Johnny Ace on the chitlin circuit at the Elk's Rest Club in Tuscaloosa, Alabama. Though the specific facts of her story are wrong, the general drift as she remembered it—the legend of Johnny Ace preserved in the oral tradition of southern African American culture—is closer to the truth *in spirit* than almost everything ever written about him.

1

Rock historians did not begin to appreciate Johnny Ace until he had been dead for a quarter-century, and then they focused on the sensational quality of his Russian roulette death—which they invariably got wrong—not with the remarkable story of his career as a rhythm and blues recording star. With no real interest in his accomplishments, different rock constituencies constructed the legend of Johnny Ace from their own perspectives and out of their own needs and purposes, revealing more about them than about him. In his reconstruction, Johnny Ace became a sign and symbol representing all those things that white people hoped, or feared, about black culture—that it was wild and animalistic, primitive and lustful, careless and decadent. Ace's dramatic death finally made him acceptable to white critics, who never found enough "rawness" in his music.

Johnny Ace was, after all, not a blues moaner or a blues shouter. He was a crooner, a straight-ahead ballad singer, an unknown Memphis singer on the unknown Duke Records label who suddenly appeared on the rhythm and blues scene in 1952, performing with a band that B.B. King had put together and then abandoned. Ace's soft and romantic performance of "My Song" on Duke was such a hit with the limited audience that heard it that it attracted the attention of Don D. Robey of Houston, who then acquired controlling interest in the label and aggressively promoted Ace's record to the top of the R&B charts, grooming him as a national headlining R&B act. Ace's shy and easy demeanor and his slim, good looks produced a perfect romantic figure for black women, who purchased most of the R&B records.

"My Song" stayed on the national R&B charts for almost five months, holding the number one spot for an impressive nine weeks. Next came "Cross My Heart," "The Clock," and "Saving My Love for You" in 1953, all "heart ballads" and all top three national hits in the restricted world of rhythm and blues. By that time Ace was on the road virtually twelve months a year, playing one-nighters not only in the Deep South but also in clubs and theaters in the West, Midwest, and New England.

The rhythm and blues field was notorious for one-hit wonders, but Ace's consistency and the professionalism of his management were notable. His third hit, the hypnotic song "The Clock," galvanized his reputation in the African American community. Rhythm and blues performers did not enjoy television exposure in the early 1950s, nor were their records played on white radio stations. Though few white Americans had ever heard of Johnny Ace, by 1953 he was an established national celebrity in black America.

"Please Forgive Me," a sad and dreamy ballad, and "Never Let Me Go," a sad and slow one, accounted for Ace's fifth and sixth straight R&B hits in 1954. The entertainment columnists in black newspapers acknowledged him, trade magazines like *Billboard* tracked his personal appearances, audiences from Billy Berg's 5-4 Ballroom in Los Angeles to the Apollo Theater in New York thrilled to his performances, and Willie Mae "Big Mama" Thornton opened his shows. Though Ace's career was still circumscribed by the narrow parameters of performing and recording African American music for an African American audience, rhythm and blues material on a national level was becoming recognizably popular with white teenagers.

About the time that the major record labels began to copy, or "cover," successful R&B songs for the predominantly white "pop" market, Johnny Ace succumbed to the perils of the road. He conked his hair, drank too much, and gained forty pounds. He became depressed and self-destructive, purchasing a 7-shot .22 pistol and playing with it recklessly. Ace's biggest hit, "Pledging My Love," was first advertised in *Billboard* on December 25, 1954. That same night he killed himself in Houston between sets in the North side dressing room of City Auditorium in front of Big Mama Thornton. He was twenty-five years old.

The level of emotion that the memory of Johnny Ace still inspires, especially among black women, is remarkable. In 1990, during a National Endowment for the Humanities Seminar at the University of Alabama titled "African American Literature, Art and the Search for Identity in Twentieth-Century America," I met sixty middle-aged black women who taught social studies or English in Alabama high schools. They not only knew all the words to "Pledging My Love," but sang them out loud, with their peers, in the middle of my formal presentation "Mainlining Black Music." Ace had been dead for more than thirty-five years by this time, and I had at least forty songs cued up that day to play, but the seminar stalled on "Pledging My Love." When I made a movement toward the cassette player one woman said, in a voice teeming with authority: "Don't you *dare* stop that song." Southern black women of their generation, I learned, have the kind of affection for Johnny Ace that southern white women have for Elvis Presley.

Johnny Ace was a black man who sang in a predominantly white style, and Elvis Presley was a white man who sang in a predominantly black one. Though Elvis spent much of his boyhood in Mississippi, both singers were products of Memphis, a Deep South city in the heart of the region of post-war America undergoing the greatest transition. In Memphis, blacks and whites lived in close proximity to one another, owed one another favors, knew one another's culture, and admired one another's music.

Elvis, for example, habituated the black area known as Beale Street, where he was known not by name but by face.[1] He sneaked into Beale Street's black clubs at night, felt as comfortable in black churches as in white, may have performed on "all-black" Amateur Nights at the Palace, and, in a well-documented event in 1956, appeared at black radio station WDIA's Goodwill Revue. He even wore Royal Crown Pomade on his hair, a product black men used to affect white hair styles. Elvis was an example of "cross-cultural collision," Nelson George says, "adapting black styles from blacks adapting white looks."[2]

Johnny and Elvis had a lifetime in common. Their fathers had come to Memphis from north Mississippi, struggling to survive and trying to keep their sons on the straight and narrow, and their mothers were dominant and imposing figures. Though Elvis was an only child and Johnny had a houseful of siblings, it was the white son who lived in project housing and the black son who was known to come from a "substance family" in predominantly black South Memphis.[3] Elvis was a frequent visitor to South Memphis as well, especially to McLemore Avenue, where he was known to hang out at Leonard's Barbeque and attend church at the First Assembly of God. Johnny Ace's widow still lives on McLemore.

Johnny and Elvis shared both time and space. Elvis was thirteen in 1948 when his family escaped from Tupelo to Memphis; Johnny was nineteen that year, unemployed, a high school dropout with a failed experience in the navy, and an aspiring musician. According to Beale Street photographer Ernest Withers, Johnny was "a look-up" for Elvis. Did they ever meet? It is unlikely that they were ever formally introduced, but evidence suggests that Elvis heard Johnny play with B.B. King's original band, also known variously as the Beale Street Blues Boys, Bee Bee's Jeebies, or the Beale Street-ers. It may have happened on a summer evening, perhaps in 1951, in the black club on Beale Street above the Mitchell Hotel. Elvis was then sixteen, experimenting with the feeling he got from live black music. Something of a misfit in the white community, he was already buying his clothes at Lansky Brothers on Beale Street and dressing like a black man. Johnny, who had just turned twenty-two, had a wife and son he rarely saw and a mother he deliberately avoided; he practically lived on Beale Street at the Mitchell Hotel.

Their immediate futures also ran along parallel tracks. Within the year Johnny had inherited the Beale Streeters Band and composed and performed "My Song," which changed his life. In 1952, when Johnny left for Texas to become a rhythm and blues legend, Elvis was a senior at Humes High School, wearing pink and black, and attempting to help out the family by working the swing shift in a furniture-assembly plant in South Memphis. While celebrity drew Ace to Houston, prosperity eventually drove the Presleys from their public housing at the Lauderdale Courts.

There is more. Just as Elvis fell into the clutches of the notorious Col. Tom Parker, the ex-carnival barker who promoted him shamelessly, drove him incessantly, and robbed him blind, Johnny fell into the hands of Don D. Robey, the Houston gambler turned entrepreneur who made him a celebrity in black America, kept him on the road twenty-eight days out of thirty, and made sure he never knew how the business worked. Public adulation, the pressure to perform, too many women, too much food, and too many nights away from home took their toll on both men. They lived too fast, played carelessly and dangerously with guns, and sought solace in alcohol and/or drugs.

As musicians, the careers of these two young Memphis men began to coincide in July 1954. Johnny was on a tour of one-nighters in Texas, Louisiana, and New Mexico. He was featuring his fifth straight R&B hit sung in essentially a white, crooning style. Elvis was going into the Sun Records studio for the first time.[4] After several false starts, the session ended up refining "That's All Right," a black song Elvis sang in a style that caused many white listeners to believe "he was colored" when they heard it on local station WHBQ.[5] This song would become his first Sun record and cause *Billboard* to name "the youngster with the hillbilly blues beat" as the nation's eighth "Most Promising" hillbilly talent. A year later, Johnny was dead and Elvis was on his way to immortality.

In March 1955, Elvis was on the road performing one-nighters as part of a Parker-promoted package called "The Hank Snow Jamboree." Elvis had not yet cut "Baby Let's Play House," his first record to make the national country and western charts, or "Mystery Train," the record that would top the *Billboard* national C&W charts and lead to national exposure on RCA Records. Johnny's "Pledging My Love," on the other hand, was the number one record on all R&B charts, a surprising Top 20 record in pop sales, and the number 11 song in *Billboard*'s prestigious Honor Roll of Hits. Did Elvis appreciate Ace's record? Apparently he did. Just as Johnny's "Pledging My Love" was the last record he released before his death in 1954 (the "B" side was called "No Money"), "Pledging My Love" was the last record Elvis released before *his* death in 1977 (the "A" side was "Way Down"). Though the Elvis single became a number one C&W record, it never reached as high on the pop charts as Johnny's.

But Johnny Ace did not live to turn forty, or even thirty. He left no estate worth millions. People all over the world do not come to Memphis to see his home or pay tribute to his final resting place. Nor is his the most thoroughly documented life in the history of American entertainment. Johnny Ace left no recorded or published interviews, no film or video footage, no costumes, awards, public acknowledgments, or personal mementos. Ed Sullivan never shook his hand, and neither Richard Nixon nor any other president knew his name. Even photographs of Ace are rare. To evaluate his achievements we must rely on his twenty-one recorded sides, the documentation of his career in the music trade magazines and the black newspapers, and the memories of his life recalled by family, friends, fans, and business associates.

Elvis Presley and Johnny Ace were part of the movement in the 1950s that permanently and dramatically changed popular music in America and the world. The source of their cultural innovation was the same fertile musical soil that W. C. Handy mined so successfully a half-century before them and Stephen Foster a half-century before that. It is not surprising to find talents like Elvis and Johnny emerging from the rich and unique cultural mix of the Mississippi Delta in general and Memphis, Tennessee, in particular. It turns out that postwar Memphis and, by extension and inference, the rest of the United States as well, was a city of at least *two* tales. The Library of Congress lists over four hundred books that detail the story of Elvis Presley; this book is an attempt to tell Johnny Ace's story for the first time.

Memphis

Chained in the

Backyard

The personal histories of Johnny Ace and his parents epitomize the
history of Memphis itself. Johnny's father, John Marshall Alexander
Sr., became a resident of Memphis in 1893 or 1894, contributing
to the increase in black population in the 1890s that established
Memphis as America's most African American city. Though he
"knew nothing" of his own parents, the senior John Alexander believed he was born in the Mississippi Delta town of Hernando,
thirty miles to the south, and sent to Memphis as an infant, where
he was passed around from relative to relative until he was old
enough to make his own way. "I didn't have parents," his daughter
remembered him saying. "My relatives took care of me until I got
to be a man in the eighth grade and got my first job."[1] Like thousands of other new black residents of Memphis, Johnny's mother,
Leslie Newsome Alexander, was originally from the east Arkansas
Delta. She was born in Lansing, a farming community between
Crawfordsville and Earle, about thirty miles west of Memphis. Her
parents worked with her aunt and seven uncles as tenant farmers

on a former plantation. The entire Newsome extended family lived in the "big house," with other tenants residing nearby.

The hardships experienced by the parents of Johnny Ace were mirrored in the history of Memphis in the nineteenth century. The period following the Civil War had not been particularly kind to the city. Though spared the devastation of invasion by the northern army, it was captured by the Union fleet after falling in a short battle with Confederate gunboats on the Mississippi River. As a consequence, Memphis did not suffer the kind of physical ruin experienced by other southern cities.[2] It did, however, experience all the dislocations of other southern communities adjusting to the new political, social, and economic realities in the years following the war. Its first crisis came as a result of some fifteen thousand new freedmen congregating in Memphis, leading to a race riot lasting several days in May 1866 (of forty-eight people killed forty-six were black)—apparently precipitated by abusive Irish policemen who feared economic competition from blacks and may have resented the compassion in Memphis often expressed in regard to ex-slaves. The Ku Klux Klan became active in Memphis a year later.[3]

As it turned out, however, the primary peril for the city lay in its neglect of sanitation. The city of Memphis in the 1870s was said to be "the dirtiest in the country," and perhaps the world, where a traveler could have knowledge of the dirt of Cairo and the foul smell of Cologne but still conclude that "they all back down before Memphis."[4] Memphis drinking water was polluted, as was its milk supply; uncollected garbage and dead animals filled yards, streets, and gutters; sewage collected in stagnant pools. According to historian Gerald M. Capers, the stench produced in Memphis "but for the adaptation peculiar to the olfactory sense, would have driven human life from the town."[5] Yellow fever, cholera, and smallpox were "calamitous" for the city in 1872–73, but especially devastating was the 1878 yellow fever epidemic, which either killed or frightened off most of the city's white population.

Thousands of people failed to return to the city after fleeing the 1878 disaster in which 17,600 blacks and whites were stricken (75 percent of white people who remained in Memphis died of yellow fever but only 7 percent of the Negroes), and many who did return left for Nashville or St. Louis the following spring and summer when more outbreaks were reported.[6] Memphis had an estimated population of 55,000 before the plague and only 14,000 afterward; more than 12,000 of these citizens were black. "White traditions were destroyed almost completely," Stanley Booth says of the population shift, making twentieth-century Memphis "a blank page."[7] The city, in fact, found itself burdened by such insurmountable debt that it surrendered its charter, reducing its status to a lowly taxing district of the state of Tennessee.[8]

Yellow fever permanently changed the relationship between blacks and whites in Memphis. Southern black writer George W. Lee pointed out in 1934 that the heroism displayed during the plague from "fearless black men" softened the racial attitudes of whites in Memphis—"the feeling lingers even until this day," he says.[9] Historian William Barlow argues that African Americans "were responsible for bringing prosperity and growth back to Memphis" after the plague,[10] and indeed the large black population was reinforced during the Reconstruction era by thousands of poor, rural blacks from Tennessee, Mississippi, Arkansas, and Alabama. Robert R. Church, who became "the most successful black businessman in Memphis," also arrived during Reconstruction, operating saloons at first, acquiring properties in the Beale Street area next, and eventually opening the city's first black-owned bank.[11]

Becoming a successful black businessman in Memphis was not without peril, however. White resentment flared up against a black grocer named Thomas Moss and two associates in March 1892. Moss and his partners were charged with shooting three white men who were part of a night mob that attacked their business, People's Grocery. The three black men were taken from their jail cells, transported by switch engine out of the city, and lynched. (An additional one hundred black men were charged with conspiracy in the attempt to protect the store, which was later successfully looted and destroyed by whites.) The real crime, apparently, was that People's Grocery was guilty of attracting black customers who had previously patronized a white-owned business.

The Memphis murders comprised only one percent of the lynchings in America in 1892, but they had wide impact. Mary Church Terrell, the daughter of Robert Church and a childhood friend of Tom Moss, protested the outrage when, in the company of abolitionist Frederick Douglass, she met with President Benjamin Harrison at the White House. And Ida B. Wells, a close friend of Mr. and Mrs. Thomas Moss and godmother to their daughter, wrote inspired and persuasive editorials in the (black) Memphis newspaper *Free Speech* calling for local black action against the recent white lawlessness.

As a result, many black customers returned major installment purchases to white merchants (the music houses could not find storage space for all the returned pianos and other instruments), the city's trolley system was boycotted and almost ruined, and hundreds of black citizens left Memphis permanently and moved west, as her editorials advised. Whole families, indeed whole church congregations, left the city. "So many Blacks took the advice of Wells," Paula Giddings says, "that the White business community began to panic." Nationally, the lynching of Tom Moss and the subsequent indignation of Ida B. Wells led to the first anti-lynching campaign in America. President Harrison, however, did not, as she implored him to do, publicly condemn lynching in his annual Congressional address.[12]

Nevertheless, in the period between 1890 and 1900 the increase in the black population in Memphis created a city of over 100,000 citizens that was almost 50 percent black, making Memphis the most African American big city in America. Birmingham was only 43 percent black at the time, Washington, D.C., 31 percent, and Chicago 2 percent.[13] The substantial black labor force was not unappreciated by the city fathers, who became concerned after World War I with the continuing problem of black out-migration to the North and West (the city's black population dropped to 38 percent of the total by 1920). After studying this problem in 1919, the Memphis Chamber of Commerce raised funds to help improve the quality of black working and living conditions, promised seed money to black organizations, and concluded that the availability of "negro labor is one of the best assets of this community."[14]

E. H. Crump, the political boss who ruled Memphis politics for a quarter of a century, was apparently the first Memphis politician to understand the value of including black voters as a central constituency. For its cooperation (staying in its place) Crump offered black Memphis a token voice in city government, said to be "the best deal African Americans could get." In addition, at election time Crump found great leverage in courting Beale Street saloon owners and the customers they could deliver.[15] Supporters of Crump would be loaded on trucks, provided with poll tax and registration receipts, and driven around the city for repeat voting.[16] W. C. Handy was hired to write the campaign tune that helped bring Crump to power in 1909. Crump was running on a strict reform platform during that election, so Handy's song, titled "Mr. Crump," began with the line, "Mr. Crump don't 'low no easy riders here" and ended with "Mr. Crump can go and catch hisself some air!" "I knew that reform was about as palatable to Beale Street voters as castor oil," Handy says in his autobiography. "Mr. Crump" was retitled "Memphis Blues" when Handy published it in 1912.[17] Three quarters of a century later the song was still being performed by black Memphis singers.

John Alexander, father of Johnny Ace, a virtual orphan from Hernando, Mississippi, did not frequent Beale Street saloons, however, nor did he serve as a repeat voter for political bosses. Alexander was a sober and serious young man with a steady job. He worked as a packer for the Plough Chemical Company, which manufactured patent medicines and toiletries aimed at both black and white markets, leaving his job to serve in World War I and resuming it after the Armistice. Later, his service connection helped him get a better paying position as a packer with the Army Depot in Memphis, where he was employed for twenty years.

Leslie Newsome, the only child of Arkansas tenant farmers who had found the means to send her to a boarding school in Memphis, met and fell so deeply in love with John Alexander that she was persuaded by him to leave school in the tenth grade and marry. For John, Leslie was exactly what he had asked the Lord for: "I wanted a good wife," he would tell his children, "and the Lord had been talking to me." For Leslie, who planned on becoming a teacher, the marriage represented the end of a dream. "She was disgusted with herself" for leaving school, she confided in her daughters:

> She just used to tell us how she made the fatal mistake after she met my father. She had gotten to the tenth grade, and he was wanting to marry. He talked her into getting married. And after she married he told her she would be able to go on and finish school so she could teach. What happened was, she just completed the tenth grade, and when she got ready to go back to the eleventh grade, she was pregnant. And then every year she was having a child. She was always sad about that and depressed, and always talked about how she just messed up her life marrying. She told us, "I said if I have any girls I don't care if they fail, fail, fail! They can get twenty years old—they're not going to receive company! They're going to get out of high school!"[18]

Leslie Alexander may have had sufficient power to guarantee that her daughters behaved as she wished, but she would have almost no control over her son, Johnny. The future Johnny Ace was born John Marshall Alexander

Jr. at home in Memphis on 9 June 1929, the sixth child in a family of eleven children, ten of whom survived. The family house, at 899 Fisher Street (now called Ferry Court) is still standing in a part of town known as South Memphis. Though Memphis was not "entirely segregated residentially by race" at this time, neighborhoods south of the downtown area had the heaviest concentration of black residents.[19] Published accounts of Johnny growing up in the economically depressed Binghampton area of Memphis are simply in error.

The elder Alexander was thirty-five years old when he named his second son after himself and became John Marshall Alexander Sr., and Leslie, his wife, was twenty-six years old and an experienced mother and homemaker. She was still a pretty woman with long hair (braided and worn on top of her head) and smooth skin. She was short, 5'4", and heavy set. John Sr., on the other hand, was very tall and lanky, a handsome man in the 6'4"–6'6" range, but solid, industrious, and religious. Sometime in the early 1920s, when he was in his early twenties himself, he informed his wife that the Lord had "called him to preach." He did not give up his day job at Plough Chemical Company, which he needed to support his rapidly growing family, but he did take on essentially a second job—serving small Baptist churches in the poor, outlying rural areas of the city. "This is not a career for me," he would say. "I have a family to feed."[20]

There is no question, however, that the service he provided as a pastor also helped him feed his family. Many rural congregations could not support a full-time pastor; indeed, they often did well to find a part-time minister to share with one or several other rural churches. Norma, the sibling closest in age to Johnny (sometimes referred to as his twin sister) and a repository of Alexander family history, understood even as a child the limited financial resources of her father's parishioners: "He always had two churches. He had to have. They were just common people, and they had all this food. And at hog-killing and cow-killing we had all the food we needed. They didn't have funds. When they would have a pastor's anniversary, he would get money—two or three hundred dollars. He was just rendering a service to man."[21]

To the congregations the Rev. Mr. Alexander served and to whom he dedicated himself, "he was their Father." After working a ten-hour day at Plough Chemical, Alexander would sometimes drive to Arkansas to minister to the emergency needs of his parishioners, described by Norma Williams as "just country people, and they didn't have nothing else to do and nowhere to go. There was no outlet for them," she says. "The only thing they would do is work all the week in the fields and then on Sundays [my father] would give them enough gas to go back and get that cotton the next week." According to his children, Alexander was an excellent preacher. "They just went wild about him," says Norma. "He was the best," says St. Clair Alexander, Johnny's younger brother, who traveled with his father almost every Sunday until he was thirteen or fourteen.

Alexander pastored briefly in Hernando, Mississippi, but the family remembers him most as the commuting pastor of two east Arkansas churches near his wife's birthplace: Macedonia Baptist Church in Lansing and Mt. Zion Baptist Church in Parkin. On the first and third Sunday he would preach at one church, on the second and fourth at the other. Mt. Zion Baptist no longer exists, but the Rev. John Marshall Alexander's photograph is still prominently displayed at Macedonia Baptist Church in Lansing, where he is remembered fondly as the pastor whose replacements never did "measure up."[22]

While the Alexanders may have been technically poor, they certainly did not live in poverty. "They were poor," says Johnny's widow, who lived with the Alexanders for several years, "but they weren't *poor* poor."[23] For one thing, they always had food on the table, and invariably the main meal included cooked greens and cornbread. While the family was large and relied upon a single wage earner for support, Mr. and Mrs. Alexander were, according to daughter Norma, "do-ers":

> They were really a good team, because he was the only one working, the bread-winner. And she was the manager. And she had clippers of all sizes to take care of the boys—they cut the boys' hair. And she had this little oil stove with some pullers, and she kept our hair. They did all of this. They were just gifted for doing, you know, with their hands. The children would laugh at us for the way daddy fixed our shoes. "Your daddy's a shoemaker!" they would say. Sometimes they would cut the boys' hair a little closer, and the children would make fun, call them "Butter Bowl." But there were so many of us.[24]

The Alexanders economized by not paying for things they could do themselves, but they also saved money by instituting household rules designed to prolong the life of purchased goods. For the children, the most humiliating conservation measure had to do with the preservation of shoes. "We had to get out of our shoes when we come home from school and put on them flops," St. Clair remembers. "They had a sole tied with wire and everything." He recalls being teased for this but only "at a distance," since the Alexander children generally ran together and stuck up for one another. Of course, the Alexanders were not the only family to sew, patch, mend, fix, and otherwise attempt to "make do" during the Depression, nor the only family living on the edge.

A WPA survey in 1940 found that 77 percent of Memphis blacks and 35 percent of whites lived in substandard housing; less than 11 percent of black families had a bathroom.[25] Norma remembers an indoor toilet during the Depression and the three Number 3 washtubs that the family set up in the kitchen for bathing. "We were always thinking we had the worst," she says, "but at least we had our indoor toilet." No one seems to remember the sleeping arrangements in the three bedroom house except that Mr. and Mrs. Alexander had a bedroom of their own that they shared with the newest baby in the family. Still, the Alexanders were better off than other families. "So many of the children [at school] would have to go home to cook, clean up, wash, and iron," Norma says. "My mother was there. She did that."

The family's stability and status made the Alexanders, according to Memphis photographer Ernest Withers, a "substance family." Withers, who knew the Alexander family members, had been a photographer for Negro League baseball teams and served briefly as a Memphis policeman (he was one of the first blacks hired and the first fired). He established a studio on Beale Street in 1948 and helped document the rich Memphis blues scene. Sometimes called "The Dean of Beale Street," Withers took the early publicity photographs of Johnny Ace, and helped arrange his funeral at Clayborn Temple in Memphis.[26]

The Alexander household was a large and extended one (both of Mrs. Alexander's parents once shared the house at 899 Fisher), characterized by sister Norma as "a devout Christian home." For the Alexander daughters, especially, the household was so devoutly Christian that it seemed as if all of life was church: "The girls just went to church all the time. We didn't know what movies were, going to dances, spending the night or weekend with a friend. We just went to church all the time. But the boys kind of had it made because when they got to the fifth or sixth grade and they started getting little jobs throwing the paper for the CD [*Chicago Defender*]—they just got wild."[27]

The children's grandmother and mother were members of the African Methodist Episcopal (AME) Church, and their grandfather a member of the Church of Christ. Father of course, was a Baptist. Since the Rev. Mr. Alexander had to commute to Arkansas in a model T Ford that couldn't carry the whole family anyway, most of the children ended up going to the AME Methodist church with their mother and grandmother. Leslie Alexander sang in the Bethel AME Church choir, as did the children, including Johnny. The Alexander family, in fact, was the "backbone" of the tiny Bethel AME Church, the reason why Johnny's funeral in 1955 at the larger Clayborn Temple AME Church in Memphis was an appropriate place for his last rites and not symbolic of any feud with his Baptist father.

Johnny and the other Alexander children attended nearby LaRose Grammar School, where their father had received his entire formal schooling. Like him, they received a strong, fundamental education. "Johnny Ace was a pretty good schoolboy," Ernest Withers says. "Literacy was his greater advantage over the rest of the boys [in the Memphis blues scene]."[28] He was also a natural musician. There was always a piano at home, says his sister, "and he just had this raw talent—he just started when he was a small child, playing. He picked it up by ear." When his mother and father were home, the piano was used to play church hymns and Christian songs exclusively, but on the first of every month when dad was at work and Mrs. Alexander left the children alone to go to town to pay bills, "the house would be rockin' because we would really let our hair down, and Johnny would be playing the blues. He couldn't do that when [our parents] were there."

St. Clair remembers serving so successfully as the lookout for his mother that the most secular tune she ever heard played on that piano was "Nearer My God to Thee." He also remembers his brother's strength, his wrestling ability, his penchant for horseplay, and his love of linguistic play. "Anything come out of his mouth, it was always fun," he says. "He would just joke a lot, and he would just come out of his mouth with anything."

When Johnny moved on to Booker T. Washington High School in the ninth grade, he "started having problems," according to Norma. "When he got to Booker Washington and saw all this equipment—well, they would be looking for him and he'd be down in the bandroom on the piano."[29] His talent was recognized by Nat D. Williams, a high school social science teacher and something of a Memphis legend. Williams wrote a newspaper column for the *Pittsburgh Courier* and the *Memphis World*, directed the festivities at the annual Cotton Jubilee, and emceed the famous Palace Theater Amateur Nights. After World War II he was "Nat D.," the South's first "publicly promoted black man on the air as a disk jockey" on the all-black sound of Memphis station WDIA.[30] As Ace's sister Norma remembers:

> And because [Johnny] was the child that had all of this raw talent, he was not only gifted with the ear of playing music but he composed, he was a composer, and he was an artist—when the school noticed he had this gift of playing, Nat D. Williams talked with my mother, wanting to get him enrolled in music, and she tried, but he didn't finish the first grade in music. He didn't want to study music; he just wanted to play. After she tried, and he didn't do anything with the music teacher, then Mr. Williams told her about his ability as an artist. He said, "He's an average child, but he's gifted, and when we're looking for him in science, he's somewhere in the music room playing the piano or he's over in the art building, drawing." So she sent off for this art course, but he wasn't interested in that. She ordered this course in the mail and he never completed the first lesson.[31]

Nor did he complete high school, dropping out of the eleventh grade to join the navy. Family members agree that Johnny had no illusion about saving the world from tyranny (World War II had been over for two years), no heightened sense of patriotism, and no strong conviction about serving his country when he enlisted in the navy: he merely wanted to travel and see the world. What he did not know at the time was that the U.S. Navy, by reputation the most racist of the services, had little it was willing to offer to young black sailors that did not involve kitchen or custodial responsibilities. Johnny's mother had the notion that military training would help her son adjust to the real world, and his father, who was proud to have served in the army during World War I and who believed that military experience could lead to civilian vocational opportunities, appears to have been unaware of the restricted prospects his son faced in the navy. "Oh you get in service, they'll make a man out of you," Norma remembers her father telling him. As for mother: "She thought he was going to come out, you know, responsible, and he would be stable. And they couldn't even keep up with him. The navy had trouble with him. They would look for him, and he would be in a small town somewhere. I think he was using the navy to travel. And he would be in a small town in a tavern or in one of those night spots playing. And a lot of times those MPs would be looking for him, and they came to our home on numerous occasions thinking my mother and father knew where he was."

Sometimes Johnny came home, saying he was "on a furlough," and a few days later the family would put him on a bus back to his base. "But then," Norma says, "he got off at that first little town." When it became clear that the navy had no influence over him, his mother was furious. She told him, "You wanted to be in the navy. This was your way out. And you got in there. Now they can't keep up with you! I can't keep up with you, and *they* can't keep up with you!"[32] Altogether, his navy service was brief (members of the family remember it in terms of weeks, not years), ending in an undesirable or dishonorable discharge in 1947.

The navy's practice at the time was to purge itself of recruits like Ace as soon as possible. "There wouldn't be any question about it if the man wasn't working out to be of any benefit to the navy," says retired navy Captain Rodney Badger, who acknowledges that until the end of World War II, official navy policy specifically restricted black recruits to jobs as stewards or mess attendants. Even after the war the practice continued. "You could no longer officially restrict them from certain kinds of jobs," he remembers of the immediate postwar era, "but it took time for [a change] to work through."[33] Accounts of Ace serving in the U.S. Navy during World War II are erroneous.[34]

Johnny not only confounded the navy establishment, whom he would not serve, but he also successfully evaded the massive bureaucracy of the United States Navy and its penchant for accurate record keeping. A military personnel record does not appear to exist for John Marshall Alexander Jr. in the navy archives. As a measure of just how free-spirited Ace was, it is also quite possible that he never had a social security number.

Discharged from a failed experiment in the navy in 1947, instead of finding a job Johnny took to the streets of South Memphis, especially the corner of Mississippi and Walker, where black men shot pool and killed time. One day on that corner he and his friend Cleveland Williams were picked up by a white man in a truck filled with scrap iron and hired to ride to Hernando, Mississippi, to help the man unload. The scrap iron had been stolen, it was revealed when all three men were arrested in Hernando, and though the white man admitted to authorities that his black helpers were innocent of the crime, they too had to remain in town until the monthly circuit judge came through.

In the tense postwar days of the segregated South, the idea of a black man arrested in Mississippi evokes images of chain gangs, railroaded labor, brutal oppression, and physical violence. For the future Johnny Ace, however, the experience may have put him on a path leading to a career as a rhythm and blues performer. He and Cleveland Williams were free to go anywhere during the daytime, even to Memphis if they wanted, but they had to go back to jail at night. According to St. Clair:

> And they'd go out and cut grass, cut people's lawns around there, make a quarter, two quarters, something like that, and then they had to go back and stay in the jail at night. They could come to Memphis, but dad wasn't going to ride up and down the highway. John Jr. had daddy bring him a guitar—we used to call it a Gene Autry guitar. They didn't have a lot of electric guitars back then, so daddy took him one of those Gene Autrys down there. I don't think it was more than five or six dollars or something like that. And he would play the guitar while Cleveland Williams would be dancing, on the street down there. And people going to work, coming to work, would throw money down there. They were making money while they was in jail![35]

St. Clair rode with his father from Memphis to Hernando to deliver the guitar to Johnny, and in the period of the late 1940s he is the most reliable witness of his brother's life. There is no doubt that Norma knew more about the family as a unit during this time, but virtually all of the Alexander boys' activities in the outside world were hidden from her as well as her parents—especially her mother. St. Clair, however, born in 1932, was old enough to envy his older brother's lifestyle, which he attempted to emulate. "I tried to follow my brother," he says, "but he ran with older guys, and they didn't want me around."

St. Clair is convinced that the experience of playing guitar on the streets of Hernando gave his brother the idea of becoming a blues musician. "That's really what started him playing in the band," he says: "Then when he came back [to Memphis] he got with some little old band playing the guitar—a little blues band that went from Memphis to Arkansas. I forget the guy's name, but he used to go from here and play all over Arkansas with that band, a blues band like John Leé Hooker, Muddy Waters, stuff like that. They had a separate name, you know, their own name."[36] At least one source credits Joe Hill Louis, "The Be-Bop Boy" who was a one-man band, as the person who started Johnny out as a professional musician in Memphis.[37] St. Clair doesn't think that Johnny was singing then, nor is he even sure that he got paid. He does believe, though, that playing guitar with the blues band led directly to playing with the Rev. Dwight "Gatemouth" Moore in his church. Like Johnny, Moore had been one of Nat D. Williams's former students at Booker T. Washington High School, but Moore was also an experienced winner of Amateur Nights at the Palace Theater. According to him he always won "except the night he lost to the blind singer Al Hibbler." By 1949 Moore was recording blues songs and earning $1,500 a week in clubs. Then, in a Paul-like experience, he was virtually frightened into a religious conversion. He was playing the Club DeLisa in Chicago, trying to sing a blues song, and, "nothing came out." "I tried it again," he remembers, and "nothing came out." When he attempted the religious song "Shine on Me," however, his voice returned, though the nightclub audience "thought [he] had lost his mind."

The experience caused Moore to give up his blues career, enter the ministry, and return to Memphis, where he joined station WDIA as a religious personality.[38] Nat D. Williams welcomed him back to Beale Street in his newspaper column ("He's one of the Avenue's own sons") and vouched for the new direction in his life. Some had looked suspiciously at Moore's "long black Cadillac," he wrote, his "ultra-modernly-cut suits," and his "very hepped manner of expression." But Moore, he said, was "offering his penance in the only manner in which he is most adept . . . he is a showman."[39] Later, the Rev. Mr. Moore spoke at Johnny Ace's funeral.

Lois Jean Palmer, the woman who married Ace, then still known as John Marshall Alexander Jr., was an impressionable ninth grader at Booker T. Washington High School in 1950 when she met him, a 5'7" handsome charmer who was out of school and out of the service. He was at Booker T. Washington every day, she says, as if he didn't have anything more important to do than to work at "messing up her life." "He was at school messing around with all the young girls," she says, "and he should have been working somewhere instead of messing with the young girls."[40] He was fun, though, and shy, and "he was nice." Jean was living with her father at the time, but Johnny was "in and out" of his home at 899 Fisher and not really living there.

Favorite places for the couple were the neighborhood movie theater at the corner of Walker and Mississippi (the Ace Theater) and the juke joint next door.[41] According to Jean, Johnny's parents did not know they were dating until she got pregnant. The couple drove across the Mississippi River on July 17, 1950, to get married in Earle, Arkansas, because Arkansas did not require waiting for the results of a blood test. The Rev. W. E. Battle conducted the ceremony. Johnny was twenty-one; Jean was sixteen. As she remembers, he was wearing "wild clothes" and singing down on Beale Street at this time but was not yet, to her knowledge, in a band.

The new husband, who apparently never had a real job in his life, did little to find one after the wedding. Norma was under the impression that her brother had been employed at the Memphis Furniture Company after he married, but Jean has no recollection of it. "They say he worked at Memphis Furniture Company," she says, "but I don't think he did too much and not too long."[42] In addition, the marriage alienated Jean from her father. "Her daddy didn't want her [anymore]," Norma says. "[The marriage] was against her father's will."[43] Without other resources to fall back on, Johnny moved his bride into the crowded Alexander home at 899 Fisher. Though there was a separate full bathroom now to complement the indoor toilet, it was still only a three bedroom house, already overcrowded with adults and overrun with children.

"There was a lot of peoples in there," Jean says. She was provided sleeping space, but her husband was not made part of the arrangement, and she doesn't know where he stayed. "Since John wasn't doing right, his mother didn't let him stay" at 899 Fisher, she remembers, "so I slept in the living room. She wouldn't let [Johnny] sleep there because he wasn't working, and she didn't want him in this music scene."[44] The hostility toward the son did not apply to Jean, however, who was made to feel at home immediately in the Alexander household and quickly became just another member of the family, going along with the rest to Mrs. Alexander's Bethel AME Church. "His mother was real nice to me," she says. "I guess I was just like a girl, her daughter. Because really, she wanted me to go back to school. The sisters were real good to me and treated me like a sister."[45]

After a son, Glenn Alexander, was born in 1950, the senior Mrs. Alexander encouraged Jean to return to Booker T. Washington for her high school diploma, revealing to her daughter-in-law her own bitterness at being a dropout. "She kind of blamed [her husband] for her marrying him and not finishing her education," Jean says.[46] More than forty years later, Jean still regrets turning down her mother-in-law's offer to help her return to school.

As for Johnny, she saw little of him. He felt he had to "dodge" his mother even more than he had dodged her before, existing as a night person and living at the Mitchell Hotel on Beale Street. He was not faithful to her, she knew perfectly well, and she saw that women found him very attractive. Sometimes she knew where he was, and sometimes she did not. "We never really had a marriage," she says.

Norma understood how impossible it would be to keep a husband like her brother: "Johnny had a talent with girls. Just like today. If a man is gifted, girls just go for them."[47] To make matters worse, Jean found it impossible to engage Johnny in serious conversation. "He was always so jolly," she says. "Of course now I realize he was just hiding his feelings, because, you know, he couldn't have been *that* happy." He was "living real fast," doing things "on the spur of the moment," and of course neglecting his wife and son.

By 1952 he was also neglecting a second child, a daughter, named Janet Alexander. By that time Johnny had already left his wife and children and was alienated from the whole family. "He was our prodigal son," explains Norma. "I found out before I got pregnant with Janet that he wasn't no husband," Jean admits. "But I loved him."[48] According to Ernest Withers, Johnny's behavior is not accurately defined by such a middle-class term as "desertion": "Young fellows like that—they're wild and woolly. It's not really a philosophical desertion—they're just wild and go."[49]

Besides Jean and the children, Johnny's mother was the person most "hurt" by her son's irresponsibility toward his family and his career choice as a singer of secular music. Especially troublesome for her was his connection with rhythm and blues. The Alexander family had never permitted blues in the house. Mrs. Alexander listened to the radio during the day, but only to stations programming gospel music. (When Jean lived with her father, blues was permitted during the week but not on Sundays.) The taboo against the blues was a familiar pattern in the black community: there were not only moral and religious objections to blues music but class objections as well. Julian Bond, civil rights pioneer and Georgia politician, remembers from his own boyhood the extent to which R&B "was looked down on. It was low-class music, it was wild music, it was sexual music, it was 'dirty' music," he says. "So far as we were concerned, it was the most glamorous life in the world."[50]

"Our father was understanding because he was a man of the cloth," says Norma. "But all mother would say [about Johnny] is, 'He strayed from his training. I brought them up in the church—in the church choir—and he just drifted on out there in the world.'" Ironically, it was the minister-father who defended his wayward son (according to the family he defended everybody), who would maintain that God had a job for Johnny, a calling for him. Mrs. Alexander was the strict parent with the children, some of whom believed at the time they had "hung so much on the cross" they would never go to church again if they "ever got grown." This was especially true of the male siblings. Johnny and his brothers would "do anything to get out from under bondage. But they just drifted out too far," says Norma, "and they didn't come back." The man who lived next door to the Alexanders ("the one who used to tell on us all the time") is said to have observed that "when those boys got up to be adults they had been chained in the back yard so long they just went wild like a dog."[51]

Birth certificate of John Marshall Alexander, Jr. His mother later corrected the spelling of her first and last names, though the birthplace of his father (it was Mississippi) remained uncorrected.

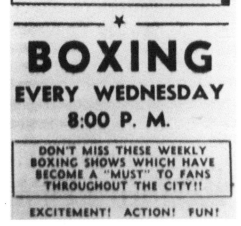

Publicity still of Ace taken in Houston in 1953 and first used in ads promoting "The Clock." (Courtesy of the Victor Pearlin Collection)

Above left: *The Beale Streeters at the WDIA studios in Memphis, late 1951 or 1952. Earl Forest, drums; Adolph "Billy" Duncan, saxophone; Bobby "Blue" Bland, vocals; John Alexander (Johnny Ace), piano. (Courtesy of Ernest Withers, Photographer)*

Left: *First appearance of Johnny Ace's name (misspelled) and photograph in his hometown Tri-State Defender (23 August 1952), in a display ad coupling two sides of the entertainment coin. The newspaper published the results of the boxing matches the next week, but it did not mention the Ace concert. (Courtesy of the Tri-State Defender)*

Facing page: *Johnny Ace at age twenty-three, in a publicity still taken in the spring of 1952 by Ernest C. Withers at his Beale Street studio. (Courtesy of Ernest Withers, Photographer)*

No		Title	45-3'.25:53	Artist	Label	Reference
	2274	Rosco's Mambo		Roscoe Gordon	Peacock	16382 B1
	2275	Three Cent Love		"	"	16382 B2
	2276	Meyers Bread Spots		Tommy Sands J Norman	Meyers	
	2277	Too Much		Roy Harris	Cobanian	16383 B4
	2278	Called You		" "	"	16383 B3
	2279	Make a Little Love With me			Diamond	16383 B2
	2280	Gonna Find my baby			"	16383 B1
	2281	Lonesome Blues		Hammond KB	Leiss	16384 B2
	2282	Take a Trip with me		"	Veisy	16384 B1
	2283	Why don't You Love me		Julius Tubb	Leisy	16384 A8
	2284	Any Time at all		"	Leiss	16384 A7
	2285	Cross My Heart		Johnny Ace	Duke	16385 A2
	2286	No Bread No Show		Bobby Bland	"	16385 A4
	2287	Wise Man's Blues		Bobby Blue	Duke	16386 B1
	2288	Burlycutie		Johnny Ace	"	16386 B3
	2289	Rockabye		Earl Forrest	Duke	16384 B3
	2290	Leaving Memphis		"	"	16384 B4
N-1	2291	Night Mare (openings)			John Norman	JN 105A
N-2	2292		33-34-35 30-37-38 16393	68	John Norman	JN 105B
N-3	2293	Night MARE!	39-40-41 47-4-43 16394	16-17	John Norman	JN 105B2
N-4	2294		44 45-46A 16395	18-19-20	"	16390 A
N-5	2295	Night Mare	50-32A-52 16375B 47-48-49 16389B	21-22-23	"	16390 B
N-6	2296		51-55 16396A -12- 16375	24-25-	"	16391 A
N-7	2297	Night MARE!		26-27	"	16391 B
N-8	2298	Night MARE!		27-28-29 30-31-2	"	16392
	2299	Hit & Run Drive		K.D. Houston		16387 A4
	2300	Blues Boogie				16387 B1

Audio Company of America (ACA) logbook page from August and September 1952. Numbers 2285–2290 document sessions in Houston by three members of the Beale Streeters, including Johnny Ace. Probably, all of these songs were first recorded in Memphis by David James Mattis and then re-recorded in Houston by Don Robey. (Logbook courtesy of Bill Holford)

Johnny Ace Orchestra on the road, 1953. The special Pontiac with Texas plates is equipped with a homemade luggage carrier. Ace's sisters, who were surprised to see this van one day in Memphis, flagged him down and asked him to go by the house to see his mother, wife, and children. (Courtesy of Ernest Withers, Photographer)

Headed For The No. 1 Spot

JOHNNY ACE
Vocals and Piano
Duke Records
From his first release, this silvery-voiced blues chanter has kept his name on the R&B best-seller charts. His "My Song" topped the retail list in September 1952, while "Cross My Heart," released this past January, is still riding high. Johnny's latest, "The Clock" b/w "Aces Wild" on Duke 112, is already clicking in the territories, and promises to be yet another smash.

TOP TEN

Collector's postcard from R&B Stars of 1953
(Milford, N.H.: Big Nickel Publications, 1987).
(Courtesy of Galen Gart, Big Nickel Publications)

"You've Been Gone So Long," a typical "B" side of an Ace record, is an Ace blues composition that sounds and feels like the regional rock 'n' roll style Charlie Gillett calls Chicago rhythm and blues. (Author's collection)

Above left: "Midnight Hours Journey," the first song John Alexander recorded, released in 1953 after he became famous. Ike Turner arranged this session for musicians associated with the Beale Streeters in 1951 at the Memphis YMCA for the Bihari brothers of Los Angeles. Drummer Earl Forest's "Trouble and Me" is the flip side of this rare record. (Author's collection)

Above right: "Saving My Love for You," Ace's fourth consecutive hit. The Duke Records logo, "borrowed" from the front end of a Cadillac, and the colors, purple and gold, represent the original design by David James Mattis, the label's founder. Eventually, Don Robey would eliminate the tagline "PEACOCK RECORDS AFFILIATE" but would retain "—Houston, Texas." (Author's collection)

ACA#	Title	Safety	Artist	W.O.#	Label	78's	Others	Remarks
2767	Feel Just Like I'm In love	M12364 B4	Jerry "Boogie" McCain	1049	TRUMPET	10" 1-19-54	45 1-19-54	TR 218 Dec 192
2768	Wine-O-Wine	M12364 B3	" "	"	"	10" 1-19-54	45 1-19-54	TR 217 Dec 190
2769	Going In Your Direction	M12364 B2	Sonny Boy Williamson	1048	"	10" 1-19-54	45 1-19-54	TR 216 Dec 188
2770	Keep It To Yourself	M12364 B1	" "		"	10" 1-19-54	45 1-19-54	TR 215 Dec 186
2771	Red Hot Kisses	M12364 A4	" "		"	10" 1-19-54	45 1-19-54	TR 216 Dec 187
2772	Getting Out of Town	M12364 A3	" "		"	10" 1-19-54	45 1-19-54	TR 215 Dec 185
2773	Tyke Police	M12365 A3	Ray Coats · Cotton Cracker Pen	1099	Shamrock	10" 11-18-54		
2774	My heart I	M12365 A4	" "	"		" "		
2775	I'm Gonna Get You Baby		MARY ROBERTS	1101	PEACOCK			
2776	I've Got A Li'l Man		" "	"	DUKE			
2777	Baby What's Your Truth Don't Want		" "	"	DUKE			
2778	If You Had Realized		" "	"	DUKE			
2779	Since I've Changed The Heart of Mine	M12380 A1	Bells of Joy	1105	Peacock	9-27-54	9-27-54	
2780	Go Down Sinner	M12380 A2	" " "	"	"			
2781	So Hard Remember Me	M12380 A3	" " "	"	"			
2782	When I end Began	M12380 A4	" " "	"	"			
2783	There's A Hand Leading Me	M12380 B1	" " "	"	"			
2784	Live Right Every Day	M12380 B2	" " "	"	"			
2785	Step By Step	M12376 B1	The Charriettes	1106	Duke	6-3-54	45 6-3-54	
2786	The God I Serve	M12376 B2	" "	"	"			
2787	Drop Me Jesus (Cause you Brought up	M12376 B3	" "	"	"	6-3-54	45 6-3-54	
2788	Rest In Heaven	M12376 B4	"	"	"	6-3-54	45 6-3-54	
2789	A Home Up Yonder	M12376 A1	" "	"	"			
2790	Destination Heaven	M12376 A2	" "	"	"			
2791	New Pray it Dear	M12380 B3	THE SULTANS	1108	Duke	10" 3-8-54	45 3-8-54	
2792	Good Time Baby	M12380 B4	" "	"	"	10" 3-8-54	45 3-8-54	
2793	I Cried My Heart Out	M12381 A1	" "	"	"	10" 8-10-54	45 8-10-54	
2794	Baby Don't Put Me Down	M12381 A2	" "	"	"	10" 8-10-54	45 8-10-54	
2795	Lost My Baby		Junior Ryder	1109	Duke			
2796	Don't Tell Nobody		"	"	"	1 1-10-55	45 1-10-55	
2797	Every Star I See		"	"	"	1 1-10-55	45 1-10-55	
2798	Anymore	M12386 B3	Johnny Ace	1112	Duke			No Master Cut Tape Filed org
2799	So Lonely	M12386 B4	" "	"	"			
2800	You've Been Gone too Long	M12386 A3	" "	"	"	4-14-54	45 4-14-54	
2801	Pledging My Love	M12387 A1	" "	"	"	12-2-54	45 12-2-54	
2802	THE SHAPE I'm In		Marie Adams	1111	Peacock			

Audio Company of America logbook page from January 1954, the session that included "Pledging My Love" (ACA 2801). Note the columns at the right: Bill Holford mastered both 78 and 45 rpm versions of "Pledging My Love" on the same day. This record was the first for Duke or Peacock to sell more 45s than 78s. (Logbook courtesy of Bill Holford)

Beale Street

Five Dollars a

Night and All

the Chili You

Can Eat

The perfect place for a young black man to go wild in Memphis
was Beale Street, the tenderloin area black Memphis businessman
George W. Lee called in 1934 "the Main Street of Negro America." "There are many other streets upon which the Negro lives and
moves," he wrote, "but only one Beale Street. As a breeding place
of smoking, red-hot syncopation, compared to it, Harlem, State
Street, and all the rest of the streets and communities of Negro
America famed in story and song are but playthings."[1] Daytime
Beale Street was a seven-block section from the Mississippi River
to Wellington Street (now Danny Thomas Boulevard). At night, virtually all of the "social action" took place on two Beale Street blocks
bordered by the Hotel Men's Improvement Club on Third Street
and Handy Park on Hernando Street. The Palace and Daisy Theaters, the Harlem House, the Midway Cafe, the One-Minute Cafe,
the Mitchell Hotel, the Club Handy, and Robert Henry's Pool Hall,
were all in this area.

According to William Barlow, post-Reconstruction Beale Street
was "the major thoroughfare in the Memphis red-light district,"

with the same "musical and cultural dynamics" as legendary Storyville in New Orleans. "Black migrants were an integral component of the red-light districts of both cities," he says; "they brought the rural blues with them and adapted the music's style and content to their new urban setting." The "outlaw subculture" that dominated Beale Street in Memphis was another characteristic patterned after New Orleans, Barlow says: African Americans "were seldom the owners of the tenderloin establishments and vice operations; mostly they were employees or customers."[2] "The saying on Beale," according to Margaret McKee, "was that the Jews had the pawn shops and the dry goods stores, the Greeks had the restaurants, the Italians had the entertainment—the theaters, the saloons, the gambling—and the blacks were the customers."[3]

Beale Street also served as a kind of beacon for African Americans, says McKee, becoming "as much a symbol of escape from despair" as the underground railroad. Invariably, black unemployment in Memphis was high, standard pay for black labor low, and black housing substandard and crowded. But on Beale "you could find surcease from sorrow; on Beale you could forget for a shining moment the burden of being black and celebrate being black; on Beale you could be a man, your own man; on Beale you could be free."[4] Especially, George W. Lee wrote in his *Beale Street: Where the Blues Began*, the pulse of freedom quickened on weekends:

> All day long every Saturday Beale Street is thronged by country people from Arkansas, North Mississippi and West Tennessee who arrive in the early morning in their wagons, their fords [*sic*], or on horseback. They bargain with the Jews for clothing, buy groceries at the Piggly-wiggly and fish and pork chops of the Greek, and sometimes moonshine in the "blind pigs." They leave at sundown to cross the Arkansas bridge or journey down the Hernando Road to their homes sleeping along the banks of the muddy Mississippi. Saturday night belongs to the cooks, maids, houseboys and factory hands.[5]

Despite Lee's assertion that Beale Street was "where the blues began, the birthplace of America's most popular music,"[6] there is no evidence that the blues *as a form* was invented on Beale Street. W. C. Handy only claimed credit for the composition and publication of blues tunes, but it is true that Memphis had been a blues town since the blues began. One of the first published blues song was Handy's "Memphis Blues" (1912), and his "Beale

Street Blues" (1916) certainly helped launch the form's popularity on a mass level. The first major venue for black music opened in 1899—a two thousand seat auditorium at Church Park, built by Memphis millionaire Robert Church specifically for the African American community.[7] The blues were performed at Church Park first, but by the 1920s the music showcased further down on Beale Street: at the Palace Theater and the saloons, restaurants, and brothels. According to Memphis Slim, Memphis was already famous by that time as a "piano city," and Beale Street was unique because its blues featured more pianos than guitars. "In most cities in the South it was guitars and harmonicas," he says, "[but] in Memphis it was pianos because the Italians were running everything and they had all these little houses with a piano in there and a piano player."[8]

During the Depression, Beale Street flourished. Businesses attracted large crowds, live music continued to be performed in saloons (one owner supported a soup kitchen with his profits), and Boss Crump, in an attempt to protect white public facilities, dedicated a park on Beale and Hernando to blues great W. C. Handy.[9] But it was also Crump who was responsible for shutting down the "high life" on Beale Street in 1940, Margaret McKee says: "Beale's joints were told to ply their trade in other cities, the bookies were ordered to fold up shop, and Beale entered into a new era."[10] George W. Lee called the change "the mysterious police shut-down order that made Beale Street like a graveyard and drove its bootleggers and gamblers into panhandling."[11]

The blues culture survived, however, and by the end of World War II the Beale Street area of Memphis remained a flourishing center of blues activity—second only to Chicago. Chicago, said to be the urban blues capital of America, had a blues culture influenced by the recent wartime migration of southern blacks to the city, but the postwar Memphis scene represented the unique Deep South consequence of a historic and large African American population existing within the framework of an official social system of racial segregation.

The 1950 census revealed that white median income in Memphis was $2,264 and black income $986—figures comparable to Atlanta, Birmingham, and New Orleans.[12] Memphis supported separate black schools and parks, required separate black restrooms, ran water to separate black drinking fountains. Its residents ate in separate restaurants, frequented separate businesses, read separate newspapers, rooted for separate minor league baseball teams: the Memphis Chicks (white) and the Memphis Blues (black). Stores downtown offered separate white and black lunch counters. There was even a black version of the official Memphis Cotton Carnival called the Cotton Maker's Jubilee—a knockoff of the white original that became in the postwar era more popular with both black and white citizens than the white version. There was the predictable situation on Beale Street of businesses being owned by whites catering to an exclusively black clientele, but there was at least one black-owned business for white-only clients: Jim's Barber Shop, at the corner of Beale and Main, where all the employees were black but who refused to barber, manicure, or shampoo anybody who was not white. Louis Cantor calls such aberrations "strange accommodations between the races."[13]

Jim Crow laws prohibited whites and blacks from attending the same indoor shows, but some Beale Street clubs offered special "white-only" performances, and white audiences could see the all-black Midnight Rambles at the Palace Theater on Beale every Thursday night. "On Thursday nights the block belongs to the white people," George Lee observed. "They come in evening dress in high-powered cars, in overalls and Fords, to see the scantily clad brown beauties dancing across the stage in the midnight show at the Palace."[14] The Midnight Rambles virtually reversed the power relationships in a Jim Crow world. "Of all segregation's peculiar manifestations," Louis Cantor says, "this has to be one of the most bizarre. Taking a cue from New York's Cotton Club, here was an all-black show, performed right on Beale Street—in the very heart of the black community—restricted to an all-white audience."[15]

Sometimes the color line caused serious logistical problems for management. Andrew Chaplin Jr., a drummer, remembers a gig he played "out on the highway" with an all-black band for a white-only audience. "And they had this white stripper," he says. "And we'd play up until the time for her to come on. Then they'd put this sheet up in front of us, so we couldn't see her dancing, you know. They didn't want blacks to see the naked white woman."[16]

Mostly, however, Beale Street represented black entertainment for black people, "a black man's haven," according to Rufus Thomas. Thomas, best known as a soul singer, was a WDIA radio personality who wrote, recorded, and emceed in postwar Memphis. "That was a neighborhood down there," he says. "It wasn't just the one street. You had thousands and thousands of people living in that area. Lights never go out down there. It was just a way of life."[17] To B.B. King, it was "a fantasy coming true. . . . It was a place kind of like a little world all of your own. I didn't think of Memphis as Memphis. I thought of *Beale Street* as Memphis."[18] For Evelyn Young, a saxophone player with the Bill Harvey Band that toured with B.B. King, Beale was like Harlem. "You had to ask folks 'Excuse me,' there was so many people down there," she says. "So many people on Beale Street it was just like New York."[19]

Another similarity was the regular Tuesday night Amateur Night at the Palace Theater, believed to have drawn a more demanding audience than New York's Apollo Theater. The Apollo may have had a man with a hook who pulled offending talent off the stage, but the Palace, nicknamed the "Graveyard of Champions," had a Lord High Executioner of Beale Street who "executed" them on the spot with a pearl-handled revolver that fired blanks.[20] Clearly, black culture in Memphis was not only rich in tradition but full-seasoned in heritage. Harry Martin pointed out in his foreword to *Beale Street Sundown* that Beale "was Afro-American when Harlem was still paying homage to the Dutch."[21]

Beale Street covered the spectrum of African American popular musical sounds. "You got it all on Beale Street," Rufus Thomas says. "If you wanted rhythm and blues, gut-bucket blues, medium blues, like when B.B. came along, you got it all. Everything you wanted when it came to music, you could get it on Beale Street."[22] What Thomas calls "medium blues" and attributes to B.B. King is, in fact, a unique postwar style that caused Memphis to challenge Chicago as a blues center. As Charles Keil explains: "Although older singers in Chicago were for the most part maintaining the country and city traditions in the bars and clubs of the South Side, a younger group of men in Memphis were in the process of creating the blues style that is most popular among urban Negroes today [1966]. Johnny Ace, Gatemouth Moore, and [Rosco] Gordon were the first major talents."[23]

In his phylogenetic order of blues styles Keil calls the Memphis contribution the "Memphis synthesis," a term denoting the bridge between two separate sounds: the hard urban blues of the "Territories and Kansas City" represented by Louis Jordan, and the softer "Postwar Texas" sound of T-Bone Walker. The "1st phase" of this Memphis synthesis, according to Keil, was represented by Ace, Moore, and Gordon; the "2nd phase" included B.B. King, early Bobby Blue Bland, and Junior Parker.[24]

By the 1950s Beale Street was not only "the Main Street of Negro America," but Memphis itself was "the Mid-South capital of black entertainment." In October 1948, Memphis radio station WDIA began to change its white audience format ("classical, pop and country-western music in 15 to 60 minute segments")[25] to all-black music serving the area's almost 47 percent black population. "As the first radio station in the country to beam its signal exclusively to a black audience," Louis Cantor says, "WDIA began a media revolution that not only drastically changed radio formats throughout the country, it inevitably uplifted the dignity of the black people living within the sound of its huge broadcast voice."

While the decision to change to an all-black format was purely a business one (the station immediately raised its advertising rates) and while management was convinced that the "station could do its best work by concentrating less on integration . . . and more on showcasing the separate accomplishments of blacks on the air," the voice of WDIA generated black pride and "fostered positive black identity at a time when there was very little opportunity in the country for blacks to demonstrate it."[26]

This historic moment in southern radio came at 4:00 P.M. on 25 October 1948, when Nat D. Williams began his "Tan Town Jamboree" with what Cantor calls a "guttural belly laugh" that was "highly infectious, instantly putting his audience at ease."[27] Nat D. became the "Jackie Robinson of radio" and the South's first black male disk jockey publicly promoted as such on the air.[28] According to Cantor, WDIA represented "a celebration of firsts": the first radio station in America "with a format designed exclusively for a black audience," the first "to present an open forum to discuss black problems," and the first all-black station "to go 50,000 watts," permitting WDIA by 1954 to claim that it could "reach an incredible 10 percent of the total black population of the United States."[29]

The station's successful R&B and Gospel format was studied and copied so heavily that WDIA deserved to call itself the "Mother Station of the Negroes."[30] "I can recall how Beale Street and WDIA was so closely related," Rufus Thomas says. "People like B.B. King, Johnny Ace, who was on his way, then there was Gatemouth Moore and Hot Rod Hulbert. There was nobody, nobody like Hot Rod. And Rosco Gordon, Nat D. [Williams], the father of all the black disk jockeys here in the South. And Bobby Bland, who today is one of the premier blues singers of the world. Even me. But I think WDIA played the most important part of all of our careers."[31]

The story of B.B. King's "second bid for success in Memphis," as told by Charles Sawyer, is a good example of how important the WDIA connection was for Beale Street performers: live music and WDIA airplay were synergistic. Riley B. King had tried to establish a musical career in Memphis in 1946. At that time he was a twenty year-old Mississippi sharecropper with $2.50 in his pocket and in trouble with his boss, to whom he owed money. After ten months, he returned to Indianola and raised another crop of cotton. But the next year, 1948, everything seemed to click. King booked his first Memphis gig across the river at the Sixteenth Street Grill in West Memphis by performing on Sonny Boy Williamson's radio show on KWEM, a station famous for featuring the electrified Delta blues of Howlin' Wolf. King then became a regular featured artist at the Sixteenth Street Grill by securing his own radio show on WDIA and promising to plug his live engagements on the air.

At first, his radio show was only ten minutes long, but he was heard daily as an advertiser for the health tonic Pepticon. As he developed a following in the Tri-State area of Tennessee, Arkansas, and Mississippi, he promoted his radio show wherever he played live, and promoted his personal appearances on WDIA. His popularity grew, leading to a longer radio show, "Sepia Swing Club," which required a catchier name than "Riley" for a full-fledged WDIA disk jockey host.

According to his biographer, King became "Beale Street Blues Boy," later modified to "Blues Boy King," and finally shortened to "B.B. King."[32] There is another story as to how King got his name, however. In early 1952, the *Tri-State Defender*—the local newspaper serving the Memphis black community—reported that King's "public had christened him the 'singing black boy' from Mississippi," and that this "public-donated nick-name of 'Black Boy'" led to a shortened "B.B."[33] Whatever the genesis of his stage name, his celebrity as WDIA radio personality "B.B. King" produced more lucrative opportunities for personal appearances, some of which required the support services of a backup band. When King began to assemble a suitable group of sidemen, one of the first Memphis musicians he hired was pianist John Alexander Jr.[34]

The precise origin of this band, known finally as the Beale Streeters, is unclear. In an interview with Arnold Shaw, King recalls that he first performed on WDIA alone, then added pianist John Alexander and drummer Earl Forest to make a radio trio; later, sax player Adolph "Billy" Duncan made the group a quartet.[35] "I guess you could say this was the first little-bitty B.B. King band," King says in his autobiography.[36] For live performances in the clubs, there was apparently no set lineup, only a loose confederation of musicians who came and went. Charles Sawyer posits one explanation for the irregularity: King was so musically crude at the time that many musicians were embarrassed to play with him in public.[37]

Nick Tosches suggests that by the end of 1949 the lineup included King on guitar, John Alexander on piano, Robert Calvin Bland ("Bobby 'Blue' Bland") on vocals, and Duncan on tenor sax.[38] No bassist is ever mentioned in connection with the group, but it is generally agreed that Earl Forest was the regular drummer. Ernestine Mitchell, who with her husband, Andrew "Sunbeam" Mitchell, ran the Mitchell Hotel and the Club Handy on Beale Street, remembers Rosco Gordon as a member of this group (Bobby Bland drove for Gordon as his chauffeur) that played throughout the Tri-State area,[39] and Peter Grendysa also lists Gordon as one of the "loosely-knit bunch of musicians and singers called the Beale Streeters."[40]

Charles Keil attempted to establish major dates and events in the late forties/early fifties Memphis scene for his *Urban Blues* (1966) but was unsuccessful. Though he was able at that time to interview B.B. King, Bobby Bland, and Junior Parker, he found himself "still confused about developments in Memphis during this period" and attributed that to the reluctance of the musicians to reexamine the "wild oats" phases of their careers.[41] St. Clair Alexander believes his brother "got hooked up with B.B.'s band in 1948 or '49." He tried on several occasions to see the band perform at the Mitchell Hotel, but he was only a teenager, and "the people at the door knew he was." The women in the Alexander family had almost no information about what Johnny was doing in this period. His wife knew he was "singing down on Beale Street" in 1950 but had no knowledge of him being part of King's band. Bobby Bland, however, remembers the group performing at "Sunbeam" Mitchell's Club Handy for "five dollars a night and all the chili they could eat."[42]

Andrew "Sunbeam" Mitchell was a beloved figure in postwar Memphis, especially among Beale Street musicians. "Sunbeam Mitchell was the godfather for the musicians in Memphis," B.B. King says. "Anytime you didn't have any money, or anything, you could always go get a room and a bowl of chili."[43] According to Mitchell, "Musicians didn't have nowhere to go. . . . And so we had to take them and put them up in the hotel and give them that chili, the best you could eat. Give 'em that chili and then sometimes they'd play a gig."[44] Mitchell was the proprietor of several businesses during this period, including the Mitchell Grill at 195 S. Third and the Club Ebony at 500 Beale Street. His primary enterprise, however, was the Mitchell Hotel, which occupied the third floor above the Pantaze Drug Store ("You Never Pay More, Often Less") at the corner of Beale and Hernando.

The Mitchell Hotel opened in 1944 and was billed as "Memphis' Leading Colored Hotel." After Mitchell got into the nightclub business, it was natural to use the facility to lodge visiting musicians. Ernestine McKinney (later Mrs. Andrew Mitchell) kept the books and managed the hotel. During the fifties, the Mitchells opened Club Handy on the second floor of the Pantaze Building, below the hotel, with an entrance at 195 Hernando. Club Handy turned out to be the last blues nightclub on Beale Street to book headline acts on a regular basis before development and restoration of the district as an Urban Renewal Area in the 1970s.[45]

The family of John Alexander Jr. felt that he practically lived at the Mitchell Hotel, and he may have. After leaving his pregnant wife at his parents' house at 899 Fisher in 1950, Johnny did not have, in the four years remaining of his life, a residence more permanent than the Mitchell Hotel. When he died it was the Mitchells who were left with his clothes and personal effects. Many other Memphis blues musicians called the Mitchell Hotel home as well; it was the place on Beale Street famous for ending the day. "We never did close because somebody was constantly coming in," Ernestine Mitchell remembers: "Like all the fellows play on gigs someplace else? When they got off they'd come and get some chili. I don't care if it was West Memphis or where ever they was, they would come. I don't care how far they was, all of them, carloads of them, would stop by. Then they'd get to talking, drinking, then jamming. That was just a nightly thing."[46]

"I can remember many nights sitting back and watching the great jam sessions," B.B. King says, "because after the show usually everybody would go up to Mitchell's." According to Evelyn Young, musicians in those days "played all day, and we played all night. No stopping. . . . Nobody ever got tired of playing." Rufus Thomas remembers that the players, mostly men, would come in with their instruments and listen to the jam session before deciding to join it. If it was "too hot for him," he says, he would "take that horn and ease right back out the door."[47]

The leader of the Club Handy house band was Bill Harvey, a tenor sax player whose all-Memphis horn section began a seven year association with

Don Robey's Peacock Records in Houston in 1950.[48] Later, Harvey's band would tour with B.B. King, and some of his players would end up in Johnny Ace's road band. "Harvey was a learned musician with a passion for teaching," Charles Sawyer says, "and the Club Handy was a kind of Academy of Rhythm and Blues. . . . The joint was small, and it was combined with limited hotel accommodations: in fact, some of the sleeping rooms opened directly into the barroom itself. Harvey's musicians lived in the hotel and ate in Mrs. Mitchell's kitchen, while Harvey schooled them in basic musicianship. Over the years, dozens of young musicians cut their chops in Harvey's makeshift school."[49] "Bill played a band like Willie Mays played the outfield," B.B. King says. "He had it covered."[50]

For performers and audiences in the postwar era, all of the Beale Street club accommodations were on the primitive side. Booker T. Laury remembers what it was like in the summer to play piano in Beale clubs before air conditioning: "They had standing fans and fans to sit on top of the piano, and sometimes they'd be waving, fan you with paper, you know, with the newspaper. And it'd be hot and sweat'd be rolling off and they'd be out there dancing wringing wet, and the little room'd be hot—no air stirring through the windows. It was uncomfortable but it was real enjoyable. The ladies'd support me and they're pouring that corn whiskey in me."[51]

Unsatisfactory working conditions on Beale did not represent a unique Memphis phenomenon, however. *Billboard* reported in 1946 that the hardships "suffered by Negro bands touring the South" were well known, and while the trade magazine specifically condemned the lodging problem ("they often have to choose between vermin-infested hotels or the band bus"), it also criticized general logistics as well. "All of this, in addition to filthy cafes, third-class hotels, poor or no valet service, long jumps on tar-gravel roads, crippled pianos and buzzing p.-a. systems," the magazine concluded, "make the South the least attractive hinterland area to musicians."[52] In Memphis, Beale Street clubs may not have measured up to the professional standards of all the clubs in Harlem, but the Mitchell Hotel provided quite desirable housing for black performers on the road.

The pay scale on Beale Street was not good either. It was common knowledge that musicians made reputations rather than money in Memphis. In B.B. King's words, it was like "dropping the pebble first on Beale Street and then the wave started like that. So if you was talked about well on Beale Street, you could always get a job. But the better jobs, the better paying job, was after you left."[53] There was, however, something else special about Beale Street for black performers headquartered in the city—an umbilical relationship that held them physically and emotionally, requiring their physical presence by the end of the day. George W. Lee attempted to describe the feeling in *Beale Street Sundown:*

> So, when the long quiet day is done, night falls from heaven on a blues heaven all packed with brown humans who rise as if out of a miasmic dream to dance and grimace in the streets; blind men on the corner drag their souls up from the dusk covered street and sing out the blues beneath the stars; dark humans lift their faces up to the moon; dark forms sway to street songs, banjo songs, songs that pulse with life—the kind of life known to Beale Street and its crowded honky tonks; then a delicate flush of gold comes into the Eastern skies like the flush on the face of a rose, and one last song comes rushing with the drift of the wind: "I'd rather be there than any place I know."[54]

"In other words," says B.B. King, "if we went to West Memphis, if we went to Hernando, if we went someplace, you'd go and play, but you'd still try to get back to Beale Street before everything closed." Ernestine Mitchell, who was usually at the hotel at night, recalls how the musicians would come in and say, "We know Mitchell's open. We can go up there and get sober now."[55]

A band consisting of B.B. King (guitar), John Alexander (piano), Earl Forest (drums), Billy Duncan (sax), and Bobby Bland, (vocals) comprised the group known to have eaten well and to have played at the Mitchell Hotel. The Beale Streeters were, according to Nick Tosches, "the premier band of Memphis throughout 1950 and 1951."[56] Louis Cantor recalls that WDIA could always count on a musical group that included B.B. King to perform at the popular WDIA Goodwill Revues during this period.[57] On 21 November 1951, the secular part of the third annual revue featured, among others, Nat Williams, Joe Hill Louis, Ford Nelson, Onzie Horn and his Vibraphone, and B.B. King's aggregation, probably the Beale Streeters with John Alexander on piano, who were billed as "Bee Bee's Jeebies." For the "hour of religious music," the Spirit of Memphis Quartet received top billing, with other performances by the Rev. W. H. Brewster's Brewsteraires, the Southern Wonders, and the Songbirds of the South.[58] According to one eyewitness, B.B. King's group stole the show: "Dr. King cures headaches, heartaches and backaches . . . corns, bunions and onions, give sight to the blind . . . and at last nite's GOODWILL REVUE he was called on to raise the dead. He's the only doctor in the world who carries his pills in a guitar case and who operates wherever he finds the patient . . . Yes, Dr. King cures everything with his now world's famous . . . Bee Bee's Jeebies . . . on WDIA at 1 o'clock Mon. thru Fri."[59]

The postwar Memphis sound of the Beale Streeters had more than just local appeal, however, since it was considered more modern and sophisticated than blues performed in other regions. "The Beale Streeters," Gary Giddins says "were more sophisticated. King knew about Django Reinhardt as well as T-Bone Walker and Scrapper Blackwell; Bland had grown up listening to country music before he was seduced by gospel; [John Alexander] knew the pop singers as well as Joe Turner."[60] Eventually, all three Beale Streeters would register Top 20 pop hits. Bland began to penetrate the pop charts in the early 1960s, when soul music turned mainstream. His biggest hit, "Ain't Nothing You Can Do," was released during the frenzy of the British Invasion in early 1964. King's success came later, after the blues revival of the late 1960s created room for black urban bluesmen. "The Thrill Is Gone" (1970) represents his greatest pop achievement. John Alexander paved the way for both. His "Pledging My Love" would cross over to pop in early 1955—before black pride, before soul, before the blues revival, even before Bill Haley's "Rock Around the Clock" began the rock 'n' roll explosion.

This child didn't do nothing but
go somewhere and get on a piano.
—Norma (Alexander) Williams

Signing Your Mama Away

A Name from the Devil's Game

In spite of the sophistication of the musicians and the rich musical heritage of the area, Memphis did not have a local record label until 1950. Of the hundreds of new independent record labels made possible by the technology of the tape recorder in the postwar era, few were established in southern cities. The most active southern recording location in the early 1950s was Houston, where three labels operated in the blues field (Macy's, Freedom, and Peacock) and one had already folded (Gold Star).[1] Besides Jackson, Mississippi (Trumpet), the only other southern cities with independent labels were in Tennessee: Nashville (Nashboro-Ernie Y and Bullet) and Gallatin (Dot), an operation that eventually became famous for releasing white versions of black records. While it appeared that independent record making had ignored the plethora of musical talent on Beale Street and left Memphis behind, there was, in fact, significant recording activity going on in the city, though it was being released on out-of-town labels.

Sam Phillips, owner of Memphis Recording Service at 706 Union ("We Record Anything—Anywhere—Anytime"), and Dewey Phillips (no relation), the "Red, Hot, and Blue" disk jockey on station WHBQ, launched a record company called Phillips in the summer of 1950 ("The Hottest Thing in the Country"), but it folded after releasing one record by Joe Hill Louis. Louis, known as the "Be-Bop Boy" on WDIA, sang in a primitive, country blues style and played three instruments (drums, harmonica, and guitar) at once.[2] What is revealing in the Louis venture is not the failure of the project but Sam Phillips's instinct to record an authentic blues performer. Black music had been part of his youth in the Florence, Alabama, area, and he had discovered Beale Street as a high school boy in 1939. "I was 16 years old," he remembers, "and I went to Memphis with some friends in a big old Dodge. We drove down Beale Street in the middle of the night and it was rockin'! The street was busy. It was active—musically, socially. God, I loved it!"[3]

Sam Phillips at the time was more interested in recording music than in making records. He had already recorded songs by Memphis blues and country performers for the West Coast label 4-Star. He established Phillips Records in 1950 only when that relationship withered. He had also been recording another musician and WDIA disk jockey, B.B. King, whom he offered to the Biharis brothers in Los Angeles. Joe, Saul, and Jules Bihari already owned Modern Records and were planning a subsidiary label, RPM. According to Colin Escott, the Biharis "were looking for new music with a down-home feel." They found enough of that in the King material to contract for ten of the songs recorded at Memphis Recording Service. Phillips also placed Joe Hill Louis with RPM, but after falling out with the Biharis brothers less than a year after he started doing business with them he moved Louis again to Chess Records in Chicago.[4] One result of the dispute between Sam Phillips and the Biharis was that Modern/RPM established its own presence in Memphis to compete with Memphis Recording Service.

The conflict with the Biharis began in March 1951, when Phillips recorded Ike Turner's band performing several blues numbers, including "Rocket 88," a shuffle-blues that featured the voice of Turner's cousin and saxophone player, Jackie Brenston. Instead of sending dubs to the Biharis, Phillips sent them to the Chess Brothers in Chicago. "Phillips probably thought he could supply repertoire to both Chess and Modern without conflict," Colin Escott believes, "and hoped to impress Chess with a strong initial cut."[5] The Biharis apparently believed that they had a monopoly on Phillips's Memphis sessions, and they were furious when "Rocket 88" hit the national R&B chart in May—finally becoming the top R&B song in the country—for a competitor.

While the success of this record convinced Phillips he could quit his day job at station WREC and devote full-time effort to the recording business, one problem that continued to complicate his new career was the new, hostile relationship with the Biharis brothers. When Phillips attempted to shift some of the other artists he recorded from RPM to Chess, he found himself embroiled in another conflict. For a few months, in fact, both RPM and Chess released sides by Rosco Gordon and Howlin' Wolf, sometimes even the same songs. (The compromise finally reached gave Gordon to RPM and Howlin' Wolf to Chess.) In addition, Ike Turner, angry at Phillips for not getting him a record of his own, denied the use of his band for a Jackie Brenston follow-up to "Rocket 88." As a result, Brenston failed, and Turner left Phillips to join the Biharis' Modern/RPM operation as their Memphis-based talent scout and producer.[6] In his new role, Turner arranged for the Biharis to audition a Beale Streeters lineup of B.B. King, John Alexander, Bobby Bland, and Rosco Gordon.

Though the Biharis brothers traveled around the country in late model Cadillacs, they had a reputation for "scrimping" on expenses—for paying their out-of-town production costs, for example, but avoiding hotel bills by sleeping overnight in the recording studio.[7] For their first set of recording sessions in Memphis, the Biharis set up their portable tape recorder at two locations selected, perhaps, for their economy: the Memphis YMCA on Lauderdale and Vance, and local music teacher Tuff Green's house. The YMCA, Joe Bihari remembers, offered "a large room with an out-of-tune upright piano," altered acoustically by hanging rugs over the windows.[8] This session is famous for producing King's "Three O'Clock Blues" and Gordon's "No More Doggin'"—records that reached the number one and two positions on the national R&B charts in early 1952.

John Alexander played piano on some of the more obscure sides cut by Bobby Bland and B.B. King at this session,[9] and he also recorded his first vocal track: a smooth blues ballad, "Midnight Hours Journey." It was not released until 1953, when it was coupled with Earl Forest's "Trouble and Me" and issued on the Biharis' Flair label. "Midnight Hours Journey" was clearly not a priority cut at this 1951 session at the YMCA because it is so seriously flawed. The introduction to the soft blues number is inappropriately short (due probably to musicians talking at the beginning of the song), the speakers delivering the vibraphone sound are overdriven, and the microphone level on the vocal is set too high, distorting the singer's voice. The song itself, credited to "Josea" (most likely a cryptographic pseudonym for Joe, Jules, and Saul Bihari) is a precursor of the kind of sad and soft material for which the singer would eventually be famous.

"When those midnight hours journey," he sings, "I was in my bed alone." He came home in the evening, he explains, and his woman was gone. "It's a miserable old feeling," he says, "when you lose the one you love." Though in his life John Alexander was better at leaving loved ones than losing them, he is absolutely convincing as a casualty of love; the blues are simply getting him down. "To get the blues at midnight," he sings persuasively, "it's one thing you can't describe. When you look at your woman's picture, tears will fall from your eyes." Though imperfect from an engineering standpoint, "Midnight Hours Journey" is a good example of what would later be described as the "Memphis Transition." Billy Duncan's saxophone work is effective in the arrangement and Onzie Horn's vibraphone solo is lovely. As for John Alexander's vocal debut, it is a good start. While his interpretation of this soft blues lyric is appropriately mournful, his voice clearly communicates professional confidence.

When "Three O'Clock Blues" hit *Billboard*'s R&B record chart after Christmas in 1951, B.B. King became the first Beale Streeter to develop a following outside of the Tri-State area. Of course he was a Memphis celebrity at this time, and local businessman Robert Henry had seen his promise. Henry signed him to a personal management contract and bought him some decent clothes at Nat Epstein's, a leading establishment in Beale Street's noted pawnshop district.[10] When "Three O'Clock Blues" became the number one R&B song in the nation in early 1952, Henry was able to sign King up with a big-time booking agency: United Artists of New York. King joined other acts, all to be backed by the well-known Tiny Bradshaw Band, on a tour that included appearances at the major black theaters in Washington, D.C. (Howard), Baltimore (Royal), and New York (Apollo).

King, who had never been as far north as Washington, D.C., soon discovered that the Beale Street pawnshop clothes he wore on stage were inappropriate for an artist at his new level. He also recognized that the expense of expanding his seven-piece musical charts into arrangements for a full, eighteen-piece orchestra was not only necessary but unavoidable. It didn't take King long, however, to "look hip," sound "like a million bucks," and take "the audience with him like a Pied Piper."[11] With King having gone on to bigger and better things, John Alexander essentially inherited the Beale Streeters band. Johnny's good looks "left the girls swooning," Charles Sawyer observes, and his good voice was essentially wasted in King's band. "It was natural," he says, "for B.B. to turn the band over to Alexander when he left Memphis for his first big gig in the real urban North at the Washington Howard [Theater]. John Alexander put the opportunity to good advantage."[12]

David James Mattis, the program director at WDIA and the founder of Duke Records, is the man generally credited with changing John Alexander's name to Johnny Ace and launching his recording career. According to Mattis, known in Memphis by his radio name, David James, he not only named the act ("Johnny" for Johnny Ray and "Ace" for the Four Aces) but the backup band as well ("I named them [the Beale Streeters] because I thought it'd look good on the label").[13] It may have happened differently. Robert Palmer suggests that the name Beale Streeters was given to the group by people who observed the musicians' "taste for the high life of black Memphis's main thoroughfare."[14] In the case of the singer's stage name, St. Clair Alexander's understanding is that when David James told his brother, "We can't call you John Marshall Alexander, Jr." and changed his first name to Johnny, Johnny said, 'Well, just call me Ace, but don't let my momma know, because I'm the ace in the hole. Don't let her know, cause the first thing she'll want to know is what is an ace.'"

With the strict, Christian life pursued by Mrs. Leslie Alexander she would have known little about cards, but she certainly would have despaired had she known that her son was singing the devil's music, sporting a name from the devil's own game. Worse, perhaps, was the aura of death that the name implied within the gambling culture of postwar Beale Street. "Ace was always a dead man's card, a dead man's hand in poker," says St. Clair Alexander. "You come up with a bunch of aces, they think you're cheating, and you'd be killed. They called that a dead man's hand." There is understandable speculation concerning the effect that singing rhythm and blues had on the relationship between John Alexander Jr. and his father, much of it centering around the stage name "Johnny Ace." Nick Tosches claims that "it was understood from the beginning" that the Alexander surname was not to be used on Johnny's records "so that his father, the Reverend, might be saved from any shame,"[15] but according to the family, the Rev. Mr. Alexander never felt shamed, and father and son were never personally estranged.

David James Mattis, the man who "discovered" Johnny Ace, taught cadets how to fly during World War II at a civilian aviation facility in Tuscaloosa, Alabama, before enlisting himself and flying missions in India and Burma. After his discharge from the Air Force he attended broadcasting school, taking his first radio job as an announcer at KYJK in Forest City, Arkansas, where he became "Cousin Jesse" for his hillbilly show and "The Boogie Man" when he played blues records. It was in Forest City that he learned that many black performers were so eager to be on the air that they would pay for the privilege.[16] "That's where I met Howlin' Wolf and Sonny Boy Williamson and Little Jr. Parker," he recalls. "They used to come over and buy fifteen minutes once a week. They'd pay for this time. That was the standard thing in black radio. They'd make all that noise and leave happy."

When he joined the staff of WDIA in Memphis in 1950 or 1951, he used his middle name as his surname, keeping, he says, "my identity at the radio station completely separate from my private one."[17] As David James, he became WDIA program director and the driving force behind the Memphis "Goodwill Station." He pushed himself and others during the day (he was a "human dynamo—a self-starter") and developed a reputation for monitoring the programming from sign-on to sign-off. Rufus Thomas believes it didn't matter what time it was, "if you boo-booed, he'd know it. You'd hear from him." David James became a mentor to all of the on-air personalities at WDIA, particularly to Rufus Thomas and B.B. King, who still praise his discipline, perseverance, and professionalism. He was hard on his employees and subjected them to his own high standards, but he was also patient, building confidence in those who lacked it, and generally acting like a coach. "He was my mentor . . . because he would always take time with me," King recalls.[18]

Louis Cantor was employed by WDIA in the 1950s and witnessed James turn the station's studios into a "musical mecca for talented black artists hungry to make a record and 'be discovered.'"[19] At the time, there were almost no opportunities for unknown black talent. Facilities that recorded black music and released the masters to larger record companies, like Sam Phillips's Memphis Recording Service, were necessarily prejudiced toward established artists who already had strong reputations. "Dave, on the other hand," says Cantor, "used the new WDIA recording studios to capture talent right off the streets—complete unknowns, who usually had come into the studios just to get on the air and who had little, if any, exposure as professional artists."[20] In addition, by 1952 the Memphis recording scene was beginning to get crowded. Sam Phillips's feud with Modern/RPM continued to provoke regular visits to the city by the Bihari brothers until a fourth brother, Lester, established the Meteor label in 1952 as Los Angeles's permanent "outpost" in Memphis.[21] In addition, the relationship between Memphis Recording Service and Chess Records, which had grown up "on a handshake deal," became strained in early 1952, prompting Sam Phillips to launch his own Sun label. "I truly did not want to open a record label," he says, "but I was forced into it by those labels either coming to Memphis to record or taking my artists elsewhere."[22]

Mattis knew in 1952 that there was an abundance of black musical talent in the Tri-State area served by Memphis: WDIA was a magnet for promising blues performers. He knew too that they were desperate for recognition. As Jerry Wexler points out, "They had very low expectations in the beginning. You know, they figured, 'Gee I can make a record?' And in those days somebody would give them $25, you know, and an orlon sportshirt, and they'd think the heavens had opened up."[23] What would a black performer do to make a record in the mid-1950s? According to black disk jockey Shelley the Playboy, "He would sign his mama away."[24] Mattis was not interested in taking advantage of anybody, but he had observed that much of the Memphis black talent was already being successfully exploited by other white men. B.B. King, of course, whom Mattis had really known first through his connection with WDIA, had already slipped through his fingers. He was aware that the music business had its grubby side (Rosco Gordon told him he was getting "hosed" by both of his record companies, Modern and Chess), but he believed it was possible to make money and deal fairly with black musical talent. "I was very careful how I did this," he says.

Mattis started Duke Records "on a shoestring," with Bill Fitzgerald of Music Sales, a local record distribution business. "It won't cost us anything," Fitzgerald promised, "because I'll see that we get rid of everything." Mattis put up $1,500, arranged to use the WDIA studios on Union Avenue as a recording facility at night (the station, 250-watts at that time, was permitted on the air only from sunrise to sunset), and set up a system to pay union scale to the musicians, which was unheard of at the time. It was not as if he did not have his own financial needs, however. When he suggested the idea of starting a record company to his wife he remembers her saying, "Well, the kids need their teeth straightened, so let's take a shot at it."[25] Mattis called his recording operation Tri-State Recording, but he wanted a name for his record label that sounded famous and would provide instant name recognition, even though it was a new and essentially one-man operation. There already was a King label, he reasoned, and a Queen, so he chose the name Duke thinking it "the best of the bunch." Mattis even designed the Duke logo: "Then I set about on the label itself which I made myself. Purple and gold were the signs of royalty and it was eye-catching. The design was simply the front end of a Cadillac: the two headlights, the V design. I bought myself a little drafting set and sat down and did it. It was a creative effort that was fun."[26]

At the first Duke recording session, probably in April 1952, Mattis cut "God's Chariot" by the Gospel Travelers, a song about a tornado that took up both sides of a single record. Mattis used sound effects to put tornado-like wind behind the vocals, and since he envisioned a whole series of gospel songs (a gospel, or "G" series) he cataloged the record as Duke G-1. Rosco Gordon cut the second record, consisting of two R&B tunes, "Hey, Fat Girl" b/w "Tell Daddy," cataloged as "R-1," but when Bill Fitzgerald pointed out that the notation R-1 gave away the fact that the business was new, Mattis patterned the numbering system after that of his personal checkbook and changed the Gordon record to R-101.[27] In addition, since Gordon's experience with both the Modern and Chess labels had left him convinced that he should never rely on promises of future royalties, Mattis paid him in cash up front.[28]

The third session at the WDIA studios was scheduled to record Bobby "Blue" Bland, a singer Mattis didn't "think much of" at the time because he "never saw the soul there." Bland had recorded previously for both Chess and Modern, but his vocals were always "sort of forced," Mattis says. "I don't think he really felt it inside of him. He just wanted to *sound* like he felt it."[29] Bland had been given the lyrics to the songs he would cut at least four days before the session, but when the night arrived Mattis discovered that Bland didn't know the songs because he was illiterate—he didn't learn the lyrics because he couldn't read them on his own. Mattis was furious. The drummer, Earl Forest, offered to sing, but in order to save the session Mattis decided to record the piano player, John Alexander, instead. Mattis knew Alexander as a "really splendid, gentle, kind young man," and when he heard him "diddlin' around" with the Ruth Brown hit "So Long" (Atlantic, 1949) Mattis says, "I just happened to recognize something that I hadn't heard before." The way that Alexander sang this I–vi–ii–V AABA ballad sounded so good that Mattis wrote some new lyrics and Alexander "faked out the melody"—that is, invented or made-up a new melody for the chord progression. "It was a fifteen minute job," Mattis says. "It was beautiful and you couldn't tell what [the original song] was."[30] The result, "My Song" (Duke 102), was released in June 1952.

Mattis changed Alexander's name at this point to Johnny Ace, apparently without argument from him, and credited the Beale Streeters as the backup band. The song was then registered for copyright as a Mattis/Alexander collaboration, representing one of the few times Ace would get songwriter credit on the "A" side of a record. Instead, the remainder of his career patterned itself after "Follow the Rule," the "B" side of Duke 102—a shuffle blues with lyrics written by Ace that were neither protected by copyright registration nor filed for BMI logging. At the same session and with the same Beale Streeters group of musicians, Earl Forest performed the vocal on "Baby, Baby" and "Rock the Bottle," which Mattis released as Duke 103. As the owner of Tri-State Recording Co., Mattis charged the account of Johnny Ace $82.50 and the account of Earl Forest $82.55 for session expenses to be deducted against future record royalties.[31]

While the production on both sides of Duke 102 is remarkably rough, with an amateurish sound featuring drums, tenor saxophone, and an out-of-tune piano (Arnold Shaw says "it sounded and still sounds like a home recording"),[32] the record was an immediate hit with the limited audience that had access to it. In his attempt to meet the demand for the first four Duke records, especially Ace's "My Song" but also the Gospel Traveler's "God's Chariot," Mattis found out what all small independent record labels of the period quickly discovered: the way to go broke in the music business was to have a hit—to sink precious capital into the manufacture and supply of product wholesaled to a distribution system that never intended to pay for it.

The problem wasn't getting rid of records, it turned out; the problem was getting paid for them. There were "an awful lot of thieves back then," Mattis says. "They used to wait till you were broke to pay you and then say, 'Well, you're broke. No sense paying you now.'" When he reached the point beyond which he could not afford to sustain the Duke operation he remembers telling Bill Fitzgerald: "I've got five thousand dollars in this thing now and we're selling records, but nobody's paying. Either I'm going to go broke or I've gotta quit."[33]

Although the Memphis black community still believes that Mattis "made a fortune out of what those young black kids did" for the Duke Records operation,[34] the evidence clearly shows that he treated Johnny Ace and the other performers with remarkable fairness and generosity. It was incumbent upon him, as program director of WDIA, the Goodwill Station, to be scrupulously honest with black musicians. Mattis had, however, heard complaints of deception and observed firsthand the other side of things: "Well, the Bihari brothers in Los Angeles stole [black performers] blind. That's why I started recording Rosco Gordon right off the bat because he was being stolen from. The same with B.B. King, who cut a couple of sides with them, and Bobby Bland had a deal. Everybody. They'd come through with a Magnacorder and every black guy who could play a guitar or sing they would record."[35]

It is only fair to point out that the R&B music business in the early fifties was exceptionally primitive, remembered at BMI as an era in which people didn't know "exactly what to do so they did anything they could."[36] "There never was an industry," asserts Jerry Wexler, the A&R man at Atlantic Records at the time. "There was a collection of individual record companies run by individual people with different ethics, different morality, different needs, different greeds."[37] The man that Mattis found to bail him out by becoming a partner in Duke Records, Don Robey, was a man with dramatically different needs and different greeds. While Don D. Robey was not the first black man to own his own record company (Peacock), he was certainly a pioneer in the history of black music in America, and he may have been, as Galen Gart suggests, "the first successful black entrepreneur to emerge in the music business after World War II."[38]

Bill Fitzgerald, Mattis's Memphis partner, apparently led Mattis to a doomed relationship with Don Robey. As part of Fitzgerald's work for the record distribution company, he handled many labels, including Peacock Records out of Houston. Everyone at Music Sales knew Irving Marcus, a white man who was the sales manager for black-owned Peacock, because he made regular trips to Memphis to promote Peacock acts and call on the Music Sales staff. Marcus, who was from Los Angeles, had worked for Peacock since 1950. His previous experience included working for the president of King Records in Cincinnati and handling the distribution of Mercury Records in Atlanta. The way Mattis remembers it, Bill Fitzgerald's suggestion for handling the financial crisis resulting from the inability of Duke

Records to collect its accounts receivable was in the form of a question: "Why don't you talk to Irving Marcus?" Mattis did, and Marcus gave him "this pitch." "You just gotta come to Houston with me," Marcus said, "you just gotta. Robey wants to see you."

Mattis believed he was going to be flown down to Houston to meet the Peacock boss, but instead Marcus picked him up in a 1948 Plymouth one evening in July 1952, and the two drove all night. Mattis claims the 700-mile trip took almost twenty-four hours the way Marcus drove, including embarrassing stops at the "worst greasy spoons." He never even got to see Robey, he says, just the Peacock office and facilities, including a "pissy little pressing plant with four pressing tables." Nevertheless, he agreed to a partnership that he thought would end his problems. Randy Wood of Dot Records told Mattis that he didn't think the Robey partnership was a good idea and offered "to work something out" with his label, but Mattis felt he was already committed to the Peacock deal. "Isn't this nice?" Mattis says he thought at the time. "This bleeding heart liberal [referring to himself] is in partnership with a black man and he's showing that inter-racial activity could really work."[39]

> *When we started out, it was about being sure that [Peacock artists] took a bath, and that their clothes were clean, their shoes were shined. We had to make them from scratch.*
> *—Evelyn Johnson*

Las Vegas in Houston

The Bronze Peacock

The concept of "inter-racial activity" envisioned by Mattis in Memphis in 1952 was equally alien to postwar Houston. Like Memphis, Houston had been a cotton port in a black belt area with Old South slaveholding traditions. In the 1830s, black workers (and Mexicans) cleared the area that became Houston when it was still a "mosquito-infested swampland," since at the time it was feared that white men could not endure the malaria, snakes, contaminated water, and physical hardship.[1] Like Memphis, Houston experienced yellow fever epidemics—especially one devastating outbreak during the summer of 1839, when one-third of the residents were infected.[2] Like Memphis, too, Houston experienced an influx of black residents immediately after the Civil War. The 1860 census reported only 1,069 slaves and eight free blacks, but as slavery collapsed, the rumor in Texas was that the Union Army in Houston would provide food, housing, and jobs. Some blacks believed no work would be involved in the new era, and many had heard that the federal government would give land to freedmen on 25 December 1865.[3]

The city was unprepared for the increase in its black population after Emancipation Day in Texas (19 June 1865), a Texas holiday still celebrated annually as "Juneteenth," and rural blacks from Texas and Louisiana continued to migrate to the city for economic opportunity and leave it for the same reason during the next seventy-five years, making Houston what sociologists later called a "stage" city. "This situation," says historian Robert V. Haynes, "revealed the racially crippling ceiling upon achievement, a ceiling high enough to attract rural Negroes but too low to retain ambitious blacks."[4] Former slaves settled primarily in an area southwest of downtown Houston called "Freedman's Town" in the Fourth Ward. By 1900 Houston was almost one-third black, the largest African American city in Texas; by the 1920s over 95 percent of Houston black-owned businesses were located in the Fourth Ward, making the area around West Dallas Street the "heart" of black business, commerce, social life, and culture in Houston.[5]

Emancipation Park, the home of the annual Juneteenth Celebration, was located in the Fourth Ward, along with black restaurants, saloons, clubs, movie houses, theaters, schools, service businesses, and institutions. Segregated facilities, Houston scholar Cary D. Wintz points out, led to a "self-contained black community."[6] African Americans in Houston had their own exclusive holiday with the Juneteenth Celebration (so many maids, butlers, chauffeurs, and domestics were absent from work on Juneteenth that in 1917 the Rice Hotel held a "rescue party" for "stranded housewives who might otherwise have had to prepare the family dinner themselves"),[7] and then, like African Americans in Memphis, appropriated a white festival as their own.

Houston white businessmen established No-Tsu-Oh (Houston spelled backwards) in 1899 as "a week-long festival designed to attract fall buyers to town." Black Houstonians established De-Ro-Loc (colored spelled backwards) in 1909—a fall carnival "on a smaller scale."[8] The simultaneous coexistence of No-Tsu-Oh and De-Ro-Loc in Houston repeated the same Jim Crow realities as that of the Cotton Carnival (white) and Cotton Maker's Jubilee (black) in Memphis. Likewise, the same traditions of white superiority also governed the lives of African Americans in Houston, where schools, parks, waiting rooms, drinking fountains, and lunch counters were racially segregated. Like Memphis, Houston had white newspapers and black newspapers, white movie houses and black, white theaters and black, a white minor league baseball team (Houston Buffaloes) and a black one

(Houston Black Buffaloes).[9] Black Houston, however, never developed the cultural power symbolized by Memphis's Beale Street.

Race relations in Houston were peaceful for the most part, though considerable tension was felt during the Jack Johnson–James J. Jeffries heavyweight boxing championship bout in 1910. The actual match was almost two thousand miles away in Reno, but three to four thousand people of both races waited at Houston newspaper offices for the results. When Johnson won (he was not only a black man but a black Texan from nearby Galveston), scattered fighting broke out, but "bystanders halted the incipient riot." (Actual riots did occur in at least six northern and southern cities.)[10]

While black and white Houstonians may not have been at one another's throats, "ominous signs of discontent" were revealed in the summer of 1917 when thousands of black laborers suddenly left the city, recruited by agents of northern industries. White businessmen in Houston properly feared the economic loss of the city's large, cheap, black labor force, much like their counterparts in Memphis would fear immediately after World War I.[11] The real racial problem in Houston that summer was revealed, however, not by black men who were leaving the city but by black men who were arriving: the 654 enlisted men of the Third Battalion, Twenty-Fourth Infantry—career soldiers who assumed that after a temporary assignment in Houston they would be sent to the war zone in France.

Houston businessmen and Chamber of Commerce members had lobbied aggressively to profit from World War I opportunities, and though the city had failed to secure one of the sixteen permanent training camps authorized by Congress, it succeeded in being named as a site for the construction of one of the sixteen temporary "tent camps" for training National Guard units. Camp Logan, to be built by a Houston-based firm, would bring two million dollars a month to the city economy. The only unfavorable part of the plan was that a battalion of Negro troops would be sent to Houston to guard and protect federal property at the construction site. Houston officials attempted, but failed, to get the War Department to use the all-white Texas National Guard instead. The black troops, they were told, would be in Houston less than two months.[12]

At the time, Houston had approximately thirty thousand black residents, and the soldiers of the Third Battalion were, "glad to be stationed in a community with a sizable Negro population": "Few of them could remember the day when they had mingled freely with civilians of their own race or had experienced the satisfaction of being looked up to by admiring citizens. At a time when there were practically no black entertainers of national reputation and even fewer well-known black athletes, Negro soldiers were about the only hero types of their race, and the black citizens of Houston seized every opportunity to communicate appreciation to them."[13] In an effort to boost morale, the unit's commanding officer encouraged civilians to visit his men at camp between the hours of 1:00 P.M. and 10:45 P.M. According to Haynes, "Black Houstonians of all ages flocked to the camp to witness first hand the life of a soldier and to exchange anecdotes with these veterans of the Pershing campaign."[14] When troops went into the city on the first weekend, however, there were immediate signs of trouble. Black soldiers, some of whom "had seldom encountered any form of discrimination," were appalled by the conspicuous Jim Crow signs on the trolley cars (several were ripped off the streetcars and thrown out the window) and by the discourteous manner of the conductors (some soldiers used profanity to communicate their resentment). At the same time, "white passengers sat in disbelief as they watched these unforgivable violations of southern mores."[15]

To make matters worse during this critical time in the summer of 1917, local movements advocating virtuous living, police reform, and prohibition combined to force the closure of "the reservation," Houston's red-light district, which occupied a ten-block area in the heavily black Fourth Ward. Police reportedly concentrated "almost exclusively" on arrests of black prostitutes, gamblers, and bootleggers during this period, when "the number of incidents involving police brutality reached frightening proportions."[16] One such incident involving an arrest by two of the "meanest" policemen on the force, one of whom was well known as a "negro baiter" and "brutal bully" on the morning of 23 August 1917, provoked the dramatic event known as the Houston Riot. The officers, attempting to run down two teenage crapshooters, burst into a black woman's home, slapped her around, complained about "these God damn sons of bitches of nigger soldiers," and arrested her. When a Third Battalion soldier on leave protested her treatment, he was pistol-whipped to the ground and arrested as well. Early in the afternoon on the same day, a member of the provost guard heard of the arrest and asked the two policemen about their version of the encounter. He, too, was struck in the head with the barrel of a gun. When the soldier attempted to get away he was shot at, beaten, and subsequently thrown in jail. Back at camp, "exaggerated and distorted stories of the incident" swept through the installation, including the false report that a black soldier had been killed by Houston policemen.[17]

Later that night, responding to rumors and in retaliation against local civilian police brutality, racial hostility, and Jim Crow customs, between 75 and 100 black regular army soldiers of the Third Battalion, Twenty-Fourth Infantry armed themselves, marched into town, and in a two-hour mutiny killed fifteen whites—mostly policemen, white soldiers mistaken for police, or civilians acting as police. The court-martial testimony from three subsequent trials reveals that as they marched through Houston the soldiers were cheered on by residents of the Fourth Ward ("This is what we call a man!").[18] Nineteen black soldiers were executed for their roles in the mutiny (thirteen were secretly hanged before the public knew of the first court-martial verdict and before the president or secretary of war could review the sentence),[19] and 110 black soldiers were imprisoned—almost half of them with sentences for life.[20]

Though both blacks and whites participated in booster campaigns for the city in the years immediately following the Houston Riot (the Houston *Informer*, a black newspaper, sold the city to African Americans as "Heavenly Houston" in 1919),[21] racial tensions inspired by the riot resulted in rigorous enforcement of Jim Crow laws and contributed to a wave of Ku Klux Klan terror in the 1920s: the Klan brutalized a Houston black dentist in 1921 and tarred and feathered a black doctor in 1925. And though the Klan lost influence in the city, in a 1928 incident Houston registered its only "documented lynching." Robert Powell, a black man who had killed a white policeman in a Fourth Ward shoot-out, was kidnapped from his hospital room by a white mob and hanged from a bridge. "Both black and white Houstonians expressed shock and outrage over this incident," Cary D. Wintz says.[22]

The Houston *Informer* took the lead in promoting black business development in the city and urged readers to patronize local black-owned companies. By 1929, though Houston had only the nation's thirteenth largest black population, it ranked tenth in black-owned businesses and seventh in sales per black business.[23] Most of these establishments were located in the inner-city Fourth Ward, which had the highest proportion of black residents. Houston's tenderloin district (saloons, honky-tonks, cabarets, eating places, bordellos) was in the Fourth Ward, but so were the more legitimate venues of black entertainment: the two TOBA theaters (the Lincoln and the Key), the Eldorado Ballroom, and the Emancipation Park Dance Pavilion, where

Juneteenth was celebrated.[24] Dowling Street was the main thoroughfare in the Fourth Ward, described as "a low-rent shopping and entertainment district for black Americans who lived in the shotgun shacks and wood-frame houses of the surrounding streets. There were hairdressers, barbecue pits, clothing stores, barber shops, barrelhouses, dance clubs, and bars. The sidewalks were hot with street-life—hobos, blues singers and everyday folks doing what they could to survive, and maybe, better themselves."[25] Indeed, the Fourth Ward was a virtual city in itself. "As a consequence of racial estrangement, manifested in laws, customs, and outbursts of violence, white men and black men [in Houston] lived almost separate lives with social and intellectual contact kept at a minimum," says urban biographer David G. McComb. "The dichotomy of the races was greater in 1930 than it had been in 1875."[26]

By 1930 Houston was the largest city in Texas (26th nationally), with an African American population of 22 percent, down considerably from the 39 percent it had been fifty years earlier.[27] Since Houston had no ordinance on segregation in housing, blacks lived in all of the city's wards, but "large black enclaves" developed not only in the Freedman's Town/Fourth Ward area but also in the Fifth Ward (northeast of the business district) and the Third Ward (southeast of downtown). Black residents of all three wards could remember the "small-town atmosphere of black neighborhoods" as late as the World War II years,[28] but in fact such a small-town atmosphere had already been undermined. In crime, Houston was near the top of the list for per capita murders in 1934, and in development the city destroyed some of the Fourth Ward's oldest churches and schools to build the thousand-unit San Felipe Courts in 1938, a low-income housing project.[29] More than 75 percent of Houston's black workers were employed in the three lowest paying job categories during this period (domestic, service worker, common laborer), with less than three percent rated as professional or semi-professional.[30]

It was only after World War II that the city began a long boom period, becoming in 1948 the "fastest growing city per capita in the country."[31] By that time, Houston already possessed a lively blues culture. Though there were only two black radio stations in Houston (KCOH and KYOK), there were plenty of performance venues: the Eldorado Ballroom, Shady's Playhouse, the Diamond L Ranch and the Double Bar Ranch, and the Club Matinee, Club Ebony, Club Savoy, and the Bronze Peacock Dinner Club.

In addition, concerts and dances were held at the black high schools and at the City Auditorium.[32] Two Texas blues pioneers who performed regularly in Houston were Sam "Lightnin'" Hopkins and Aaron "T-Bone" Walker. Lightnin' Hopkins, whose ankles were scarred from leg-irons from time served at a prison farm during the Depression, had been Houston-based since the late 1920s, playing Fourth Ward honky-tonks and saloons.

T-Bone Walker, who grew up in Dallas, migrated west to Los Angeles during the Depression like many other Texas bluesmen. When his records hit the national race music charts in the late 1940s, he was able to tour with his own band, playing black clubs and ballrooms and "breaking down" audiences in much the same way that Elvis Presley would later do. Mariellen Shepphard, who grew up in nearby San Antonio, told Texas R&B historian Alan Govenar what the experience of a T-Bone Walker performance was like for a working-class black woman in the 1950s:

> Well, I'll tell it like it is. I was sneaking off to the Avalon Grill on Maid's night out. So, I was up there as close as I could get, and T-Bone comes out in his white, white suit with big diamond rings. He comes out there and strikes up his guitar, v-rooom, v-rooom. Oh, Mistah T-Bone! He couldn't even get through the first song before the purses started flyin' with everyone goin', "Play my song, Mistah T-Bone!" The purse started goin', "Take all my money!" and he was cool, but then after he got hot, he put that guitar behind his head. Then he'd start to really get pluckin'. He'd turn around and swing. And then everything went: shoes, rings, bracelets, everything. Honey, he'd play them blues all night long. But sometimes the men got mad at the girls for throwing their money and purses or whatever else they could on stage. T-Bone would come back out and start playing again and they threw anything they could get loose.[33]

"Most of the black clubs were small then," Houston blues performer Joe Hughes recalled. "A lot of houses were converted into clubs. That gave you basic two- or three-room structures, but there were so many of them around the city." In addition, he believes that the "little clubs would be jumping" because the simplicity of the sound systems at the time made the music purer. "People felt the music more back then because the music was about them," he says. "And the musicians played with more feeling."[34]

There were no opportunities for recording black music in Houston until after World War II. Bill Quinn, who established Gold Star Records as a hillbilly label in 1946 to record Cajun music pioneer Harry Choates, record-ed local blues performer Lightnin' Hopkins in 1947 but could not keep him exclusively on his label. Gold Star ceased operations altogether in 1952.[35] In 1949, three labels were launched in Houston: Freedom by Saul Kaul, Macy's by Macy Lela Wood, and Peacock by Don Robey.[36] Of the three, only Don Robey's would survive the transition from race music to rhythm and blues to soul.

Don Deadric Robey was born in Houston on 1 November 1903, the son of Zeb and Gertrude Robey. The family, originally from Louisiana, lived in Eagle Lake, Texas, a community less than fifty miles west of the city. Because the Robeys were never known for the closeness of their household, little is known of Don Robey's early family life or childhood except that he had a sister, Ella, and two step-sisters, Gertrude and Margaret. His father may at one time have operated a restaurant, and his paternal grandfather may have been a doctor.[37] Like Johnny Ace, Robey left home early to be-gin his own life and dropped out of high school in the eleventh grade. While Ace's intention was to escape from the world, Robey's plan was to manipu-late it: he reportedly pursued a career as a professional gambler. Before the age of twenty he was married for a short time and fathered a son. Accord-ing to one account, Robey gave up gambling in Negro nightspots for a day job as a sales representative for a Houston liquor distributor, calling on the same local nightclubs and beer joints he had been freelancing at night.[38]

Except for a three-year stay in Los Angeles during the Depression, Robey lived and worked in Houston all of his life. At one point prior to World War II he established a taxi business in Houston and was the first to put radios in his cabs (eighteen of them), monopolizing the local taxi business for sev-eral months until the competition could follow suit.[39] Some evidence sug-gests that his gambling activity may have made him a major partner in the Houston numbers operation. What is certain is that Robey always had cap-ital to invest and knew how to use it, which is how he came to be involved in promoting dances. A local promoter who was short on money asked Robey to help him bring an attraction into town. Robey consented and quickly saw the possibilities in that field for a man with capital who was willing to take a chance.[40] Robey, who had been taking chances all his life, soon developed a reputation as a band promoter. He brought to Houston, Dallas, and other cities in Texas, Louisiana, and Oklahoma such territorial bands as Milt Larkin and Jack McVea together with such name bands and singers as Louis

Armstrong, Duke Ellington, Count Basie, Nat Cole, and Ella Fitzgerald. He also brought "produced shows" into the area, attractions built around a celebrity like Joe Louis, with dancers, comedians, and other acts.[41]

Robey's first connection with the nightclub business began in 1937, when he opened the Harlem Grill on West Dallas at Heiner Street. But it was the Bronze Peacock Dinner Club on Erastus Street, which Robey built in 1945 and opened in 1946, that he parlayed into a series of entertainment-amusement businesses that made him, according to the Houston *Informer*, one of Houston's "foremost black business wizards," and a local Horatio Alger.[42] According to Evelyn Johnson, Robey's business partner who ran the club, the Bronze Peacock was named by one of Robey's friends. "Bronze was to denote our people," she remembers, "and Peacock, a very proud bird. So Robey goes out and gets a neon company to do a whole peacock in neon up on the sign board."[43] Actually, Robey was himself a kind of peacock. "He was flamboyant and a showoff," Johnson says. "He stood out like a sore thumb. I remember seeing him driving down the street in a Buick that was yellow, and nobody was driving a yellow car. And he might have on a green hat with a red band on it."[44]

Galen Gart suggests that "peacock" was slang for the well-dressed, upscale "'Beautiful People' of black society" and that "bronze" was a term to denote "a lighter-skinned Negro of presumed urbanity or higher-class upbringing, in contrast to the darker complexion of his less sophisticated 'country' cousin."[45] Whatever the intentionality, Robey himself was a light-skinned African American frequently taken as a white man. "To be very frank," Evelyn Johnson says, "there were years whenever I would pick [Robey] up at the airport, if he happened to be on one of those salesmen's flights, I'd have to stand there to pick him out."[46] The rumor in Houston was that Robey represented "a racial mix of Negro, Irish, and Jewish ancestry."[47]

The location of the Bronze Peacock was also significant. It was in the Fifth Ward—the newly emerging center of Houston black business and activity and the last black area of the city to prosper under a system of racial segregation. By 1950 the Fifth Ward, dominated by the Lyon Avenue Commercial Corridor and the largest African American population in the city, was the hub of black social life in Houston.[48] The Bronze Peacock contributed to the vitality and importance of the area: it was a "plush" nightclub that quickly became "the mecca of entertainment in the Southwest."[49] Evelyn Johnson calls it "Las Vegas in our category. There was everything but the chorus line at the Peacock. We had an emcee, comedian, band, featured singers, the whole nine yards. White people, important people came there. Segregation laws were not enforced with those people."[50] There was also casino gambling, which was not legal. Robey used his skill as a promoter to bring in Louis Jordan, Ruth Brown, Johnny Otis, T-Bone Walker, and other popular black acts.[51] In fact, booking talent for the Peacock got Robey first into the talent management business and then into records and music publishing.

About the time that the future Johnny Ace, discharged from the navy for being worthless and hopeless, was wasting his time hanging out with the boys at the corner of Mississippi and Walker, Don Robey was positioning himself to take advantage of business opportunities. His moment of inspiration came one night in 1947, when Clarence "Gatemouth" Brown, an unknown guitarist from San Antonio, substituted for T-Bone Walker at the Peacock and ended up finishing Walker's engagement. Brown was a hit with the Peacock crowd, "inventing" on stage that night the tune known as "Gatemouth Boogie." "I made six hundred dollars in fifteen minutes," he remembers, "from an all black audience."[52] No gambler like Robey could mistake the cards that he had been dealt. He was so impressed that he took Brown on as a client and launched his career. Evelyn Johnson says that within months Robey had equipped Brown with "a new car, a great guitar, tailor-made tails (black, white, red, green) with matching top hats, and Robey became his personal manager."[53] Later, Robey was convinced that Brown would be a better draw if he were a recording artist, so he flew him to Los Angeles and arranged a recording contract with Eddie Mesner of Aladdin Records. With Robey pressing the deal, Brown was guaranteed four released sides in a twelve-month period with the "unheard of" artist royalty of four cents per record.

Aladdin recorded the four sides in November 1947 and issued the first record, but did not promote it to Robey's satisfaction. When the second record was released on the last day of the year merely to fulfill the contract, Robey was angry. He told Evelyn Johnson he was going into the record business himself: " 'We don't need Eddie Mesner to make records on Gatemouth Brown. We'll make them ourselves.' I said, 'We will?' He said, 'Yes.' I said, 'Tell me this. How do you make a record?' He said, 'Hell, I don't know. That's for you to find out!' " Johnson calls this conversation "the minutes of the formation of Peacock Records."[54] The response to the problem and the escalation of the solution was typical of what Evelyn Johnson had come to expect from Robey. "He knew nothing about music," she says, "he knew nothing about records, he knew nothing about anything. The only thing he knew was that somebody had made a contract with him, and when the contract expired he challenged it, because that was what his whole life was built about—challenging and competing. He was a gambler. I mean he was a *gambler* gambler."[55]

The formation of Peacock Records in 1949 led Robey into the few music related businesses he had not yet attempted. He had already booked talent, managed talent, and showcased it at his Bronze Peacock nightclub. When he turned his package liquor store at 4104 Lyon Avenue into a record store, Peacock Records, he also became a retailer. None of these activities, however, would provide the challenges and opportunities that were to come through the launching of a race record label to exploit the talents of Gatemouth Brown. In a session that may have taken four days to complete, Robey and Johnson rented a small studio on Hamilton Street and arranged for Brown to record six tunes with Jack McVea's band: "Didn't Reach My Goal," "Atomic Energy," "Mercy On Me," "Ditch Diggin' Daddy," "My Time Is Expensive," and "Mary Is Fine."[56]

The six tunes provided Robey with enough material to release four records in a way that would have been completely unacceptable to record label professionals: after releasing the first record, "Didn't Reach My Goal" b/w "Atomic Energy" (Peacock 1500), he released "Didn't Reach My Goal" b/w "Mercy On Me" and cataloged *that* as Peacock 1500. As Peacock 1501, actually the third release, Robey dumped the "A" side of the previous record and substituted "Ditch Diggin' Daddy," keeping "Mercy On Me" as the flip side. As unconventional as the releases were, Robey was developing an audience for Gatemouth Brown. "My Time Is Expensive," the "A" side of Peacock 1504, received sufficient radio airplay to sell some records, and when the disk jockeys started to play the flip side, "Mary Is Fine," the record started to sell again. Robey looked at his bank account, saw $35,000 in it, and decided that this was the business for him. From that point on the Bronze Peacock nightclub ceased to be his primary interest.[57]

The Peacock Recording Company was initially operated out of the Peacock Records store; the label featured a peacock as the company logo with three stars in the background. It has been suggested that Robey's peacock may have been modeled on the plumed bird of historically important black-owned record labels like Black Patti or Black Swan, but Robey had neither knowledge nor interest in the history of the recording business. What he did know how to do, however, was to trust his instincts and the instincts of Evelyn Johnson. From the outset, even when the audio engineering was primitive, the decisions made about the material to record and the musical arrangements, the sound of the songs, were invariably correct. "Gatemouth Brown's early recordings on Robey's Peacock label are classics," says Alan Govenar. "The electric guitar sound is modern: quick single string runs with a driving rhythm backed by tenor saxophone and trumpet. On some of the early sessions the horn section is enlarged to give a big band sound with swing era solos in a call and response pattern with the progressions of the electric guitar."[58]

As far as the business of music was concerned, however, Robey was clearly a novice. "Robey didn't know a record from a hubcap," Evelyn Johnson says about the early days of Peacock,[59] nor, in fact, did she. At first, the songs on Gatemouth Brown's records were not even registered for copyright, but Johnson was a resourceful person. She soon learned that Broadcast Music, Incorporated (BMI), the licensing society with the open membership policy with whom virtually all race/rhythm and blues writers and publishers affiliated, and the Library of Congress, which formally registered song copyrights, had all the forms pertinent to the record business. She asked everyone to send her a form, and then she decided whether the company needed it or not. If it appeared that the form wasn't necessary she kept it anyway, in a file she called "It Could Be In Here."[60] When she didn't know how to do something she would call the Library of Congress. Someone there knew everything, she discovered, and would direct her to the right office or agency or person.[61] On the telephone, she learned, Houston could be as close to the center of action as New York.

The independence to operate as she saw fit, to explore opportunities and break new ground thrilled Evelyn Johnson. She was intellectually and emotionally ready for such a challenge. A few years earlier, she had sought a career in the field of medicine, but X-ray technology was considered the province of white males in 1940s Houston, and she was denied the opportunity to take the certification exam.[62] The music business may have been just as male-dominated, but the pure entrepreneurial spirit that existed in her partnership with Robey gave her hope, and the business education courses she had taken at Texas Southern University gave her confidence.

Still, for all Robey's intuitive skill and Johnson's brash initiative, the Peacock operation faced one fundamental problem. While it had a retail sales outlet, a local venue to showcase the talents of Gatemouth Brown, and a record company to release his records, the city of Houston was not a large enough market to support the company. In order to generate record sales for Gatemouth Brown, Robey needed his star to make personal appearances before a wider audience; but in order to create demand for Gatemouth Brown's personal appearances, Brown needed record sales in a wider market. The company had no choice but to expand the base of support for Peacock Records and to do it on its own. "There were no booking agencies interested in the likes of Gatemouth Brown," Evelyn Johnson says, "because there were no clubs, there was no market for him. But he needed to work more than most, because you cannot be known sitting on logs. And he has to be in a position to make some money because we can just take care of him for so long—buy the groceries and all."[63]

At the time, no national agency was interested in booking Brown's personal appearances and no regional agency either. So it was Evelyn Johnson, and not Don Robey, who applied to the American Federation of Musicians for a booking license in order to "act as agent, manager, or representative for members of the association,"[64] and it was Evelyn Johnson who gave the booking business the name Buffalo Booking Agency. At least now there was an entity that could reasonably seek personal appearances for Peacock artists, even if the entire roster consisted only of Brown. "Gatemouth Brown was the reason there was a Peacock Records," she says, "and Gatemouth Brown is the reason there was a Buffalo Booking Agency." Since neither Brown nor Buffalo Booking was in a position to attract large audiences to a 2000-seat city auditorium, the organization built from the bottom up by creating a circuit of small clubs and venues. "Every little town has a dance hall, or a juke joint," Johnson reasoned. "Now every town has a band, because the band plays at the local club, so they are really high on the hog when they get somebody for a traveling band coming in. This is the way we started the agency, and built from there."

It was only later, after consolidating the smaller venues, that the operation moved on to bigger clubs in larger towns. By that time the eastern establishment already referred to Buffalo Booking venues as the "chitlin circuit" and credited the booking activity, as well as everything else, to Don Robey. "They called it Robey's Booking Agency," Johnson says.[65] Nevertheless, Johnson went about her business as a "go-between," booking Brown into areas where Peacock could sell records and getting Peacock Records into places that were potential markets for Gatemouth Brown's personal appearances. "One hand," she says, "washed the other."[66] The result was the establishment of a market area that eventually included not only Texas but Arkansas, Louisiana, Mississippi, Alabama, and Georgia. By 1951, in fact, Buffalo Booking could send Gatemouth Brown and his band on a series of one-nighters in California.[67] Eventually, when the artist roster grew with both secular acts (Floyd Dixon and Willie Mae Thornton) and sacred acts (Original Five Blind Boys and the Bells of Joy), Johnson arranged appearances for Peacock artists in St. Louis, Kansas City, and Chicago,[68] though she did not receive credit for her contribution.

Robey and Johnson may have been unique in their attempt to create a touring circuit for their performers, but they were not the only entrepreneurs trying to establish a record company in the postwar era. More than a thousand new record labels were founded between 1948 and 1954, a phenomenon attributed to affordable technology that permitted entry into the popular music business for an initial investment of under a thousand dollars. "Recording costs, operating expenses and performer royalties," Marc Eliot says, "could now be paid from sales as low as fifteen hundred units."[69] The technological advance was the reel-to-reel tape recorder, a product of "war-stimulated research," developed in Germany and discovered by the Allies during the invasion of Germany in 1945.

The new equipment brought mobility and capability to document sound outside the power culture centers of the period—not only in Houston but in New Orleans, Memphis, Jackson, Cincinnati, and other secondary markets. "The tape recorder," according to W. T. Lhamon Jr., "thus helped break down the concentration of culture production in its established locations."[70] Of course in the postwar era, investment capital was still easier for white Americans to accumulate than African Americans. Galen Gart estimates that of approximately four thousand record companies active in the 1940s and 1950s, "fewer than three dozen" (including many backroom and one-shot operations that were short-lived) were black owned.[71]

For a black businessman with capital, however, the postwar period was a particularly good time for a self-motivator to start his own business, be his own boss, and reap the rewards of his own efforts. And the social system of segregation in the South generated even more opportunities for a black man engaged in the business of black music. "One of the things that defined the R&B world," Nelson George points out, "one that separated it from most other American businesses, was the ability of blacks to form businesses and profit from a product their own people created."[72] Booker T. Washington certainly would have approved of the self-sufficiency inherent in the production and distribution of black music for a black audience by black-owned companies. The professionalism of the Peacock operation surprised everyone, however. "It was unheard of that a Negro group would come through this way," Evelyn Johnson says.[73]

Most of the other R&B independent labels with whom Don Robey competed nationally were white-owned in general and Jewish-owned in particular: Chess (Leonard and Phil Chess) in Chicago; Savoy (Herman Lubinsky) in Newark; King (Syd Nathan) in Cincinnati; Aladdin (Eddie and Leo Mesner), Modern (Jules, Joe, and Saul Bihari), and Specialty (Art Rupe) in Los Angeles; and Atlantic (Ahmet Ertegun and Herb Abramson) in New York. While all the white competitors were established before Peacock, the oldest of them, Savoy in Newark (established in 1942), had a mere seven years head start on Robey, who caught up with some of them immediately and most of them eventually, building what Nelson George calls "an empire worth millions in a city far removed from the main line of entertainment." Robey's location, in fact, helped him to succeed, giving him the opportunity to become "a big fish in a pond that hadn't held any that big before."[74]

Dave Clark, arguably the first independent promotion man in the record business and the first African American columnist to write for *Down Beat*, worked for Robey in the fifties. He understood not only the particulars of Robey's operation but the context in which it prospered as well. According to Clark, Robey was not only a maverick, a gambler, an entrepreneur, and a capitalist but "one of the greatest black record manufacturers who ever lived." He was "a pioneer who gave black talent a shot," a man with "toughness to survive in a racist industry." While the kind of toughness the business called for in those days is frequently seen today as evidence of gross exploitation of the artists, Dave Clark insists that the heroes of the time were the label owners who took the economic risks:

Some of [the artists] didn't tend to be too smart; some of them were so smart they outsmarted themselves. Back in those days a guy would go out and make him a record. First thing you know he wanted a Cadillac. Don Robey said, "All right, I'll get you the Cadillac, but you got to pay me just like you pay the man." And when royalty time came and you ain't made enough money out of the record to pay for your Cadillac [Robey would charge it against your account]. Guys would come get $4000 to $5000 at a time. You see all the artist [*sic*] wanted to be big shots. They all wanted big cars. They all wanted fine clothes and everything that went with it.[75]

Robey also wanted these material things for his artists. Beginning with Gatemouth Brown, the Peacock operation invariably "groomed" performers before sending them out on the road, investing money up-front that it expected to recoup through record royalties. "Peacock supported them," says Evelyn Johnson, "bought their clothes and their transportation and so forth and so on. That went along with contracts. [Robey] bought all of these things for them. In the contract, so far as the recording industry was concerned, all of this tended to be an advance against future royalties." The label literally took the artists on board and supplied them with life's necessities. According to Johnson, "as a result of that the next thing you knew you were paying for the birth of the baby, and the girl, and the grandmother, and paying for the divorce and the whatever. I used to tease them all the time. I'd say, 'This is not a contract—this is an adoption paper.'"[76]

Adoption, of course, ideally works for the benefit of both parties. If Robey and Johnson were taking on children, it follows that the children were getting parents. In another era, Berry Gordy of Motown would teach his male groups manners and send them to choreography classes and teach his female groups choreography and send them to finishing school. At Peacock, in the early fifties, a broader and more basic approach was required. "When we started out," Evelyn Johnson says, "it was about being sure that they took a bath, and that their clothes were clean, their shoes were shined. We started from scratch, making sure that everybody had a toothbrush. We started from the ground up. These people—we had to make them from scratch."[77]

Robey discovered virtually all of his talent, beginning with Gatemouth Brown, in this raw stage. Not surprisingly, when *Billboard* began reviewing Peacock records in February 1950, it mostly panned the obscure performers Robey had recently launched: R. B. Thibadeaux, Edgar Blanchard, Bea Johnson, Norman Dunlap, and Silver Cooks—artists who would never have a hit for Peacock or any other label.[78] It is understandable that during this period, in the infancy of Peacock Records, Robey might come to believe that his chances with the big time would improve if he were to record artists who were already known. He claimed to have signed Louis Jordan that year, which would have represented an extraordinary accomplishment, though the assertion proved false when Jordan renewed his contract with Decca Records.

Louis Jordan (1908–75), played alto saxophone and sang with Chick Webb's band until Webb's death in 1938, when he formed his own band, later known as the Tympany Five. His first hit, "I'm Gonna Leave You at the Outskirts of Town," was recognized in 1942 upon publication of the Harlem Hit Parade—the first popularity chart to measure race music. His records began to cross over to pop in 1943 ("Ration Blues"), and by 1944 he occupied the number one position on both charts with "G.I. Jive" b/w "Is You Is Or Is You Ain't (My Baby)," tunes from the hit movie *Follow the Boys*. In 1946 alone he had an unprecedented thirteen hits on the Harlem Hit Parade, and by the time Robey claimed to have signed him he was a giant in the world of rhythm and blues with more than fifty hit records, almost twenty of which had crossed over to pop. Jordan was proud to have straddled the color fence. "I made just as much money off white people as I did off colored," he told Arnold Shaw.[79]

The success of Jordan's Tympany Five (actually a band with six, seven, or sometimes even eight members) popularized the R&B combo. "With my little band, I did everything they did with a big band," Jordan said. "I made the blues jump."[80] Nelson George believes Jordan actually "standardized the size of the postwar black dance band," consciously recording song material that reflected the experience of urban blacks whose lives were often "not one generation removed from life in the rural South."[81] "Ain't Nobody Here But Us Chickens," "Barnyard Boogie," "Beans and Cornbread," and "Saturday Night Fish Fry" represent songs employing this approach. In addition, Jordan's crossover appeal was enhanced by his affiliation with a major record label. His producer, Milt Gabler, was white, his writers were frequently white, and he was able to record duets with other Decca stars, notably Bing Crosby and Ella Fitzgerald. According to John Chilton, his biographer, "only Fats Waller and Louis Armstrong had previously been able consistently to appeal to both black and white mass audiences."[82]

Robey could not have succeeded in exploiting the talents of Louis Jordan at this stage in Peacock Record's history, but he was able to acquire veteran musicians Memphis Slim (five previous hits) and Floyd Dixon (two previous hits), whose "Sad Journey Blues" was the first Peacock record to make a *Billboard* R&B chart.[83] Robey also signed the Original Five Blind Boys of Mississippi (formerly the Jackson Harmoneers), a "hard" gospel group with much experience but little success in the studio. "Our Father," the group's third release, is still famous for the shocking blood-curdling scream by lead singer Archie Brownlee that caused the song to become a juke box hit—unprecedented for a religious record. "You drive down the so-called bad streets," Evelyn Johnson remembers, "and coming out of the juke joints you would hear Lightnin' Hopkins and Smokey Hogg and that kind of thing and then the next thing you would hear would be 'Our Father' by the Blind Boys and then behind that you would hear 'Tennessee Waltz' [by Patti Page]. Those two records hit the juke boxes in areas where it was unbelievable."[84]

Robey's strategy in signing performers with at least some experience not only paid immediate dividends in sales, but the extraordinary success of the Blind Boy's gospel record ("Our Father" sold an estimated half a million copies) inadvertently established a winning formula that he used for almost a quarter-century. Robey learned the marketing advantage of alternating the release of his secular records with religious ones. Later, he claimed that it was he "who put the [rhythmic] beat into religious records." "I was highly criticized when I started it," he said, "but I put the first beat—which was not a drum—and then after the public started to buy the beat, why, then I put a drum into it."[85] In this fashion, gospel music became the mainstay of Peacock Records, the "bread and butter," according to Galen Gart, "while the occasional pop hit was its 'gravy.'"[86] Evelyn Johnson believes that Peacock actually became the "biggest gospel label in the country but never got credit for it." Ultimately, all gospel music was taken off the red Peacock label and given its own color—black.[87]

By December 1950, exactly one year since the establishment of Peacock Records was announced in *Billboard*, the future Johnny Ace was playing piano with B.B. King's band and practically living on Beale Street. He had yet to record "Midnight Hours Journey" or distinguish himself in any way. Robey, on the other hand, had recorded twenty-two different acts and had discovered many others—notably blues-shouter Willie Mae "Big Mama" Thornton. In addition, he had hired a full-time sales manager, Irving Marcus, who traveled the country promoting Peacock records and artists in the "territories," as the R&B markets were called.[88] Marcus taught Robey how to use the R&B columnist at *Billboard* to document his promotional activities.[89]

Except for the first ten sides, all of the Peacock recording sessions were conducted at Bill Holford's Audio Company of America (ACA) studio in Houston, "just a room, actually," but Holford knew how to engineer sound. Holford, who is white, developed a cordial and even social relationship with Robey, and he especially remembers the professionalism of the Peacock operation and the level of organization that Robey brought to the studio: "[Robey] had stuff well rehearsed before he even came in. And I remember he used to fine the musicians that came in late—five dollars or so. And he had the session down in his mind like he wanted it to go. He didn't hesitate telling them, either, and if he wanted to change something, he'd change it."[90] After Robey was satisfied with the sides, Holford mastered the tapes, frequently cutting multiple masters, which were sent to New Jersey, Indiana, and California manufacturers. "That was the system for smaller companies," Evelyn Johnson says. The records were then shipped to eight distributors around the country during the early years, and eventually to thirty-three distributors.[91]

In addition, Robey had learned how to keep costs down in the production of a Peacock record while at the same time increasing his own income. He began to register the copyrights for songs he was recording with the Library of Congress, filing generally as the author of both the words and the music and listing the copyright owner as the "Peacock Recording Co.," sometimes adding his own name as copyright owner as well. When it came time for Peacock Records to pay the statutory mechanical rights fee for the use of songs on a single record (two cents per side), Robey was able, essentially, to pay himself the four cents—more than five percent of the retail cost of one of his records ($0.79). In the event that one of the songs was able to log a significant number of public performances (radio airplay, for example), it was Don Robey as writer and Don Robey as publisher who would reap the benefit of the performance rights money paid quarterly by BMI.

Virtually all record companies—large and small—created publishing subsidiaries for the material they recorded, and Robey's Peacock Recording Co., which he soon renamed "Lion Publishing Co.," was established under existing industry practices. Robey was not the first record owner to demand publishing rights and a share of writer credit for the privilege of recording a song. Still, there is no doubt that he became an early master of this tactic. Floyd Dixon's "Sad Journey Blues," the first Peacock record to make the *Billboard* R&B charts, was credited fully to Robey (words and music by Don D. Robey, copyrighted by Peacock Recording Co. and Don D. Robey), as was the first Peacock big seller: "Our Father" by the Five Blind Boys.[92]

By January 1952, Robey's savvy as the owner of an independent record label was showing results in gross sales. *Billboard* announced that Peacock had purchased a complete pressing plant in Houston, justified by what Robey and Irving Marcus claimed to be a 300 percent increase in business in the preceding year.[93] Peacock Record's growth was not confined to sales alone, however. Robey's activity in signing acts and developing talent was so prolific in early 1952 that it is difficult to keep up with the exact status of Peacock Records at any moment. It appears, however, that by the end of the summer of 1952 Robey had recorded or released singles by almost fifty different performers or groups on the Peacock label and had announced the signing of several others.[94] Two milestones in the summer of 1952, however, would change the Robey operation from a regional to a national one: Willie Mae Thornton's recording of "Hound Dog" and the acquisition of Johnny Ace and the Duke record label.

Of the two events, signing Johnny Ace was not only the most significant accomplishment; it was the one that brought Robey the greatest satisfaction. All of his life he had demanded respect, pursued status, and admired class. Now he had the opportunity to achieve all three. Blues music, especially coarse "downhome" or "gut-bucket" blues, lacked all of the qualities he most admired. Indeed, it was forbidden in many black households and misunderstood in much of the white community. Evelyn Johnson contends that at the time "everything that a black person did was considered blues," even music that was clearly outside of the blues category.[95] The whole field of black music by black performers for a black audience may have been called rhythm and blues in the trade magazines, but it was, in Robey's words, "felt to be degrading, low, and not to be heard by respectable people."[96] Like W. C. Handy, Duke Ellington, and many others before him, he yearned to change the negative attitudes, create a more acceptable product, establish an upscale operation, and gain respectability.

This hunger for respectability may have been the primary motivation for Robey's aggressive acquistion of Johnny Ace's "My Song," which he heard first in July 1952. David (James) Mattis had established Duke Records only a few months earlier and had recorded only ten sides in all, but one of those, "My Song" by Johnny Ace and the Beale Streeters, was a hit with the limited audience that had heard it, creating a demand for records that Mattis's limited capital could not supply. Both Robey and Evelyn Johnson had been to Memphis on several occasions[97] (Peacock Records were played regularly on WDIA), and it was quite natural for a money-man like Robey to offer his services, especially when he heard the gentle quality of Johnny Ace's voice, singing not a blues verse but a standard AABA pop song in a fully respectable crooning style owing more to the world of white popular music.

The arrangement made perfect sense. "We already had the contacts," says Evelyn Johnson. "In spite of the fact that [Mattis] was in radio—that too might have been a hindrance for him. But we were already established. We had distributors and that sort of thing and we were already paying off disk jockeys. Our little road was open. It was just a little old path, but it was open."[98] Even the crudeness of the Duke production must have inspired Robey, who knew perfectly well how to obtain a clean, professional sound. So Don Robey, the black entrepreneur with a checkered past and aggressive business practices from Houston, formed a partnership with David James Mattis, the white radio executive from Memphis who still refers to himself as "the only blues manager with a heart."[99] "That partnership," Evelyn Johnson says, "was like oil and water. And I was standing in the middle the whole time."[100]

"Pledging My Love," Billboard's most played R&B record of 1955, a BMI "Millionaire Song," and perhaps the first rock 'n' roll record, in its 78 rpm configuration for the R&B market. The flip side, "No Money," is an Ace blues composition. Note Don Robey's songwriting credit. "ACA 2801" denotes the accession number at the Audio Corporation of America studio in Houston. (Author's collection)

8514

INQUEST PROCEEDINGS

temporarily at crystal Hotel 3520 Lyons **DECEASED.**

John Alexander known as Johnnie Ace - 899 Tucker Ave. Memphis Tenn.

Place of conducting inquest *Back stage in dressing room City Auditorium (no side)*

Nationality *negro*   Age *26*   Sex *male*

Death occurred *about*   *11:* P M; *25* day of *Dec*   19 *54*

Body discovered by *General present*   *25* day of —   19 —
Lt. W. C Dees to night clerk
Coroner notified by *Fred White*   at *11:40 P* M. *25* day of —   19 —

Cause of Death *Playing Russian Roulette - Bullet wound in right temples. self inflicted*

Location of wounds *Entrance about 1" above + 2" to right of right eye. no exit. Deceased had been drinking + playing with small 22 calibre H+R revolver + according to officers had also snapped the pistol after spinning the cylinder at his girl friend seated on his lap at the time*

Personal effects taken from body of deceased *a 3 stone yellow gold ring (diamond) a Lucerne wrist watch 2 in clip key chain, + 5 keys, lighter + $23.20 Currency (no billfold or credentials)*

Disposition of property *% y Received above — Florin K. Bradford, mc Donald Building Houston, Tex.*

Description of surroundings, condition of body, etc. *Fully clothed in gray suit, lying on floor in dressing room off stage at city Auditorium. Room in disorder + cluttered with whisky + vodka bottles, one on table with Vodka still in bottle. There had been a negro christmas dance at the auditorium + the floor of the auditorium was cluttered with empty half pint whisky*

Persons present when death occurred

Johnny Ace's Inquest Proceedings setting the time of death at approximately 11:00 P.M. *on 25 December 1954 and the cause of death as self-inflicted.*

RE/Death of Johnny Alexander @ Johnny Ace.

STATE OF TEXAS   §   December 26, 1954

COUNTY OF HARRIS   §   12:40 A.M.

Before me, the undersigned authority this day personally appeared Olivia Gibbs, who is a credible person and who after having been sworn did depose and say:

My name is Olivia Gibbs. I am 22 years old and live at 1814 Alabama. I was the girl-friend of Johnny Ace. We had been going together for about a year and a half. Johnny Ace, who is a featured singer and piano player of the Johnny Board Band. He was the leader of the band and accompanied by Johnny Board. He and the band arrived into Houst Wednesday afternoon. They came here to fill an engagement at the City Auditorrium Chri night.

Johnny Ace worked last night in Port Author, Texas and came back to Houston this mornin around 9:00 A.M. He went to sleep at my apartment and woke up about 2:30 P.M. He invi the members of the band over to my place for dinner. At that time Johnny started playi with a small 22 caliber pistol. He played the game of Russian Roulette with this gun t afternoon. The gun was not loaded this afternoon when he was playing with it.

Tonight Johnny Ace sang and played the piano at the Auditorium. At intermission he tol me that he didn't think he would go back out on the stage because of a toothache. I went and got him an asprin. There were several of us sitting in the dressing room of the auditorium. This was around 11:00 P.M. Johnny was sitting on the table and I was by hi and he had his arm around me. Some of the other persons in the room at the time were Mary Carter, Willie Mae Thornton, Earnest Easley, Joe Hammond. At that time Johnny sta fooling with this little pistol again. I did not think it was loaded. I saw Johnny lo at the gun and then he put it up to my head and pulled the trigger and it snapped. I s him look at the gun again and then he put it up to his head and pulled the trigger and the gun fired. He then fell off of the table and on to the floor. Everybody ran out o the room except Mary Carter, Willie Mae Thornton and me. I thought that he was just playing and I picked up his head and then I saw the blood. I then ran to the box offi and told Evelyn Johnson that Johnny had shot himself.

This is all I know about the above case. I have read the above statement and it is true and correct.

Signed   *Olivia Gibbs*
                   Olivia Gibbs

Subscribed and sworn to before me this 26th day of December A.D., 1954.

                         D.M. Fults, Notary Public in and
                         for Harris County, Tex.

Doc/

Deposition by Olivia Gibbs, Johnny Ace's girlfriend, who witnessed the shooting. D. M. ("Doc") Fults, the Houston Police detective who took this testimony, believes he is "probably the only one left alive on that [Johnny Ace investigation] deal."

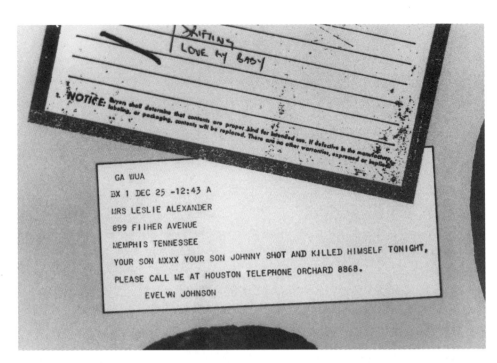

DRIFTING
LOVE MY BABY

2. **NOTICE:** Buyers shall determine that contents are proper kind for intended use. If defective in the manufacture, labeling, or packaging, contents will be replaced. There are no other warranties, expressed or implied.

GA WUA
BX 1 DEC 25 -12:43 A
MRS LESLIE ALEXANDER
899 FIIHER AVENUE
MEMPHIS TENNESSEE
YOUR SON MXXX YOUR SON JOHNNY SHOT AND KILLED HIMSELF TONIGHT,
PLEASE CALL ME AT HOUSTON TELEPHONE ORCHARD 8868.
        EVELYN JOHNSON

Ralph Matthew's drawing and rendering of the Ace shooting to accompany his article on the death of Johnny Ace for the Cleveland Call and Post, *15 January 1955. (Courtesy of the* Cleveland Call and Post*)*

Facing page, top: *The fraudulent telegram with a dateline almost twenty-two hours before Ace's death. "I sent a telegram to tell his mother on a telegram that he had shot himself to death?" Evelyn Johnson asks. "That's the most ridiculous thing! To me, that's an insult! It's degrading!" (Author's collection)*

Facing page, bottom: *Johnny Ace in state. The funeral crowd in Memphis, estimated at five thousand, could not be accommodated by Clayborn AME Temple, which seated only two thousand. This event was not considered newsworthy by the white newspapers in Memphis. (Courtesy of Ernest Withers, Photographer)*

Top: *This 45 rpm version of "Pledging My Love" for the pop market is arguably the first rock 'n' roll record. "Pledging My Love" sold more 45s than 78s, and the pace of its popularity was slowed only by the manufacturer's inability to satisfy demand for the record in this configuration. (Courtesy of the Victor Pearlin Collection)*

Bottom: *Memorial Album for Johnny Ace (LP 70), the first 33⅓ rpm album released by one of Don Robey's labels, in March 1955, contained the eight songs that Robey insisted were Ace's hits. For collectors, its value today is $600–1,000. (Courtesy of the Victor Pearlin Collection)*

Top: *Sheet music for "Pledging My Love," a first for Don Robey's Lion Publishing Company and a tribute to the song's mainstream success. (Courtesy of the Victor Pearlin Collection)*

Bottom: *A Tribute to Johnny Ace (EP 81), one of two EPs released in March 1955 after Ace's white teenage fans demanded 45 rpm versions of his previous records. Together, EP 81 and EP 80 contain the same songs as Memorial Album for Johnny Ace (LP 70). (Courtesy of the Victor Pearlin Collection)*

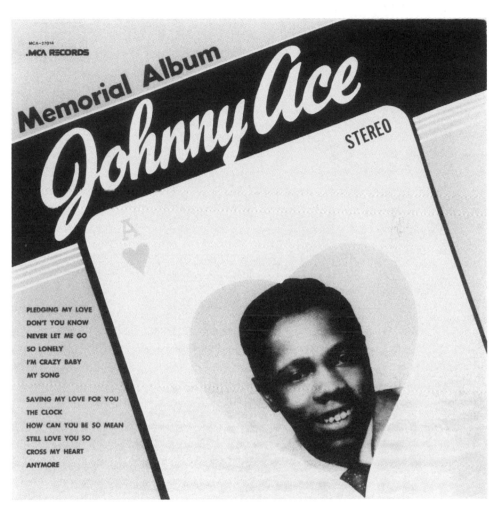

Memorial Album for Johnny Ace, *a conventional twelve-inch LP released in 1957, often referred to as "Memorial Album Number II" because it superseded the original ten-inch LP that included only eight songs. Robey sold out the Duke catalog in 1973. This 1980s version, MCA-27014, is the same album as Duke DLP-71, including front and back covers and liner notes by Dzondria LaIsac. (Author's collection)*

T. O. M. A. PRODUCTIONS
★ ★ PRESENTS ★ ★
"JOHNNY ACE LIVES"
In Honor of Black History Month
"ST. CLAIR ACE"
Will Revive The Buried History of his Brother, The First
R & B Cross-Over Artist

In A Musical Salute of His Greatest Hits
"Pledging My Love" - "The Clock", Etc.
PLUS HIS OWN COMPOSITION
"RADIATION FLU"
2 SHOWS A NIGHT
10:30 P. M. & 12 MIDNIGHT
★ MUSIC BY ★

ST. CLAIR ACE
ENERGY, TIME AND SPACE
FRI. & SAT.
Featuring The Sax Preacher

FEBRUARY 27 & 28 - 1987
—AT—
CADILLAC BOB'S SHOWROOM
105 EAST 115 STREET - DONATION $5.00
For More Information Contact: D. Wilson 723-7531 - Bob Cherry 821-9293
Sponsored By The Gene Ammons Memorial Foundation School of Performing Arts
★ ★ A NON-PROFIT ORGANIZATION ★ ★

A 1987 poster promoting a Johnny Ace tribute in Memphis by his brother, whose real last name is Alexander. St. Clair could sing his brother's songs but could never replicate his timing. "He had an off-beat singing style in all his songs," St. Clair says. "That's what made him so unique." (Author's collection)

Heart

Ballads

Robey's partnership with Mattis was as short as it was tempestuous. Only months after forming Duke Records in April, Mattis brought in Robey as a partner in July. Months after that, in November, Duke was a permanent part of Peacock Records, and Mattis was out in the cold. Between July and November the two men worked less than six hundred miles apart on the map, but the personal distance between them increased as Robey began to direct his full-time attention to the exploitation of his new Duke Records artists. And while Robey had good reason to be interested in "the whole Memphis scene,"[1] the particular property that energized his actions most was Johnny Ace and his first single record "My Song."

Robey heard in "My Song" not only the vulnerability and innocence in Ace's youthful voice but a new sound represented by the Memphis synthesis as well. A pretty blues ballad like "My Song" "would normally have demanded a pop treatment (maybe a soft chorus)," R&B historian Al Pavlow says. "Instead, it was fitted with a typical Memphis '52 track, which included piano and sax. The combination of these elements was unbeatable."[2] Mattis has claimed that "Don Robey was a black man who didn't understand his people's music,"[3] but it is clear that Robey knew exactly what he was doing when he acquired Ace, the other Duke artists, and masters of their recording sessions. Johnny Otis, whose band had produced several hits for the Peacock label and who was to become the producer of most Ace sides, remembers "the charm" of "My Song" when Robey played it for him, probably in July 1952. "When I heard it I told [Robey], 'God, that's nice.' And he said, 'I'm buying it, and I'm gonna put it out.'"[4]

"My Song" begins much like "Midnight Hours Journey." The singer is alone, depressed, and vulnerable. "You told me that you would leave me here in tears," he admits in the first verse. "Now you're gone and hours seem like years. So darling, I sing my song." "Your leaving," Ace sings mournfully in the second verse, "make my heart beat low and slow"—not quite grammatical but certainly emotionally effective. Indeed, he would become famous for making the hearts of his R&B audience "beat low and slow." In the bridge, the drums and saxophone provide rhythmic punches to highlight the insistence of the lyrics. "I still love you," the singer claims, "won't you please come back to me. Come back where you ought to be." Suddenly, his voice turns confident. "Don't stay from me," he warns, "'cause you'll always be my own. We'll be together for eternity."

Robey's intentions regarding the Duke operation were clear from the start: he would call all the shots. The first thing he did as managing partner of Duke Records was to arrange for a full-page ad in *Billboard* announcing his new acquisition: "Peacock Proudly Introduces Duke Records." The display ad described Duke as a "hot rhythm and blues line" and positioned Ace's "My Song" as a record at the cutting edge of black popular music ("Johnny Ace With the New Blues Sound"). The ad also promoted fellow Beale Streeters Rosco Gordon, Earl Forest, and a vocalist whom Robey called simply "Bobby Blue" [*sic*].[5] Within a week, Robey's connections, money, and business expertise had successfully promoted "My Song" into *Billboard*'s Top 10 "Best Selling Retail Rhythm & Blues Records," where it remained for twenty weeks, including nine weeks at the top spot.[6] In mid-August, Robey promoted "My Song" in New York so successfully at a music trade show sponsored by the National Association of Music Merchandisers that, according to one source, he sold 53,000 copies of the record "before it was released."[7] Ace probably appeared in person to perform his hit song at this gathering, and it is likely that papers for the Robey-Mattis partnership were formally signed at this time.[8]

Evidence suggests that Robey had predatory designs on Duke from the start, since he immediately began a series of maneuvers aimed at moving the entire Duke operation from Memphis to Houston. The muddy sound of the WDIA studio produced by the primitive equipment (an old Berlant tape recorder and three inadequate microphones) was completely unacceptable to a man of Robey's standards and accomplishments. Though Mattis continued to write songs, rehearse musicians, and conduct recording sessions, it appears that the only Duke recordings actually made in Memphis were the ten sides (two of them by Ace) representing activity before Robey became a partner.[9] Once Robey was involved he arranged immediately for the newly acquired Duke artists (most of whom were members of the Beale Streeters band) to travel to Houston to record at Bill Holford's ACA studio for subsequent sessions, effectively cutting Mattis out of any significant action in the company he had founded.

As a full but inactive partner in Duke Records, Mattis found it impossible to get Robey to send him any of the money now being made in Houston. So, he says, he exercised an option in their agreement to become a full and *active* partner. He quit his job at WDIA in November 1952, went to Houston, and announced to Robey, "'I'm here to exercise my partnership,' and [Robey] said, 'There'll be nothing like that.' That's when the .45 came out on the desk." Mattis stayed in Houston for ten days and began legal proceedings that took six months to resolve.[10] "He had no idea of what's right," Mattis says. "The only thing he could do was pull a big automatic pistol out and slam it on his desk. I settled with Robey for the whole share of [Duke Records] for ten thousand dollars, and I had about seven in it. He had about a couple hundred thousand on the books."[11] Evelyn Johnson does not believe that Robey pulled a gun on Dave Mattis, but she acknowledges that Robey carried one. "He *always* wore a gun," she says, "always wore a gun. I think he was impressing himself, because he had no notches in those guns. It was an image he was living up to."[12]

Gatemouth Brown has told many people the story of how Robey pulled a gun on him during this period. "When he pulled it on me, he got the shit whupped out of him, that's what happened," Brown says. "I tore his ass up." After the altercation over money, Brown ran home in a rage to get his own gun. He was going to kill Robey, he says, but someone telephoned his wife to warn her, and she hid his weapon.[13] There are other stories of Robey allegedly pulling his gun or placing it on his desk in arguments with his artists over money up through the 1960s and accounts of more ordinary physical violence on his part. "Robey was a cold-blooded man," Roosevelt Jamison told Peter Guralnick, "he wasn't scared of the fork-tongued devil."[14] Little Richard claims in his autobiography that Robey once jumped on him, knocked him down, and kicked him in the stomach. "He would beat everybody up but Big Mama Thornton," he says. "He was scared of her. She was built like a big bull."[15] Evelyn Johnson believes that Little Richard's stories about Don Robey represent "flat, bald-faced lies," but she does remember Robey slapping him once.[16]

Mattis was not the only person to start out as a partner with Robey and end up outside of the action,[17] nor is there any evidence to suggest that Robey ever meant to share power with the original owner of Duke Records. Mattis was an amateur in the record business in every way. He did not understand copyrights, mechanical royalties, or performance rights. He did not know how to launch a major talent like Johnny Ace, how to build momentum for a record like "My Song," guarantee radio airplay in the territorial markets, or secure national industry attention. Nor could Mattis put capital into Ace's career, provide him with a backup band, and send him on the road to support his record sales with personal appearances; so Robey went ahead as if he had no partner. He put up front money into Johnny Ace just as he had done earlier with Gatemouth Brown, buying him new clothes, arranging for suitable transportation, and exploiting him nationally. This time, however, he was careful to cultivate the kind of polished, first-class, uptown image that Berry Gordy would later emulate at Motown. "I remember when Johnny Ace came here," Evelyn Johnson says. "He had gathered up a little money from someplace and he had a little pasteboard suitcase, and in that suitcase was, like, a shirt, and maybe some underwear—everything in there was new—toothpaste, toothbrush, and that's about all. And of course the first thing we did was take him to a tailor, we had a couple of tailors who were in the business, and get him outfitted."[18] "In a week, he was sharp," Robey told *Ebony*. "I knew the value of the boy, even then."[19]

Robey's idea of signing the talent, cutting the records, copyrighting the songs, and then booking the recording artists in venues all over America made his new, overall operation (Duke/Peacock/Lion Publishing/Buffalo

Booking) "the South's largest recording and talent enterprise of its kind."[20] Nelson George argues that the geographical remoteness of Robey's organization was probably an asset. Harlem was a magnet for "Afro-America's brightest talents," he says, but it "never had a black-owned operation of comparable stature."[21]

It is important to note that Don Robey was in the rhythm and blues business before it was called "rhythm and blues," and that the first records he produced for Gatemouth Brown (had they charted) would have been listed by *Billboard* as "race records"; *Billboard* didn't use the term "rhythm and blues" until its 25 June 1949 issue. Moreover, the field of black popular music in black styles by black performers for black audiences was a widely diversified one by the 1950s, including country and urban blues, jump bands, blues shouters, jazz, vocal groups, torch singers, novelty songs, and crooners. Though R&B is usually thought of as loud, up-tempo music, a tradition of commercially successful soft ballad singers (generally piano players as well) was almost twenty-five years old by 1952, established by Leroy Carr (1905–35), "the father," according to Arnold Shaw, of the "murmuring, gentle *vibrato* ballad style."[22] Carr emerged in 1928 on the Vocalion label with "How Long, How Long Blues," and is also widely known for "In the Evening (When the Sun Goes Down)." He was perhaps "the first impressive blues pianist," Shaw says, with a voice employing "crystal clear" diction, whose "great forte was in creating a mood, especially of longing and loneliness."[23]

Cecil Gant (1913–52), the "G.I. Sing-Sation," continued Carr's ballad style into the 1940s (he even recorded Carr's "In the Evening (When the Sun Goes Down"), but he became famous for "I Wonder," a sad ballad sung by a soldier worrying about who his sweetheart is sleeping with back home. Gant was influenced by Bing Crosby, Arnold Shaw says, "then at the peak of his popularity, and by newly arrived [Frank Sinatra]. In short, a sepia crooner with blues inflections and a black sound." "I Wonder" was so successful crossing over to the pop market that it "promoted the rapid rise of small record companies on the west coast" and made Gant the first of the "Sepia Sinatras."[24] If Gant was the first, then Nat "King" Cole was surely the most successful, accounting for his career as a race act until his full emergence into pop music from jazz in 1948.

Charlie Gillett credits Nat Cole (1917–65) with helping originate the "club singing style," which he believes was not part of black musical tradition (Cole's race was "irrelevant to his style") but rather a development resulting from wartime racial mixing in California nightclubs, where customers wanted to hear music while they carried on their conversations. He posits that the "unusual integrated audience may have encouraged the black singers to minimize the blues content of their repertoire" and that the vocalists were compelled "to develop a style that instilled a mood without requiring that all the words be heard."[25] Cole's music "embodied the sophistication and street-smart savoir faire that was burgeoning close to both sides of the tracks in New York and Los Angeles," says Nick Tosches; "Cole was the link between the old and the new, the dungarees and the sharkskin britches."[26] When Cole gave up the club scene in Los Angeles for a more national audience in the pop field, his place was taken by Charles Brown (born 1922), the vocalist/piano player with Johnny Moore's Three Blazers, who replaced Cole's relaxed self-confidence with sadness, exemplifying singers who "had become narcissistically preoccupied with the depths of their misery, seemingly unable to find a cause for hope or gladness."[27]

All of Ace's hits, beginning with "My Song," are R&B ballads. The tone he employs—warm and relaxed—reflects the feeling of a Nat "King" Cole song, but the mood he communicates—pain and sorrow—is in the tradition of Leroy Carr/Cecil Gant/Charles Brown. Perhaps this combination of tone and mood, a synthesis of the extremes of the black crooning style, accounts for what Mattis heard as "soft purple sounds." "I just happened to recognize something that I hadn't heard before," he remembers. The industry credited "My Song" with beginning a new musical trend. "Ace's simple and unaffected style of singing, his evident sincerity and heart," *Billboard* reported after his death, "actually started the r.&b. field on a type of song that has come to be known as a 'heart ballad.'"[28] Ace's first "heart ballad" (others called this blend of vocal performance, material, and attitude the "beat ballad" or the "blues ballad") generated increased activity in covering—the industry practice of recording "covers" (performances) of the same song by other artists. "This is the first r.&b. ditty that has spurred this many [three] versions in a long time," noted *Billboard*.[29] The extraordinary success of "My Song," coming from an unknown artist on an unfamiliar label, also illustrated the vitality and openness of the R&B market at the time.

Because independent R&B hits in the 1950s lacked the extensive marketing and distribution systems of the major labels that permitted the simultaneous national distribution of a pop record, they were vulnerable to competing cover versions. In R&B especially, in which small, independent operations were the lifeblood of the genre, a single label could rarely promote a song in all of the regional markets (*Billboard* called them territories) simultaneously. Johnny Ace's first hit, "My Song," is a case in point. The recording broke first in Detroit and New York in the middle of November, then in Los Angeles, the D.C. area, Charlotte, and Philadelphia a week later, and finally, at the end of the month, in St. Louis. But it never penetrated the charts in Atlanta, Chicago, Cincinnati, or New Orleans. As it happened routinely in rhythm and blues, in some markets Ace's original version of "My Song" was introduced to an audience that was already familiar with one of the "cover" versions. "By now the first side will have proved its five-star rating by racking up five-star sales," *Down Beat* declared when it finally reviewed Ace's "My Song" in October. "Although the singing, the balance and the performance of the accompanying Beale Streeters are distinctly inferior to Dinah Washington's and other later performances, this is the [version] that started the whole thing."

Down Beat, more musically sophisticated than the trade magazines, could not resist pointing out the song's melodic and harmonic similarities with "So Long," which had been a hit, it reminded readers, back in 1946 for Johnny Moore's Three Blazers and again in 1949 for Ruth Brown.[30] "On Broadway was a big circular sign that had Johnny Ace's picture in the middle with everybody else who covered the song pictured around him," Evelyn Johnson remembers. "*Down Beat*, a magazine, said, 'Mr. and Mrs. John Q. Public want 'My Song' by Johnny Ace, bad music and all.'"[31] In addition, an R&B hit could have considerable longevity, remaining number one in the black community for five or six months, a time during which a pop artist would have replaced an old hit with a new song. Pop hits were disposable commodities; an R&B song, Johnny Otis says, "could become almost an anthem." Six months after the release of "My Song," the initial momentum had certainly faded, but the record continued to chart at number three in national sales, number five in juke box plays, and was still considered a current hit in most of the regional markets. To encourage the sales of "My Song" around the country, Robey already had Ace on the road doing one-nighters in the secondary markets and longer engagements at the Orchard Room in Kansas City and the Club Alabam in Los Angeles.[32]

Robey had vowed publicly not to be rushed into a new Ace recording session for his new star until he found the "right material,"[33] but in fact he already had the material and had been sitting on it for months, waiting for

"My Song" to play itself out. Immediately after "My Song" fell off the national R&B charts in December 1952 Robey released Ace's "Cross My Heart" (Duke 107), another AABA ballad with the same I–vi–ii–V progression as the first hit, even the same a–a–b–c–c–b rhyme scheme. "Cross My Heart" was essentially the same song as "My Song" (credited to Mattis/Alexander), only this time the writing credit specified Mattis and Don Robey.[34] The history of the recording session of "Cross My Heart" is as contentious as the Mattis-Robey partnership itself. It appears that there were two distinct Duke Records operations at work in the late summer and early fall of 1952. In Memphis, David Mattis continued to write songs, rehearse the Beale Streeters, and record material for Johnny Ace at the WDIA studios. "Johnny just sang whatever was put in front of him," he recalls about the "Cross My Heart" session: "I had had a Hammond organ put into the studio, I rented it myself for some kind of a gospel thing. And it was sitting in there, next to the piano, when we came in to cut 'Cross My Heart' and 'Angel.' And he sat down, he was playing with the thing. And I said, 'Hey, would you like to cut something with that?' He said, 'Oh yeah.' Never had touched one of the things before. We cut 'Cross My Heart' in about 15 minutes."[35]

There is no doubt that Mattis produced a "Cross My Heart" session in late summer or early fall 1952; indeed, he may have produced as many as ten sides in this period for Johnny Ace, Earl Forest, Rosco Gordon, and Bobby Bland. A typewritten memo from 2 November 1952 summarizes session charges to be deducted from royalties due to these Duke artists.[36] After the initial partnership with Robey ("the bill of goods," he calls it) Mattis is certain to this day that he cut the songs and Robey only mastered the tapes. "I would just send the tapes down to Houston," Mattis maintains. "They were not recorded there; they were just mastered there." Actually, Robey was re-recording everything in Houston. Soon after he acquired an interest in Duke Records he arranged (probably in August or early September 1952) for all the musicians Mattis called the Beale Streeters to travel to Houston to record at Bill Holford's Audio Company of America (ACA) studio on Washington Avenue. Ace recorded four songs at this session, Bobby Bland four, Earl Forest four, and Rosco Gordon six. "I don't remember these particular sessions, because I cut so much stuff for [Robey]," Bill Holford says, "but they're in the [studio log] book, and that book hasn't been touched since it was written."[37]

Since "Cross My Heart" was obviously written in Memphis, it is quite likely that Johnny Ace "faked out the melody" to the song in the same manner as "My Song," though under Robey's direction he did not get songwriter credit. Since Robey rarely released records without giving himself at least co-writer credit, it would have been perfectly consistent for him to claim half of "Cross My Heart," let Mattis have the other half, and shut the recording artist out altogether. Of Ace's seven certified R&B hits after "My Song," Robey took writer credit on all but two. Ace, however, was allowed to acquire co-writer credit with Mattis for the "B" side of the record, an AABA ballad called "Angel."

"Cross My Heart" has additional significance: it was the first Ace record to display something more than mere amateur production, and the improved quality of both sides is immediately discernible. Holford was an audio engineer who had been in the recording business since 1948. Though his ACA studio was "just a room," he knew how to engineer the sound, position the microphones (he used eight), and set the levels. With his Ampex 300 mono tape recorder there was no overdubbing, but he had an ear for quality. "We took things straight," he remembers, "and did them over until we got it right." In addition, he worked well with Robey, with whom he had a long and successful professional relationship, and trusted Robey's professional instincts. "Robey was always the producer," Holford says. "He was the one who was paying for the session, and he sat beside me and told me what he wanted and told the musicians what he wanted."[38]

The musical arrangement of Duke 107 represents a significant improvement as well, though it appears that the instrumentation of the backup band was identical to those used in the original sessions cut in Memphis (both songs feature two saxophones and a full rhythm section). On "Cross My Heart," Ace plays a Hammond organ that Bill Holford happened to have in his studio to accommodate John Norman's production of the radio show *Night Mare!* Ace's "delicate touch on that much-abused instrument, countered with lovely vibraphone work" makes the record, according to Peter Grendysa, "an R&B masterpiece."[39]

Some evidence suggests that Robey couldn't make up his mind which song on Duke 107 should be the "A" side and that he let the industry decide, suggesting in the *Billboard* advertisement on 3 January 1953 that either side might represent the next Johnny Ace hit. A week later Duke 107 was listed as one of the "New Records to Watch": "Both sides are slow-paced ballads with strong ork [orchestral] backing. 'Cross My Heart' likely side. It's cut from the same cloth as 'My Song.'" On 17 January, "Cross My Heart" was one of "This Week's Territorial Best Sellers to Watch," having broken in St. Louis and selling strong in Philadelphia, New York, and markets in the South. "Disk surging up fast," *Billboard* reported on 24 January. "Already on New York, Philadelphia and St. Louis charts. Picked up by dealers [number one] and operators [number four]."[40] By the next week "Cross My Heart" had made both national charts (number five sales, number ten juke boxes). "A solid smash," said *Billboard*. *Down Beat* was equally impressed, awarding "Cross My Heart" five stars and "Angel" four:

> Johnny Ace, coming off his big hit, *My Song*, contributes another song of the same genre which seems destined to become another hit record. Side features the plaintive Ace approach. This one should do it.
>
> *Angel* is a good song, quietly sung, and might make some noise on its own. But top deck looks like the side.[41]

"Cross My Heart" peaked in mid-February at numbers four sales and three juke boxes. The only territory in which the Ace record was not a hit was Chicago, the home of Chess Records and one of the markets that "My Song" never penetrated.

Robey later told the press that he had lost thousands of dollars on Duke 107 because the songs on both sides of the record "hit with equal vigor," causing him to send out "two hits for the price of one."[42] "We billed it as a double hit," Evelyn Johnson recalls.[43] The industry disagreed. "Angel" was never certified as a hit by the trade publications, though it apparently generated some radio airplay and juke box action after "Cross My Heart" had played itself out. Robey's assertion that "Angel" was a hit reveals more about the attention he was paying to developing Ace's career and exploiting his talents than about any loss of income. Sometime between the first Duke recording session in Houston and the release of "Cross My Heart"/"Angel" in December, Robey put together a band to back Ace for personal appearances and booked him through the Buffalo Booking Agency. Not only did these personal appearances generate their own fees; they supported record sales and maintained a system in which the artist was essentially responsible for earning his own living. One of the few ways for an R&B performer to see some actual money in the early 1950s was to make it on the road.

(Mattis claims that when Robey took over Duke Records he reduced the artist royalty from two-and-a-half cents a record to one-half cent.)[44] If hit records weren't the surest way to artistic wealth, they at least increased personal performance fees—for Ace an estimated $600 a night.[45]

Not only did Don Robey's system of interlocking music-related companies require personal performances to guarantee success, but the overall realities of the rhythm and blues business in the postwar era demanded it. Once Johnny Ace became a rhythm and blues star, it was inevitable that he would spend most of his nights on the road, becoming, according to the Duke/Peacock publicist, the "King of One Night Stands."[46] As Charles Sawyer properly points out in regard to B.B. King, to achieve a "self-sustaining career" for a black musician performing black music for a black audience in an America not yet changed by the civil rights movement, five essential ingredients were required: a suitable road band, reliable transportation, a national booking agency (King was a client of the Buffalo Booking Agency for nine years), a record company to release "a steady string of modest hits," and personal appearances to give the artist "long-term exposure to audiences who dependably patronized his music." King's career (like Ace's) was necessarily constricted by a "built-in ceiling" at the time, "beamed at the lower economic strata of black American society." Both Buffalo Booking and the R&B artists' record companies (King on Modern and Ace on Duke) "dealt with clientele who served the same market—ghetto theaters, small-town dances, country dance halls and roadside joints—called the chitlin circuit."[47]

Neither the relative small size of the venues nor the economic disadvantage of the clientele prevented the operation from being totally professional. For artists signed to the Duke and Peacock labels, Evelyn Johnson had created by 1952 perhaps the most efficient system for arranging personal appearances of any independent label in America. As she told Alan Govenar, "the acts I booked worked more than any other show on the road. Maybe for less money, but they were working for two reasons, not only for their living, but for mental stability. This was their life. So the more they did, the better off they were. And they worked more than anybody on the road." She remembers clearly how difficult it was to establish acts on the road in those days, and when she did establish them to help them keep "their heads above water until their time came. When I first met B.B. King," she says, "he couldn't move to the next town."[48]

Johnny Ace, of course, had the advantage of considerable national exposure before he even went on the road. Not only was "My Song" a number one R&B hit, but—according to *Billboard* tabulations—it was the sixth best-selling R&B record in stores for all of 1952 and the seventh most played on juke boxes. On his first time out, Johnny Ace's record ranked higher than current releases by B.B. King, Fats Domino, Roy Milton, or Joe Turner.[49] Even so, Johnson recalls the early days when "a band of his caliber" had to settle for a performance fee of $350. "It wasn't too long before we went up to $600, to $750, and $1,000," she says. "It wasn't too long because of his record sales."[50]

While his appearance fees continued to rise, Ace's supporting cast, members of his road band, continued to improve. When Milton Hopkins joined the Johnny Ace band in late 1952, it was already playing four or five nights a week. The musical director was Johnny Board, originally from Chicago, who had performed with Coleman Hawkins and Lionel Hampton and been a member of the Count Basie band after World War II.[51] More recently, Board had been a tenor and alto saxophone player with a road band backing vocalists signed to Robey's Peacock label—essentially the Robey house band. Robey named this aggregation the Johnny Board Orchestra and permitted it to receive accompaniment credit for Johnny Ace records on which the band never played. By accident or design, all of Ace's records credit a single band as backup group on both sides, and several performances credited to the Johnny Board Orchestra are actually by Johnny Otis. According to Hopkins, who played guitar, the other band members were Joe Scott (trumpet), Milton Bradford (baritone and tenor sax), C.C. Pinkston (drums and vibes), and Curtis Tillman (bass).[52] Paul Monday, who played piano, was also a member of the band, which by March 1953 was backing not only Ace but Willie Mae "Big Mama" Thornton as well.

————————

Willie Mae Thornton was born on 11 December 1926 in Montgomery, Alabama, the sixth child of George W. Thornton, a Baptist minister, and his wife Mattie, who sang in the church choir. As a child Willie Mae exhibited musical talent. She taught herself to play harmonica by watching her older brother and salvaging his discards. "Every time he would throw [a harmonica] away and buy another one she would go and get the old one and practice," her sister Mattie Fields says. "And that's how she learned."[53]

Willie Mae's musical talents found other directions, too. At age twelve her singing won first prize in an amateur program at her hometown theater. What filled her childhood hours turned out to be important as a means of support after her mother died in 1939 or 1940. For a time she washed floors in a Montgomery tavern, but she was never far from music. She dropped out of school and left Montgomery at age fourteen to become a member of Sammy Green's Hot Harlem Revue, an Atlanta variety show that toured small-market southeastern cities. She reportedly drew the attention of the group when she helped them move a piano from a Montgomery street to a second-floor dancehall. "I can sing a little, too," she told those who hooted at her tomboy actions.[54] What may appear today as a desperate act of a teen-age girl was not particularly uncommon for black girls in the Deep South before World War II. "During them days, you had to actually run away so to speak," Mattie Fields says. "Parents wanted you to work at home, in the fields and stuff. But she didn't. She left. And that's when she left school also."

The Hot Harlem Revue was a self-contained show with featured singers, dancers, comedians, and a band. "You couldn't repeat," says Billy Wright, who danced with the group when Thornton was a member. "Had to have a new show, new material every week." Essentially, the circuit was an Alabama-Georgia operation. "We'd play Birmingham every Monday and Tuesday, Montgomery on Wednesday, Macon on Thursday, then back to Atlanta for Friday and Saturday," Wright remembers. "Sometimes go to Dothan (Alabama)."[55] Thornton sang, danced, played harmonica and drums, and performed comedy with the revue until 1948, when she had a falling out with the ownership and quit in a disagreement over money.

The anger she directed at Hot Harlem served to propel her into Don Robey's orbit. Thornton moved to Houston and worked the club scene, where she sang with Roy Milton's, Joe Liggins's, and other local bands. Don Robey saw her at the Eldorado Club, signed her to Peacock Records, booked her into his Bronze Peacock Dinner Club, and began to develop her talent.[56] She had already developed a reputation for heavy drinking, crudeness, bitterness, vulgarity, and masculine behavior. Robey's "right hand," Evelyn Johnson, who as head of the Buffalo Booking Agency was supposed to prepare her for the road, considered Thornton a "female thug":

> She was very blunt, and she used a lot of bad language. She wore khaki pants, plaid shirts, all the time. Part of it was her overall mental thing.

Part of it was her exposure, and it was just her. And she was very prone to say, "I ain't wearing that." And finally it was just a matter of going to some of the stores where I shopped. She said, "Look here boss lady, I ain't going in there." So we went down to other stores, places where we could get bigger clothes. We bought her a lace dress, fixed her whole luggage up, and hired a woman to travel with her to dress her, you know. The woman got involved with one of the musicians and they didn't get along, and all. She fired the woman because she didn't want to do this.[57]

Willie Mae Thornton was Robey's twenty-seventh Peacock artist and something of a project. *Billboard* did not review her first record, "Partnership Blues" b/w "I'm All Fed Up" (1951), so Robey announced its availability himself as an example of new "Blues and Boogies" in a *Billboard* display ad of Peacock new releases.[58] But Robey had more important things to do at the time than to promote a crude woman who sang old-fashioned "gutbucket" blues. Throughout 1951, he was busy attempting to establish Peacock Records outside of the South and Southwest. *Billboard* announced in February that Peacock was "expanding on a national basis," and that sales manager Irving Marcus was setting up deals in the East and Midwest. By November Peacock had added three new distributors in Los Angeles, New Orleans, and Cincinnati.[59] Not until December, then, did Robey release a second record by Thornton, "Let Your Tears Fall (Baby)" b/w "No Jody for Me" (Peacock 1587). This time the record was reviewed ("Jump blues gets a good shouting vocal from Thornton, plus solid ork background"; and "Chanter socks over the lyrics on this better-than-average blues. Band gives good support"), but none of the four *Billboard* reviewers scored either of the sides higher than 74 ("Good"), certainly not the reception Robey hoped for.[60]

In an unusual move, perhaps because he could not find a way to launch Thornton's career with the primitive blues shouting style she brought with her to Peacock, Robey auditioned her for bandleader Johnny Otis. Otis led a traveling musical revue that was known in black communities all over the country (the Johnny Otis Rhythm & Blues Caravan, it was sometimes called, or Johnny Otis and His Barrel House Revue). Robey arranged for Thornton to travel with the Otis band as a featured singer. In addition, the bandleader was to act as her producer in recording sessions to be held in California. This turned out to be an extraordinarily successful strategy. Thornton played outside of the South for the first time as part of the Otis organization, impressing critics and audiences with her smokey, blues shouting.

The *Chicago Defender* reported that "Big Mama" Thornton "stopped the show in Tacoma, Oakland and Richmond auditoriums; in Stockton, Sacramento, Bakersfield and at Elks auditorium in Los Angeles." In San Diego, the paper declared, "they called out the fire department to cool her off!"[61] *Cash Box* noted in October 1952 that this 250-pound woman was the "show-stopper" of the Otis Revue.[62] Indeed, when Thornton made her first appearance at Harlem's Apollo Theater she so electrified the audience with her version of the Dominoes' "Have Mercy Baby" (she had no hit song of her own at this point) that the headliner, "Little" Esther Phillips, never got on the first show at all. "That's when they put my name in lights," Thornton remembered, when "Little" Esther had to move over and make room for "Big Mama" Thornton.[63]

While Willie Mae Thornton made her mark as a star performer in a package show, Johnny Ace also established himself as a national R&B recording star. In October 1952, as Ace's "My Song" was climbing both of *Billboard*'s national R&B charts on the way to the number one position, his second hit, "Cross My Heart," was ready for release. For Thornton, Ace's success would be fortuitous. "My Song" made the Duke label and Ace famous, but it also made Don Robey a major player in the independent R&B business. After its success, Robey was able to leverage his achievement by positioning his Peacock artists for national attention. Before the acquisition of Ace in August 1952 Robey had to settle for the occasional *Billboard* record review and the rare mention in the "R&B Notes" column. After August, however, the industry was more receptive to his Houston labels.

By the end of 1952 Robey was virtually assured *Billboard* reviews for his new Duke artists, his deserving Peacock secular artists, and the best of the Peacock "spiritual" acts ("spiritual" was *Billboard*'s term for black gospel in the 1950s). For example, Jimmy McCracklin was reviewed in late August and again in September, along with Marie Adams; Memphis Slim was reviewed in October; Rosco Gordon, Earl Forest & the Beale Streeters, and Bobby "Blue" Bland were reviewed in November; the Dixie Hummingbirds, the Christland Singers, the Golden Harp Gospel Singers, and Joe Fritz received December reviews. The momentum continued into 1953 with a January bonanza. Not only was Johnny Ace reviewed that month, but also

Gatemouth Brown, Sister Jessie Mae Renfro, Al Grey, Lloyd "Fat Man" Smith, Paul Monday, and the Bells of Joy. For Robey, industry attention represented a complete turnaround.

In addition to reviews, other Peacock records began to make *Billboard*'s "New Records to Watch" list, or "This Week's Best Buys," or "Coming Up in the Trade." It might have disappointed Robey that he could not interest the *Billboard* reviewers in Thornton's third release, "Everytime I Think of You" b/w "Mischievous Boogie," but the record became an "R&B Record to Watch" even if *Billboard* inadvertently mistitled it.[64] Robey corrected the error and underwrote a promotional ad for the record, associating Thornton with the Johnny Otis band and touting her as a "House Rocker and Show Stopper."[65] He was right to stick with Big Mama Thornton: her next release became a huge hit for Peacock Records.

"Hound Dog" b/w "Night Mare," Thornton's fourth single record for Peacock, not only made Big Mama famous in the national blues community but established Peacock Records as a major independent label in black secular music. Recorded in Los Angeles at Radio Recorders Studio on 13 August 1952, "Hound Dog" was produced by Johnny Otis and written, according to agreements made at the time, by Otis and two young, white songwriters from Los Angeles who loved black music: Jerry Leiber and Mike Stoller. Leiber and Stoller, of course, would eventually become one of pop music's most successful writing teams, generating among hundreds of titles "Loving You" and "Jailhouse Rock" for Elvis Presley, "Yakety Yak" for the Coasters, "Stand By Me" for Ben E. King, and "Is That All There Is" for Peggy Lee. At the time, however, they were newcomers, not even old enough to enter into contracts without a parent's signature, and certainly not able to hold their own against so powerful a personality as Willie Mae Thornton.

According to Evelyn Johnson, when Thornton began to practice the new tune the songwriters said, "No, that's not the way it goes." "You wrote it," Thornton said, "I sing it."[66] Sing she did, using a frenzied, aggressive shouting style in the simple blues, arranged almost primitively by Johnny Otis for bass, guitar, drums, and hand claps, with Leiber and Stoller barking and howling in the background.[67] "You ain't nothin' but a hound dog, quit snoopin' 'round my door," the song begins. It was "as if she had her hands on her hips and a rolling pin nearby," one writer says, and in a tone "too raw for white ears."[68] Thornton's performance is all emotion; she is the woman wronged, berating men in the classic female blues tradition of Bessie Smith and Ma Rainey. "You can wag your tail," she tells her mate, "but I ain't gonna feed you no more." The rawness of the sound combined with the overt sexuality of the lyric made "Hound Dog" an immediate smash hit in urban black America from late March to the middle of July 1953.[69]

Robey purchased the first mention of "Hound Dog" in *Billboard*. "This is a HIT, HIT, HIT," Robey promised in a Peacock display ad for the 7 March 1953 issue, "Every Commercial Effect Possible."[70] The next week "Hound Dog" was a "New Record to Watch," with a rating in the excellent range by *Billboard* reviewers: "This is a wild slicing loaded with excitement. Willie Mae Thornton hands it a sock reading, selling the tune powerfully, while the ork swings the rhumba blues with a pulsating beat that builds all the way. Thrush's vocal is outstanding, and the backing is infectious. This one is mighty potent and could bust thru quickly. A solid effort for the boxes."[71]

Almost immediately after its release, *Cash Box* made "Hound Dog" its "Rhythm 'N Blues Sleeper of the Week." "Willie Mae Thornton gives a frenzied performance," the trade paper said, and the singer was "Easy when she should be easy, and driving when she has to bang it home." Overall, there was "just enough of the spiritual feel to stir up the emotions and raise the blood pressure."[72] According to a *Cash Box* "Rhythm N' Blues Ramblings" item later in the month, "the switchboard at [station WHOM–New York] lit up like Broadway and 42nd Street after one playing on the air."[73] "One of the biggest rhythm and blues records of all time," according to *Down Beat*,[74] the song was covered by ten different artists (mostly country and western) before Elvis Presley's version in 1956. George Moonoogian claims that by 1984 there were eighty-five versions of "Hound Dog," making it the "best known and most-often recorded Rock & Roll song."[75]

"Hound Dog" put Peacock Records on the national R&B map (Robey estimated later that the Thornton version sold between 500,000 and 750,000 copies),[76] but it also brought him grief. A best-selling record featuring sexual lyrics and a gut-bucket blues performance by a crude and vulgar woman-man was not the kind of thing he had in mind to move R&B to respectability. Worse, the projected sales for "Hound Dog" were immediately diluted by the abundance of "answer records," so common in the field of rhythm and blues, especially when the music was a standard blues form. The success of "Hound Dog" generated six answer songs in 1953 alone. Sam Phillips's Sun Records in Memphis released the most competitive answer to cash in on the popularity of "Hound Dog": Rufus Thomas's "Bear Cat" (Sun 181).

Like the original, "Bear Cat" employed a rhythm section arrangement, but instead of barking and howling there was meowing and hissing in the background. In true answer form, the gender of the participants is reversed. This time the protagonist is male, directly challenging the worthless female of the original song—correcting her previous insults and re-directing them at her. "You know what you said about me woman?" says the man in open confrontation. "Well. . . . You ain't nothin' but a bearcat, scratchin' at my door." All of the irony and sarcasm of the original is captured in the answer, even the sexuality: "You can purr, pretty kitty, but I ain't gonna rub you no more."[77] *Billboard* noted in late March that answers to hit records were coming out faster than ever: "It used to be that the answers to hits usually waited until the hit had started on the downward trail, but today the answers are ready a few days after records start moving upwards. This has led some to remark that the diskeries soon may be bringing out the answers before the original records are released."[78]

By early April Robey was on the legal warpath. His Lion Music and two other music publishers had retained attorneys to protect their copyrights from the "bastardization" and infringement of answer songs. The trade magazines covered the matter fully—an indication that the field of rhythm and blues was being closely watched by interests in the larger field of popular music. "If someone does not stop this practice [of copyright infringement]," New York attorney Lee Eastman warned, "it will spread to fields other than rhythm and blues." *Billboard* reported that Robey's Lion Publishing Company had ordered the Harry Fox Agency to issue Sun Records a mechanical license for "Bear Cat" (the standard procedure for a music publisher in granting a record company the opportunity to exploit a copyright for a fixed fee) but that Sun had refused to accept it. Robey is quoted as saying he would follow through "with a court procedure if they refuse a license."[79] Although this kind of lawsuit was without precedent, Robey had good reason to believe that he was now an established power in R&B and could demand respect: according to *Billboard* tabulations in the 11 April 1953 issue, Robey's Peacock and Duke labels accounted for the number two R&B record in national sales ("Hound Dog") and three of the ten positions for juke box plays ("Hound Dog" at number three, Earl Forest's "Whoopin' and Hollerin'" at number eight, and Ace's "Cross My Heart" at number nine).

Robey clearly had a point on the matter of copyright infringement by "Bear Cat." The Sun answer to "Hound Dog" was outside the general prac-

tice and spirit of the traditional answer song; it did not flatter the original —
it was in direct competition with it for market share. By 18 April "Hound
Dog" was the number one R&B record in sales; "Bear Cat" was number
nine. On juke boxes "Hound Dog" was number two; "Bear Cat" was number ten. Though he had positioned Thornton's "Hound Dog" as "The
ORIGINAL Version" and had warned dealers, distributors, and operators to
"Beware of Imitations," "Bear Cat" continued to climb the national charts,
finally reaching the number three position. In the New Orleans and St.
Louis territories the answer song actually eclipsed the original.[80] Robey sued
Sun Records in August, successfully as it turned out, and was awarded 2
percent of all the "Bear Cat" profits plus court costs.[81] "One thing is sure,"
said the *Pittsburgh Courier*, "this is the most profitable hound dog since Eliza
slid across the ice [in *Uncle Tom's Cabin*]."[82]

By July 1953 "Hound Dog" had fallen off both national R&B charts, and
by August it had disappeared from the territorial charts. Before the record
died, however, Robey had the satisfaction of watching Johnny Ace's "The
Clock" become the number one R&B record in the country; indeed, for a
transitional period of six weeks both Thornton and Ace appeared on the
territorial lists. Unfortunately, "Hound Dog" was to be Willie Mae Thornton's only hit. Robey launched an unsuccessful campaign in September for
"They Call Me Big Mama" (Peacock 1621), a song cut at the same recording session as "Hound Dog," without success. *Billboard* gave it a lukewarm
review ("A fair side, with good instrumental support. Okay follow-up to
'Hound Dog'"). The flip side, "Cotton Picking Blues," was said to be "a
much more primitive, moody type of blues, with long piano interlude."[83]
The record did not penetrate the national or territorial charts. In fact, none
of the eight Thornton singles released by Peacock after "Hound Dog" was
commercially successful. Big Mama Thornton's ride on the top of the R&B
record charts had lasted a scant six months and was never reached again.
As a touring performer, however, she remained a popular personality and a
box-office attraction as Johnny Ace's opening act.[84]

Potent Wax

Johnny Ace's

Mid-Era Hits

While Big Mama Thornton's appeal may have slipped with R&B record buyers, Johnny Ace was clearly a star on the rise. When Robey put the two singers together on the road and promoted them as a package, it turned out to be a sound business decision that generated increased box-office revenue. The arrangement was especially good for Thornton, who was not a headliner. Indeed, few women R&B recording stars in the early 1950s could compete with male acts in either personal appearances or record sales. *Billboard* pointed out in the spring of 1953 how rare it was to have two women heading the national R&B charts: Willie Mae Thornton's Peacock hit and Ruth Brown's "(Mama) He Treats Your Daughter Mean" on Atlantic.[1]

According to Evelyn Johnson, the gender difference was easily explained by the demographics of the 1950s R&B consumer: "The women were the record buyers," she says, "and they were interested in men and what they had to say in song. They weren't concerned with what sister had to say."[2] Appearing with Ace thus enlarged Thornton's audience. In fact, Robey was able to exploit the popularity of Ace by linking him with other acts represented by the Buffalo Booking Agency as well. Ace "was so big," Johnny Board remembers, "that the booking agent insisted that you buy B.B. King and Bobby Blue Bland as a package if you wanted Johnny Ace."[3] As Evelyn Johnson explains it, "The way I booked B.B. was to put him between Johnny Ace and Bobby Bland, or vice versa. In other words, you buy this one because you want him, but you've got to buy that one to get the other one. That was the strategy. It had to be that way."[4]

Gross receipts for personal appearances were one measure of the fast track that Ace's career was on, and record sales were another, as "Cross My Heart" b/w "Angel" took off quickly at the beginning of 1953. Robey was so confident of Ace's popularity with a national R&B audience that before "Cross My Heart" ever showed up on the first *Billboard* R&B territorial chart, he already had Ace's third hit in the can. At a recording session in Houston at Bill Holford's ACA studio on 13 January 1953, the Johnny Otis Band backed Ace on "The Clock," a ballad credited to David James Mattis in the copyright registration but reported later to BMI as a Mattis-John Alexander collaboration. "The Clock," like its predecessor "Cross My Heart," had originally been recorded in Memphis. The lyric is lonesome and mournful, the chord progression borrowed from the pop standard "Two Loves Have I." The song was created in the same manner as the two previous Ace hits: Mattis wrote new words to a hit song, and Ace composed a new melody. "I told [Ace] to fake it," David Mattis says, "and that's what came out. I had the lyrics for him, so he faked it. He got the music and I took the lyrics. I thought that was fair, but nobody else thought so. Everybody thought I was stupid."[5] Mattis recalls cutting the song at the WDIA studios and sending the tape to Houston, but Robey had it re-recorded at ACA with Johnny Otis's band. "That's me making that clock noise," says Otis.[6]

The clock noise is omnipresent in "The Clock," not so much driving the song as dragging it along. The tempo is agonizingly slow, less than fifty beats a minute, as if the ticking sounds were designed to make the listener's heart beat even lower and slower than the previous Ace hits. "I looked at the face of the clock on the wall, and it doesn't tell me nothing at all," the singer complains mournfully. He has been left alone (Ace the persona is always left alone), with only the face of the clock to stare at him. "It knows I'm lonely," he says, "and always will be." The clock is lonely too, part of a long tradition of personifying objects in rhythm and blues and country and western songs, and Ace's baritone is thin and vulnerable. "I want to cry my heart out," he claims in the bridge, "want my baby back with me. Got nothing but time to step out, but time means nothing to me." Sustaining saxophones enter at verse one and at the bridge. Aside from occasional motions from the piano, the sax fills are the only sound free from the oppressive mood of the arrangement.

Time, it appears from the sound of the clock, is not only slow in passing but tormenting as well. The clock tick is supplied by a drum stick hitting the side of the bass drum, then echoing slightly. The bass plays on every beat too, but the bass and drum sounds are not always in synch. The clock ticks hesitate and drag distinctly, as if to impede any relief the singer can hope for. While the prevailing motion of the clock is deliberate—slow, then slower—Ace's lyric is at first behind and then ahead of the beat, never predictable: he is playing with time on another level.

Ace's timing here, unique to his own interpretation of the lyric, is characteristic of his vocal delivery and would prove impossible to reproduce by other singers. (Even St. Clair Alexander, who studied his brother's performances carefully, would fail in this attempt.) "If you hear me," Ace begs in the last verse, "please come back real soon, 'cause the clock and I are so lonely in this room." After a sad, almost depressing tenor saxophone solo, Ace practically cries his way through the bridge again. Then he repeats the last verse, and the clock continues to tick, and tick, and tick—a fadeout ending lasting fifteen seconds. Gloomy as it was, the hypnotic performance seemed to strike a nerve in the R&B audience.

For reasons never clarified, Robey credited the Beale Streeters as the backup band and did not take writer credit himself. His reluctance to claim authorship, perhaps, owed more to litigation than largesse. By early 1953 the Mattis-Robey partnership was in the hands of lawyers and close to dissolution. Since Robey was about to own Duke Records outright for an amount in the $10,000 to $27,000 range (Mattis claims there had been over $200,000 in collections alone but he was powerless to share in any of it), he could easily afford to be magnanimous with a single property.[7] At any rate, Robey copyrighted "The Clock" as an unpublished song on 9 April 1953, with Mattis as sole author. He did not, however, explain to Mattis that in order to receive any of the performance rights money a song earns he must register as an affiliated writer with BMI.

Whatever his motives, Robey's management of "The Clock" reflected his growing marketing skill. He had apparently learned something from his experience with Ace's second hit, because he put a "B" side on "The Clock" that could not possibly complicate his deliberate promotion efforts. In fact, the song he chose, "Ace's Wild,"[8] a composition credited to John Alexander (instrumental blues with Ace playing boogie woogie piano), had been recorded by the Beale Streeters at the first Houston session in the fall of 1952 and had originally been scheduled to be the "B" side of "Angel." "Angel," of course, had itself become the "B" side of Duke 107 when Robey permitted the industry to choose "Cross My Heart" as the most commercially appealing.

There was no ambiguity in the marketing of "The Clock" b/w "Ace's Wild" (Duke 112), released in May 1953 a few weeks after "Cross My Heart" dropped off all *Billboard* R&B charts. "The Clock" was specifically advertised in *Billboard* as the upcoming Ace hit in the 20 June 1953 issue. In a large Duke Records display ad, Robey announced new releases by two recently successful Duke artists: "The Clock" for Johnny Ace and "Last Night's Dream" for Earl Forest. In the Ace section, an alarm clock set for 3:00 was featured, embellished with a handwritten "Third Hit!" on its face. "Bong! Bong! Bong!" declared the timepiece. Johnny Ace's "The Clock" was already "Acclaimed! Third Smash Hit." Each singer was represented by a photograph, but an unfortunate transposition left Earl Forest's face promoting Ace's record, while Ace's image plugged Forest's.[9] Robey corrected the mistake for the ad's subsequent appearance.[10] *Billboard* endorsed "The Clock" immediately. "There's a lot of potential in this ballad which Ace offers up in his warm style," it suggested. "Could be a real big one."[11]

The next week its "Fast start" made it a *Billboard* "Best Buy." "Already on the chart in New Orleans with good to strong reports from New York, Philadelphia, Detroit and Southern areas."[12] According to the reviewer, "Johnny Ace, who has come thru with a number of hits in a row, has one here that also looks like a real smash. It's another heart ballad, sung by the warbler in his own meaningful style, over a moody ork backing. Tune is melodic, and the clock ticks gimmicks should help it, too. A solid coin-grabber." "Wild instrumental effort," *Billboard* called "Aces Wild." "The flip side has the power, but this one should also cull some juke loot."[13] *Down Beat* gave "The Clock" five stars: "Third hit in a row for Johnny," it said, "who came from out of nowhere within the last year."[14]

Cash Box also noticed Ace's sudden rise to the top of the R&B charts, giving the record an "Award O' The Week" notation. Don Robey could not resist the opportunity and immediately incorporated the *Cash Box* comments in a display ad for "The Clock":

> Johnny Ace, unknown to the trade one short year ago, streaked across the hot charts with a number one sensation "My Song," followed about six months later with another big hit, "Cross My Heart," and now keeps his record one hundred percent with his third, and what looks like a certain click, "The Clock." The tune is a slow sentimental item hauntingly sung by Ace in the style that has been so successful for him. The blues singer is despondently lonesome and he begs his baby to come back real soon if she hears him. Tune is simple, melodic and hummable. A real good bet for some top pop artist.[15]

As it turned out, no one bothered to cover the song until Lee Andrews and the Hearts recorded it in 1957.

By 4 July "The Clock" was on the national R&B charts for record sales and by 18 July was the number one R&B record in America. Two weeks later, at the end of July, the song was—impressively—either number one or two in all eleven R&B territories. According to Bill Holford's studio log books, the song was mastered as a 78 rpm record only, consistent with sales patterns of the R&B market at the time. Black consumers, primarily adult, were the last to change over to the newer technology of the 45 rpm player—the hardware of choice for white adolescents. Since Robey pressed records all over the country, several sets of masters were cut to accommodate the demand for this hit record, the sales of which were supported by heavy bookings of personal appearances in the South, West Coast, Midwest, and East. Robey's operation had come so far by the summer of 1953 that Duke and Peacock Records were now handled by thirty-five distributors—from New York in the East to Los Angeles in the West, and from Seattle in the Northwest to New Orleans in the South. Robey purchased an ad in *Billboard* to thank those firms and warn the others. "Your name should be on this list!" he admonished distributors who did not carry Duke/Peacock product.[16]

Robey must have seen that the producing skills Johnny Otis brought to Ace's records were invaluable, because he went to considerable trouble to bring the two together again in Los Angeles for a 13 August recording session at Radio Recorders studio. Ace and Willie Mae Thornton were on tour at the time, breaking attendance records at Billy Berg's 5-4 Ballroom in Los Angeles and helping to headline Gene Norman's "Fourth Annual Rhythm and Blues Jubilee."[17] Robey flew in to organize the session (he was "supervising waxings," *Billboard* explained),[18] where he used the arranging talent of Johnny Otis, with the Otis band backing Ace on three solo cuts plus an Ace/Willie Mae Thornton duet. He also supervised recordings by Otis alone and by Joseph "Google Eyes" August, the *Pittsburgh Courier* reported, pointing out that Robey had traveled between Houston and the West Coast "via plane."[19]

The Robey operation was unique at this point. Ace's third hit clearly established him as a star with staying power—R&B was notorious for one-hit wonders—and together with Thornton's "Hound Dog," the *Cash Box* R&B record of the year, Robey would estimate his 1953 record sales at 1,500,000 units for secular music alone. The "spiritual catalog," he said, would account for another 500,000 units.[20] In addition, Robey had signed a number of new artists, including "Little Richard" Penniman and Johnny Otis on Peacock and "Little Junior" Parker and Joseph August on Duke, had established a new label called Progressive Jazz, and had enlarged his Houston facilities to include a rehearsal studio and a record pressing and processing plant.[21] Meanwhile, the Buffalo Booking Agency now added Junior Parker and the Blue Flames to the Ace/Thornton package and kept it busy with dates across the country, culminating in Apollo Theater performances in late October.

To take advantage of Ace's national reputation, the Bihari brothers released the only Ace song they had, a mournful and soft, well-produced blues number called "Midnight Hours Journey," recorded at the Memphis YMCA in 1951, and put fellow Beale Streeter Earl Forest's "Trouble and Me" on the other side (Flair 1015). At this point in Ace's career, a record review was automatic. "This doesn't sound like the Johnny Ace now on Duke Records," *Billboard* acknowledged, "but it may have been made [awhile] ago. Under any circumstances it is an effective performance and it should pull spins and loot on the basis of the name, if for no other reason."[22] Without Robey's promotion efforts, however, the record did not succeed.

For Ace, life must have seemed a whirlwind. It had been only three years since he deposited his pregnant wife at his parents' home in Memphis, two years since he sang for the first time on tape at the local YMCA, and only a scant twelve months that he had been on the road as an R&B recording star. Not only did he fail to contact his family during this period, but he was often able to slip back into Memphis for a personal engagement without their knowledge, since his appearances were rarely announced in a way that alerted his wife or mother.

His name and photograph had appeared in the *Tri-State Defender* on 23 August 1952 (this seems to be the first time that he received any hometown recognition), but the occasion was a display ad for a one-night only concert at the Hippodrome at 500 Beale Avenue, where it was "COOL and COMFORTABLE." Big acts played the Hippodrome, with stars like Ruth Brown, the Ink Spots, Lionel Hampton, Johnny Otis, Billy Eckstine, and Count Basie, and the club sometimes held "white only" shows. Tickets to the Ace performance sold for $1.00 in advance or $1.35 at the door, and the star had to share his glory with the "Excitement! Action! Fun!" of the Hippodrome's weekly boxing shows every Wednesday night, which were said to "HAVE BECOME A 'MUST' TO FANS THROUGHOUT THE CITY!!"[23] If rhythm and blues and boxing were two sides of the same entertainment coin, there was, nevertheless, at least one difference: the newspaper published the results of the boxing matches the next week, but it did not mention the Ace concert.[24]

Johnny Ace did not contribute to the support of his wife and children before he became famous, and he made no attempt to provide for his family afterwards. While he was technically a resident of Memphis, the closest thing he had to a permanent residence in 1953 was a room at the Mitchell Hotel on Beale Street; in fact, Ernestine Mitchell kept his clothes for years after his death.[25] In an attempt to avoid the unpleasantness of confronting his wife and his mother, he made sure he stayed away from the "home house" at 899 Fisher. Once, however, his wife found out he was in town and went to see him at the Club Handy with her brother, who was home from the service. "He was there with this lady," Jean Alexander remembers. "And he really didn't want to hurt me. He was trying to get me out of there."[26] She stayed for one set and left.

On another occasion, Ace's sisters Norma and Mamie came out of the Universal Life Insurance building, where they worked, and just happened to see the van carrying the Johnny Ace Band drive by:

Some of the girls said, "Your brother! That's Johnny Ace!" And we flagged him down and asked him to go by the house. "Yeah I was going," [he said]. He wasn't going there because mother was the kind who just stayed on him. And when she told him, "You should be ashamed. Your children are here, and Lois Jean, and you don't think about your family." And, I mean, he just counted out three or four hundred dollars. He said he had to leave for an engagement. He said he had to go to the Apollo, wherever that was. He just gave up the money.[27]

The Alexander sisters may have been engaged in so many church activities that they had never heard of Harlem's famous Apollo Theater on 125th Street, but the brothers certainly had. "If you made it through the Apollo," St. Clair Alexander knew, "if you went there and sung there or performed there, you was on your way."[28]

Brother Johnny certainly was on his way, though he was not yet a polished performer. *Variety* reviewed his first Apollo Theater performance in October 1953, not as part of a package but as a single performer in an eleven-minute set:

Johnny Ace is another Negro singer who's aroused attention via his indie label recordings. In a first-time booking at Harlem's Apollo Theatre, he impresses with a smooth baritone but unfortunately his song salesmanship isn't commensurate with the quality of his voice.

Self-accomped at the '88, Ace warbles a trio of tunes — "My Song," a plaintive ballad with a touch of the blues idiom; "Cross My Heart," a syrupy item, and "The Clock," in a similar genre. His is a slow, resonant delivery that by intentional design gives each note more time to register upon the audience.

For strictly aural media such as waxings, Ace's style has good possibilities. On the other hand he's too stiff and wooden at present to cause much of a visual stir. When he discovers the value of occasionally facing the payees instead of continually fixing his optics on the mike while seated at the piano he'll increase his booking potential.[29]

It is quite likely that Ace was intimidated more than usual by the Apollo facility and crowd — this was, after all, his first engagement at the historic theater. It is surprising, however, to find such glaring symptoms of shyness after a full year of almost continuous live performances in what turns out to be the midpoint of his career. But Ace's shyness is well documented during this time, and even in the small clubs that he played most frequently and where he should have felt most comfortable, he is known to have delivered his vocals from his piano seat. "Johnny was a very, very shy, quiet person," Evelyn Johnson says. "He was shy around people, and masses of people. He was childlike." Though almost any other R&B performer would have taken center stage and been the focus of attention in personal performances, Ace just couldn't do it. "We had pianists with the band," Johnson says, "but when he'd go on he'd dismiss the pianist and sit down. That was because [at first] he couldn't face the people, but he never would admit it, you know. The band would say 'Man, why don't you get on stage.' 'Blow your horn.' He just wouldn't do it."[30]

"It didn't come natural to John Jr.," explains St. Clair Alexander, who saw his brother perform at Milwaukee's Riverview Ballroom in 1953. Johnny refused to call attention to himself, to put on a show "like Muddy Waters and all them guys, to be acting while they'd be playing, and B.B. King making all them faces and all that stuff." Johnny had no flair, his brother says. He was an "Ice Man" like Jerry Butler, a performer who would "step up to the mike and just sing—wouldn't be no movements or no motions or nothing. He'd just stand out there and sing his heart out and go home."[31] In Johnny's case it was even more subtle: he would be sitting behind his piano. Evelyn Johnson remembers the night he first took center stage: "And then one time, it was either in Seattle or Portland, one of the two, he did [stand at the microphone in front of the band]. I'd been begging him, 'Please get up there.' But he did go ahead and do it after he once started. He did it maybe once or twice that week and maybe skipped a few days and then he started to do it and then he did it. But when the mood hit him, he would just go to that piano."[32]

Johnny Ace was technically between hits on Thanksgiving Day 1953, when B.B. King joined the Ace/Thornton touring unit in Houston for what *Billboard* called a "giant holiday show,"[33] but his last record had virtually mesmerized America's R&B audience. "The Clock" stayed on the national charts from June to October and did not fall completely off the territorial charts until late November, generating a remarkable marketing life of twenty-one weeks. Of the eight certified Ace hits, older black Americans today are most apt to recall this mournful song, a "sentimental ballad of unrequited love," Gary Giddins observes, that is only twenty-eight measures long. "The Clock," he says, made Ace "a black teenage heartthrob in the same years that Johnnie Ray was shedding tears on the white market."[34] As a white male singer with an intense and emotional vocal style, Johnnie Ray had confused all record buyers in the early 1950s—in fact, some people who heard "Cry" b/w "The Little White Cloud That Cried" thought the voice belonged to a black woman.[35] After both sides of his first record succeeded on the R&B and popular music charts, his record company put him on its mainstream pop label, Columbia.

The color line was slowly beginning to erode in American commercial music in the early 1950s: Johnnie Ray was borrowing from a black model of vocal performance and Johnny Ace was borrowing from a white one. In addition, the record that replaced "The Clock" at the top of the national R&B charts in the summmer of 1953 was another mutation. "Crying in the Chapel," by the Orioles, featured a black quartet covering a country and western record so successfully that it crossed over from R&B to the popular music charts. The increase in sales of what had formerly been black music by black performers in black styles for a black audience was not universally welcomed by the music trade magazines. *Down Beat* published an article in mid-July by Atlantic Records' Jerry Wexler, who argued that R&B was merely a form of jazz. "Jazz was originally created by the Negro people for their own enjoyment," Wexler explained: "The music that the Negro people listen to for their own enjoyment today is called rhythm and blues, and is not regarded as having any esoteric significance by the critics and trade in general. However, it is certain that many of these contemporary record hits are regarded with more than transient affection by the people who buy them, keep them, and play them over and over."[36] Nevertheless, the magazine abandoned its R&B coverage two weeks later, removing not only the R&B reviews but other features as well: the "Capsules" and the "Best Bets." *Down Beat* even withdrew its R&B column for more than a year, though it continued its coverage of country and western music and polka bands. Why? There is no official explanation, but New York radio personality Buddy Bowser observed later, and probably correctly, that rhythm and blues was "just another form of segregation."[37]

It would be difficult to argue that the interest *Down Beat* exhibited in country and western music and polka bands had anything to do with musical sophistication. These were forms of white music performed by white artists in white styles for a white audience, controlled by the large white-owned record companies. Don Robey manufactured records for "the other side of town." On 5 December 1953 he introduced Ace's next record, "Saving My Love For You" b/w "Yes, Baby" (Duke 128)—two of the four sides recorded in Los Angeles in late August with the Johnny Otis band.

Like other Ace releases, the "A" side was the ballad, and the "B" side the jumper. "Saving My Love For You" features a lush albeit stringless arrangement with Otis on vibes while the singer promises his fidelity to an absent sweetheart. "Please believe me," he pleads at the end of each verse, "I'm saving my love for you." "Yes, Baby" is a celebration of lovemaking, an up-tempo blues number with the big band sound of the Otis organization. *Billboard* designated Duke 128 as one of the "New Records to Watch" on 12 December: "Two potential powerhouses by Ace. 'Saving' is in the normal Ace tradition, a fine 'Heart' ballad with a powerful reading. Flip is an up-tempo blues which also has good possibilities."[38] The record was a "Best Buy" one week later, reporting "strong action" in New York, Philadelphia, Buffalo, Nashville, St. Louis, and Dallas. "Johnny Ace has had three hits in a row; with this new disk he should stretch his string to four, and this one could be his biggest to date," said the *Billboard* reviewer. "It's another touching ballad, and the boy sings out his heart on it over a good beat by the combo. A real coin-grabber this." "Yes, Baby" was equally praised: "Ace proves on this side that he can sell a rhythm tune as well as a ballad. He really comes thru with a powerful rendition on this jump effort, while the combo and an unbilled singer swings out behind him. This side, too, has more than a chance to make it. Two fine sides for the singer."[39]

The "unbilled singer" swinging out behind Ace was, of course, his personal appearance partner Willie Mae Thornton. It is quite possible that Robey did not want to tarnish the upscale image of Duke Records by officially crediting Thornton, a blues singer signed to Peacock, on the Duke label, or perhaps he thought of Thornton's supporting vocal as just an additional instrument in the band and therefore unworthy of special mention. A live rendition of their duet, however, was destined to become famous as Ace's last public performance.

By the end of December, "Saving My Love for You" had entered the national R&B chart for juke box plays, where it remained for a month before penetrating the sales chart, reversing the usual order of success for an Ace hit. During this period there was limited opportunity for an R&B song to receive heavy radio exposure (*Billboard* did not even publish a chart to measure R&B radio airplay until after Ace's death). "The radio stations did not play what they called race, or blues," Evelyn Johnson told an audience at Indiana University. "Now you have these records. What do you do with them? How do you get them to the people?" All the independent R&B labels figured out "ways to get them to the juke boxes," she explained, understanding that "certain records go on certain juke boxes in certain places."[40]

Specific placement was essential, especially in the field of rhythm and blues, where the juke box was an indispensable link between the record label and the listening music public. Juke box owners, or "operators" as they were called in the industry, represented an important element in the diffusion of rhythm and blues music in the postwar era. Charlie Gillett estimates the number of juke boxes in America at this time to be almost half a million, accounting for up to 40 percent of annual record sales.[41] As Johnny Otis told John Broven: "At the time, to hear a record you either had to buy it, listen on a juke box, or maybe see an artist in person. There was not much air exposure. The pressure and competition which cause a record to die quickly today were not the same. The record owners used to work out deals with the juke box men. The juke box was a vital outlet but I was not aware of the details of these deals."[42]

Don Robey apparently knew these details and was doing very well in this regard. According to *Billboard*'s tabulation of the top R&B records for 1953, three Robey titles ended up in the top twenty: Thornton's "Hound Dog" (number three sales, number four juke boxes), Ace's "The Clock" (number five sales and nine juke boxes), and Ace's "Cross My Heart" (nineteen sales and fifteen juke boxes).[43] Evelyn Johnson recalls the practice of supplying free records to the organization that furnished the juke box "tags" to operators. "We had to furnish X number of records to them," she says. "It was an advertisement thing, but that was the way their system worked. It was a promotional cost, and they distributed those records—I don't know whether they sold them or not."[44] Boosted and propelled by its juke box plays, "Saving My Love For You" became a "National Best Seller" on 23 January, and Robey was quick to declare Duke 118 "another double hit" because of "Yes, Baby," the blues shouting duet with Big Mama Thornton. According to Robey's inflated accounting, Ace's four single records had now generated six hits.[45]

Johnny Ace and rhythm and blues were still gathering momentum by the end of 1953, but the American entertainment business was clearly in transition: "'54 Finds Radio & TV Healthy, Music Nervous, Vaude[ville] on Diet," declared a *Billboard* headline. In three related stories, the trade journal observed that the big question in television broadcasting related to the overall effect of color TV on the industry ("Broadcasting Has Good '53;

Worry Is Color").[46] While color TV seemed to be futuristic in the mid-1950s (the biggest boom in television ownership had yet to occur), television viewing was already displacing other recreational behaviors, especially live entertainment, which was off 35 percent in 1953, *Billboard* reported.[47] As for the music business, the forecast was for "continuing flux." Popular music had become more competitive in 1953, *Billboard* observed, and more complex in its marketing. For music publishers, the three traditional sources of income (sheet music, records, and performances) had shifted with the decline of sheet music sales. Publishers would accent performances (primarily radio airplay) as an income source, the magazine said, using records as "the prime promotional source." The value of records, it was believed, was not in the mechanical rights income that songs generated (two cents per song during this period) but in the performance income that radio airplay brought: "far and away the importance of disks to publishers continues to lie in exposure value."[48]

None of this had much to do with Johnny Ace, Don Robey, or rhythm and blues in general. Few African Americans owned television sets at this time and consequently had no opportunity to modify their traditional leisure listening activities. They did, however, have more disposable income. Between 1950 and 1953 the so-called Korean War prosperity was especially favorable to black American males, in a comparative sense, whose wages and salaries rose at a higher rate than incomes for white Americans.[49] Live entertainment was booming in African American communities in 1953. Black movie theaters were not converting to wide-screen Cinemascope and therefore had no pressure to eliminate live shows, and, indeed, the music booking business (especially Buffalo Booking) was flourishing, with acts contracted for personal appearances months in advance. Moreover, a music publisher like Don Robey was quite content to accumulate the two cents per side mechanical rights money that Duke or Peacock records generated: his publishing company had never made money on sheet music, and his R&B records did not receive sufficient airplay to warrant substantial performance rights money from BMI. For Robey and his many cohorts in the field of independent label rhythm and blues, there was good money to be made in tapping into the newly emerging general interest in black music on the part of white youth. The *Billboard* R&B columnist joked that the list of R&B firms making the charts in 1953 was so long that it could be said "as many record companies hit the charts as records."[50]

Although it had not yet become a discernible trend, sales of R&B records were going up, the R&B market share was increasing, and the industry was beginning to note early in 1954 that careers in R&B were becoming more stable. Both current retail and juke box action on the part of such relative newcomers as Johnny Ace, artists with five or six hits, "have put to rest a lot of the cliches about one-record artists," reported *Billboard*, which noted this new trend with a new term—"repeat performers": "It is evident that once the r.&b. customer okays a new artist today, he'll come back for disks by the same artist again, as long as the disk is a good one. And it is also evident that the diskeries, as a whole, once they break thru a new artist, do their best to find the right material to keep the artist up there."[51]

Certainly Don Robey was doing his best to find the kind of material that would keep Johnny Ace at the top of the charts. He was also attempting to keep Ace's name current not only in the trade publications but in the black newspapers as well. The *New York Age Defender,* for example, reported in a story with a Houston dateline that "phenomenal young Duke recording artist" Johnny "My Song" Ace had recently interrupted his tour in Columbia, South Carolina, in order to "fulfill a recording date with Johnny Otis at Peacock Studios." After the "waxing session Johnny flew via TWA to rejoin his unit in Pensacola, Fla."[52] Civilian air travel was not common in January 1954 and especially rare for African Americans. Robey wanted black America to know just how exceptional a talent Ace was. Johnny Ace was a major star, Robey was insisting, and Duke Records represented not only big business but a class act—the company spared no expense when it came to a national celebrity of Ace's status.

In addition to the public relations value, the timing of the recording session that required Ace to be taken off the road in South Carolina and flown to Houston was essential to Robey's marketing plan because he again wanted Johnny Otis to produce the music, using the Otis Band to back Ace up. The Otis Revue was on a tour of its own, arriving in Houston from a date in Dallas. "The Johnny Otis Orchestra," as Robey called the backing group, was not only a good band and a popular one at the time—it had the respect of other professional musicians as well. "Anywhere you were in earshot of Johnny Otis," Milton Hopkins, the guitar player in Ace's road band, remembers, "that's the band that was going to do the session." Otis arranged the four songs cut at this session at the ACA studio on 27 January 1954, most of which, like "Pledging My Love," featured Ace on piano and vocals, Pete

Lewis on guitar, James Von Streeter on tenor sax, Albert Winston on bass, Leard Bell on drums, and Otis himself playing vibes.[53] What no one could know at the time was that this January date would generate both of Ace's posthumous hits.

Johnny Otis is central to the success of Johnny Ace, producing eight of Ace's twenty-one recorded songs. As a musician, Otis is known primarily as a drummer, but in the transition of rhythm and blues to rock 'n' roll he is more accurately recognized as a pioneer producer. His first job as a teenager was with Count Otis Matthews' West Oakland House Rockers, an otherwise all-black band in the Berkeley, California, area prior to World War II.[54] In 1948 he opened a rhythm and blues club in black Los Angeles called the Barrel House, known throughout the city for its hot house band and large white audience on Friday nights. "Big Jay McNeely was my tenorman," Otis told John Broven, "and the crowd went wild when he played on his knees, then on his back, shaking his legs!"[55] As a songwriter, Otis is probably best known for "Willie and the Hand Jive," a Top 10 pop hit on Capitol in 1958, covered by many artists over the years, including Eric Clapton. He also wrote "Every Beat of My Heart" and co-wrote "Hound Dog" and one of the famous "Annie" songs, called "Wallflower" when Etta James sang it and "Dance with Me Henry" when it was covered for the white pop market by Georgia Gibbs in 1955. Otis's "Barrel House Stomp" (1949), "Rockin' Blues" (1950), and "Rock Me Baby" (1953) are R&B tunes often considered among the earliest rock 'n' roll records.

Otis is generally credited with discovering Little Esther, Mel Evans, and Etta James.[56] He is also said to have discovered Hank Ballard, Little Willie John, and Jackie Wilson at the same amateur talent show in Detroit in 1951.[57] His traveling band, called the Johnny Otis Revue, the Rhythm & Blues Caravan, or the Barrel House Revue, was one of the last of the great rhythm and blues touring bands of the 1950s (Little Esther and Willie Mae Thornton were among the featured vocalists). According to Charlie Gillett, Otis was able to change "the line-up and sound of his band to accommodate the shift to rock 'n' roll."[58] George Lipsitz calls Otis "the artist who best exemplifies the new cultural fusions engendered by rock 'n' roll music," since he so successfully promoted black music to mixed audiences in both white and Mexican-American communities.[59] In addition, Johnny Otis is notable as both producer and arranger, especially for Don Robey's labels. Two of the famous transitional records from rhythm and blues to rock 'n' roll were produced and arranged by Johnny Otis: Ace's "Pledging My Love" and Thornton's "Hound Dog."

What set Otis apart from his time and place is not that he was a white man making his living in black music but that he had consciously *chosen* to be black. Born of Greek parents in 1921 (John Veliotes is his real name), he grew up in an integrated section of Berkeley, California, that eventually became a totally black neighborhood. His friends were black, the high school sweetheart he married was black, and the music he loved was black. In his book about the Watts riots of 1965 Otis explains: "As a kid I decided that if our society dictated that one had to be either black or white, I would be black." It was not his attraction to R&B music that caused him to "become black," he says, or his marriage to a Negro. "I became what I am because as a child I reacted to the way of life, the special vitality, the atmosphere of the black community. Some people call this difficult-to describe quality, Negritude. Today it is more popularly known as 'soul.'" He has always been, he says, "black by choice."[60] Nelson George describes Otis as one of the postwar era "new Negrophiles" who "embraced black culture to the point that they became 'honorary' blacks and, in some cases, subject to the same discrimination as their dark role models. Johnny Otis, a Los Angeles resident of Greek descent, was one of the first of this breed. As a bandleader, songwriter, and talent scout, Otis was a real force in the Los Angeles scene. And in terms of promoting rhythm and blues, these black voices behind white faces would be more important than any single musician."[61]

In typical Don Robey fashion, the Otis-arranged material Johnny Ace recorded in January 1954 was in the can well in advance of the release dates. In fact, "Saving My Love for You," Ace's then current hit, would not peak on the *Billboard* R&B charts until the week of 6 February. Except for a "B" side that would be coupled with Ace's next hit, songs cut in January 1954 did not succeed or fail until after Ace's death. The session itself, however, is famous for recording "Pledging My Love," the rhythm and blues song by the solo black male star signed to an independent R&B label that the major pop labels could not successfully cover.

As for "Saving My Love for You," this record must have been something of a disappointment to both Ace and Robey since the hit's upward momentum took longer than the previous releases, played itself out sooner, and never reached the top of the R&B charts. Not only did the record fail to hit in all of the *Billboard* territories (it never charted in New Orleans or Baltimore/Washington, D.C., and barely made the charts in its last week in Chicago), but its life was considerably longer on the juke boxes (nineteen weeks) than in the stores (nine weeks). Though it may have puzzled Don Robey at the time, it became clear later that juke box operators had been ahead of record distributors in the business of supplying young, white Americans with the black music they appeared to favor. Juke box plays in R&B were perhaps a more reliable indicator of overall popularity than record sales. It is possible that Robey's contention that "Saving My Love for You" b/w "Yes, Baby" was a two-sided hit was also his attempt to allay any impression that Ace's career had stalled, since it clearly had not; both Ace and Duke Records were going strong.

The rhythm and blues business was down in early 1954, Bob Rolontz pointed out in his March *Billboard* column, though the "spiritual business" was holding steady, and dealers who handled both were doing fine. Of the three top-selling spirituals mentioned, one was a Robey record: the Five Blind Boys' "Jesus Is a Rock in a Weary Land."[62] Gospel records were "the main stream" of the Peacock Record business, Evelyn Johnson says. "Had Peacock been able to get its just desserts, it would have been the biggest gospel label—it really was, but it was never credited [by the industry] that way."[63] As far as the Duke operation was concerned, and Johnny Ace in particular, evidence in early 1954 suggests that Robey may have taken Ace's crooning to a new level of popularity with a black audience: at this point the name Johnny Ace begins to appear regularly in the trade magazines and black newspapers. According to one flattering story, when Hollywood radio station KRKD asked listeners to phone in their favorite Ace recording, one vote came thousands of miles away from the mid-Pacific via a ship-to-shore hook-up from a sailor on board the U.S.S. *Bryce Canyon.*[64]

Another indication of Ace's rising celebrity is the extent to which the trade magazines tracked the Ace/Thornton unit on the road. The duo played one-nighters with the C.C. Pinkston Orchestra in the Alabama-Georgia territory throughout January and February, working up to a March appearance at Pep's Musical Bar in Philadelphia with Johnny Board's Orchestra. Next, they did a series of one-nighters in Michigan and Ohio, culminating in a week's engagement at the Apollo Theater in New York beginning April 23. Promotion for the Apollo appearance was especially heavy. It was Ace's second and Thornton's fourth appearance at "the fabulous 'Palace' of r.&b.," and the Ace/Thornton unit formed a "smashing package"—Ace was "sensational" and Thornton represented "Peacock's belting lady killer of the blues." According to one account, this "stellar crew hit town with such an impact that [it] caused the whole of 125th and vicinity to just 'shake, rattle and roll' with the same blazing fire as did Joe Turner's latest Atlantic sizzler ["Shake, Rattle & Roll"].[65]

The "reigning 'king and queen of blues,'" as the *New York Age Defender* called Ace and Thornton,[66] represented the smash hit on this Apollo bill. "There's not much action on the Apollo bill this frame until the closing round," *Variety* said. "And then things really start rolling. Credit the Johnny Ace/Willie Mae Thornton unit for pulling the overlong layout out of the doldrums":

> Miss Thornton and Ace split the vocalistics with support from a driving seven-man combo (four rhythm, two reed and a brass), Femme is a heavy rhythm & blues thrush while Ace is a mellow crooner. The contrast is effective and sustains interest and excitement all the way. Miss Thornton blasts her disk faves, "Houn' Dog," "Let Your Tears Fall" and "For You My Love," with the kind of gusto that keeps the and rocking. Ace, a new disk fave in the r&b field, wins with "The Clock," "Follow the Rules," [*sic*] and "Saving My Love."[67]

It was Johnny Ace's greatest triumph at the Apollo, and his last.

During this period of Ace's fourth consecutive hit, the singer's expanding fan base was a microcosm of the increased popularity of rhythm and blues. *Billboard* acknowledged in a special section on R&B and a front-page story that the limited sales appeal of the "relatively small Negro market" music had now "blossomed into one of the fastest growing areas of the entire record business." There were now over seven hundred disk jockeys playing R&B exclusively, the magazine reported, and more than seventy-five labels releasing one thousand R&B records a year. "Teenagers have spearheaded the current swing," *Billboard* said, and the "teenage tide has swept down the old barriers which kept this music restricted to a segment of the population."

One possible explanation for this generational behavior was that this group of young people had not experienced the "rhythmically exciting dance bands of the swing era." As a measure of the dramatic nature of the change, California juke box operators reported that "machines located where young people congregate will show popular records taking a secondary position to r.&b. recordings." Retail outlets that did not previously stock R&B records had "found it necessary and especially profitable to do so," *Billboard* said, making it now possible for a white teenager to buy such records in his or her own neighborhood.[68] In an editorial, *Billboard* noted that the "rhythm and blues field has caught the ear of the nation. It is no longer the stepchild of the record business. Recent years have seen it develop into a stalwart member of the recording industry." Rhythm and blues firms were no longer "fly-by-nights," and the field itself had "finally broken itself free of its old confines," becoming a music that could "enjoy a healthy following among all people, regardless of race or color."[69]

In a related story, *Billboard* marveled at the "fabulous amount of bookings for r.&b. artists," where the top names were commonly engaged for a solid six months at a time. Rhythm and blues booking agencies aggressively sought new locations for their artists, and while venues for pop singers had diminished, spots available for R&B performers had increased. With the possible exception of gospel music, no other field of show business booked as many one-night stands as R&B artists, some of whom worked a full year "doing nothing but one-nighters from the New York area across the country to California." Finally, *Billboard* provided its analysis for success in the R&B field. Though it mentioned seven major agencies in the body of the story, it could have been describing the "special" relationship of Don Robey's Duke and Peacock Record labels and Evelyn Johnson's Buffalo Booking Agency:

> Agencies and record companies in the r.&b. field work together hand-in-glove. Each needs the other, and, of course, the artist needs both. It's the record company which brings the artist to public attention, and it's the booking agency which places the artists in clubs and on tours.
>
> An artist who hopes to make money needs two things: good records and good bookings.[70]

Additional validation of the importance of R&B in this special issue of *Billboard* is revealed in a discussion of music publishing in the R&B field — one of the most profitable potentially but "least talked about aspects." Almost every record label has its own publishing company, Bob Rolontz explained, and while artists "usually write their own material," at Atlantic, Aladdin, and Duke "the execs of the firms write material for their artists." Since the important precedent set by the court regarding answer songs (Peacock and "Hound Dog" vs. Sun Records and "Bear Cat"), Rolontz report-ed that R&B publishers had stopped using "one another's material with impunity, under the assumption that blues material was in the public do-main and therefore not in the ken of the copyright act."[71]

Don Robey took the opportunity to advertise Peacock Records and Duke Records ("RHYTHM and BLUES and RELIGIOUS Music For Millions") in this special *Billboard* issue. In a schizophrenic half-page ad that appeared to destroy the separate identities for the two labels that he had worked so hard to achieve, Robey hyped nineteen different artists, including the "Irrepress-ible Johnny Ace." Four acts are listed twice, with some Duke artists appear-ing in the Peacock side of the ad and some Peacock acts appearing on the Duke side. Altogether, the Duke/Peacock records are said to represent "SMASH-AFTER-SMASH-AFTER-SMASH."[72]

Nevertheless, Robey's attention to artist development bucked the trend in R&B. Nelson George points out in *The Death of Rhythm & Blues* that the trouble with most R&B operations was that they always went for the quick buck and the next easy hit. Few of the R&B business people, or "doo-wop capitalists," cared anything about artist development, he says. "All they thought about was capturing the moment. They recorded singers at a pace that suggested the market was going to evaporate the next day."[73] In this regard, Robey's development of artists signed to Duke and Peacock was intelligent and unusual. In early 1954 his companies were heavily promot-ing Sonny Parker, Marie Adams, Junior Parker, Little Richard and the Tem-po Toppers, Earl Forest, and Billy Brooks, among others, along with such gospel acts as the Five Blind Boys, Brother Cleophus Robinson, and the Dixie Hummingbirds. He had not given up on Willie Mae Thornton ei-ther. *Billboard* speculated that Thornton's "I Smell a Rat," released in May, "could be one of the strongest records of the season,"[74] though it failed to chart at all.

In Robey's direction of Ace's career—his deliberate development of Ace as an artist—he was especially perceptive. He released Ace records roughly every six months, promoting them fully and replacing them only when necessary. Three weeks after "Saving My Love for You" fell off the charts, for example, Robey released Ace's "Please Forgive Me" b/w "You've Been Gone So Long" (Duke 128)—a ballad on one side and an up-tempo blues on the other. The initial promotion in *Billboard* was a "History of Johnny The Ace" display ad, complete with twelve coast-to-coast markets declaring

"Ace does it again." Ace hits, beginning with "My Song," are presented in variable typeface, occupying larger and larger space, with "PLEASE FORGIVE ME" in the largest type of all. Sales figures are included in the ad, which claims sales of 100,000 units of the new record in only two days.[75]

In tone and feel, "Please Forgive Me" was patterned after the other four Ace hits. The arrangement features a soft Hammond organ (Ace), light vibes (Johnny Otis), and delicate guitar work (Pete Lewis). Lyrically, the phrase "please forgive me" is repeated four times in the first verse alone, coupled at the end with "I was wrong," presented vocally in a sad, lush, and rich baritone. *Billboard*, of course, reviewed it immediately: "Johnny Ace should do it again with this fine new release and keep his lengthy string of hits unbroken. 'Forgive Me' is a tuneful ballad which he sings with soul; the flip is a bouncy item and is handled brightly. Potent wax for operators and dealers."[76]

Before *Billboard* could make "Please Forgive Me" one of "This Week's Best Buys" it had to show up on one of the territorial charts, which it did on 5 June (number eight in Cincinnati), about the time that the Ace/Thornton unit was on a tour of one-nighters through the Carolinas.[77] In addition, the song was "reportedly strong in Dallas, Houston, New Orleans, Durham, Nashville, Los Angeles, St. Louis, Detroit, Philadelphia, and Pittsburgh."[78] Robey promoted the record vigorously in the following week's display ads, but could only show one additional territorial success — St. Louis (number five). "Please Forgive Me" appeared on the retail sales chart at number ten for only two weeks in June and on the juke box chart (highest position number six) for another two-week period in July. It was the second Ace record in a row to falter, "a hit," according to Nick Tosches, "but not of the magnitude of those that had come before it."[79] It is possible that sad and mournful Ace ballads were wearing a bit thin with the R&B audience, a market that seemed to have no interest at all in Ace as a blues shouter.

The "B" side of Duke 128 sounds very much like an early regional rock 'n' roll style, perhaps Chicago rhythm and blues. "You've Been Gone So Long," a shuffle blues written by Ace, represents the high energy side of his music ("hard-punching" and "credible," according to Peter Grendysa).[80] "You've been gone so long, I'm about to lose my mind," Ace asserts, and repeats. "Come back to me baby — everything's going to be real fine." It is a typical Ace scenario: his woman has left him and he can find no solace. "I can't sleep at night 'cause you're always in my dreams. I know you can't believe me, but it's strange as it seems." Indeed, it is "strange." From the total confidence projected by his voice there is good reason to disbelieve him: in typical blues fashion the emotion he communicates owes less to the "you've been gone" than to the "everything's going to be real fine." Ace is the victim, perhaps, but it is also clear that he may be the potential victor.

"Well, I turn, toss, all in my sleep," he says. "Tell me pretty baby what you've done to me." Ace is backed by the full Johnny Otis Band, and the guitar in the middle is a Chuck Berry–like solo by Pete Lewis well over a year before Berry's first record. Chuck Berry came up with a lot of innovations, Otis notes, but "we all borrowed from something"—Berry borrowed from Pete Lewis, who in turn borrowed heavily from T-Bone Walker.[81] Unfortunately, there is no evidence that this kind of blues material or "jump" side had any particular appeal to the contemporary black audience.

The Ace traveling aggregation returned to Houston in July 1954 for a recording session that was to be Ace's last. Five tunes were cut at Bill Holford's ACA studio at this time, all written by Ace or members of the group and performed by the road band, known variously as the Johnny Ace Band, the Johnny Board Band, or the C.C. Pinkston Orchestra.[82] Ace contributed three blues songs to this session, with trumpet player Joe Scott and drummer/vibes player C.C. Pinkston providing the ballads. With the exception of the marginal hit "Never Let Me Go," none of these sides would succeed in the marketplace.

All told, Ace's last opportunity to perform on tape for posterity was uneventful. It is possible that Johnny Ace had reached his potential as an R&B recording star in the summer of 1954 and was now on his way down. Perhaps Don Robey sensed the decline as well and attempted to renew Ace's momentum, which may explain the overheated nature of the Ace publicity machine that continued to roll on throughout the summer, claiming that the success of "Please Forgive Me" was "helping to pull in the standing room crowds" and causing Ace fans in Houston to maul him in adoration. Five hundred members of his fan club reportedly "stampeded and ripped his suit to pieces" when Ace "started handing out autographed pictures to the necessary demons."[83] Evelyn Johnson, who ran the Houston office, would have remembered such a spectacle had it actually happened. "Someone," she says, "must have made that up."[84]

Johnny Ace was the most unassuming
person. "Johnny stand up. Johnny sit
down." Sweetest thing since sugar. But he
didn't care about nuttin', honey. Life was
like a routine for him, but that's
what kept him going.
—Evelyn Johnson

Dirty Talk
and One-Night
Stands

In the middle of July 1954, while the Johnny Ace/Willie Mae
Thornton unit was making one-night tours of Texas, Louisiana, and
New Mexico, Bob Rolontz pointed out in *Billboard* that R&B was
beginning to have a powerful influence on the rest of the music industry. "Sh-Boom," he observed, a tune recorded by the Chords and
released by Atlantic Record's subsidiary Cat, had broken through
to the pop charts and was selling "solidly" in a pop cover version
by the Crewcuts. It generated a second pop cover by the Billy
Williams Quartet and was now being released in a country and
western arrangement. Nor was this just an isolated example. The
Spaniels' "Goodnight, Sweetheart, Goodnight" was being successfully covered in pop by the McGuire Sisters, Joe Turner's "Shake,
Rattle & Roll" had been cleaned up enough to be performed by
Bill Haley & the Comets, and three other hits by R&B vocal groups
were released as pop covers.[1] The notion that what was good for
the record industry was good for R&B was being turned on its ear,
according to Rolontz: "It appears that the pop and country a.&r.
men pay a lot of attention to what goes on in the r.&b. field. In fact,

according to some r.&b. execs, they pay too much attention, staying as close to the original r.&b. arrangement as possible when they cover the tune. Maybe it's time to adapt an old slogan to read 'What's good for the r.&b. business is good for the record industry.'"[2]

Whether or not the 45 rpm single was good for the industry was being hotly contested in the summer of 1954. Record companies had good reasons to switch to the smaller, unbreakable format, and the juke box industry welcomed the change. Radio stations, however, were balking at the new policy by the labels to furnish stations with 45 rpm product exclusively. Stations everywhere played more records on the air, but many could not secure or install the necessary new turntables fast enough to keep up with the new industry standard. A group of "articulate radio station men," *Billboard* editorialized, were continuing "to disregard technological and economic developments" in the music business.

Record manufacturers, on the other hand, were failing "to ease the path of progress." Both sides suffered from "general astigmatism."[3] The argument over format, or the "DJ-45 Battle," next spilled over to the music publishers, who were caught in the middle. Though publishers didn't care whether their songs were cut on 45 or 78 rpm configurations, under the new policy by the labels only the smaller records were initially manufactured and available as samples and promotional copies. Disk jockeys employed by stations that rejected the new format put pressure on the publishers to provide them with the 78 rpm records they wanted, but publishers could not provide what did not exist. One alternative for the publisher was to try to locate an acetate copy of the song and pay three dollars to have a shellac dub made. Not only was this expensive but inconvenient as well: shellac records could not be mailed—they had to be hand delivered.[4] Over the next few months some publishers would be forced to order one hundred or more acetates of new records and rush them to influential disk jockeys.[5]

Even though the 78 rpm single record would remain the primary mode of communication for R&B songs for many years (the less affluent and more adult African American market was traditionally slow to change entertainment hardware), Don Robey, as usual, anticipated the change. Six weeks after "Please Forgive Me" fell off the national charts, Robey released "Never Let Me Go" b/w "Burley Cutie" (Duke 132)—another sad and slow AABA ballad with a throw-away instrumental blues side. Curiously, the coupling of the two sides formed a pair of contrasting bookends. The ballad side had

been recorded at the most recent session; the blues side had been originally cut in Memphis by David James Mattis and then re-recorded at the ACA
studio during the first Houston session two years before. Apparently, Robey
did not even see the value in protecting the side with a copyright. Duke 132
was, however, the first Ace record to be simultaneously mastered in both
78 and 45 rpm configurations.[6]

"Just let me love you tonight," Ace pleads at the beginning of the song,
"forget about tomorrow." The pulse of "Never Let Me Go" is very slow—
slower than one beat per second. "My darling, won't you hold me tight,"
he sings with the vulnerability of a voice in absolute supplication, "and never
let me go." Barry Hansen, the musicologist whose radio name is Dr. Demento, remembers the power of the song for white teenagers after Ace's death:
"During my last two years in high school (1958–59) in Minneapolis, I was
appointed as the DJ for most of the school's sock hops (because I had the
most records.) Though the school was 99 percent white I considered it my
mission to play as many R&B records as I could get away with. Toward the
end of the evening, when slow dancing was in order, I'd always put on a
couple of Johnny Ace's ballads, and in fact 'Never Let Me Go' was the last
dance at least 50 percent of the time."[7]

Perhaps Peter Grendysa has this performance in mind when he calls Ace
"a wonderful singer with the bluest pipes around, the guy with a tear in his
voice."[8] Colin Escott observes "a profound sadness underpinning most of
Ace's work," which may be why his uptempo material was not successful.
"He managed to instill some meaning and genuine feeling into some fairly
maudlin and mediocre material," he says. "'Never Let Me Go' is a good
example. In another artist's hands it would simply be a less than memora-
ble ballad but in Ace's hands it becomes a genuinely affecting performance.
The orchestral backdrop suits the mood of the piece to perfection."[9] *Billboard* continued to review Ace favorably for essentially the same reasons.
"Johnny Ace sings this new ballad with his usual sincerity," it reported, "and
the record has a chance for the big time."[10] Bob Rolontz called Ace an R&B
"top wax name" in his column in this issue.[11]

By the end of the summer of 1954, the trend detected by *Billboard* that
rhythm and blues material was "moving strongly into the pop market" was
documented on a regular basis.[12] Independent Atlantic Records was "the
most covered label in the rhythm and blues field today," Rolontz pointed
out, "with at least 18 different record artists doing cover-jobs on Atlantic disks

within the last few months." Luckily for the label, sixteen of the songs were published by Progressive Music Corporation, the publishing company owned by Atlantic.[13] The closer that R&B came into national consciousness, however, the more resistance it encountered. On national television in September, Los Angeles disk jockey Peter Potter, "foreman" of CBS's *Juke Box Jury*, blasted the teenage popularity of rhythm and blues, placing the blame on recording company A&R men. Much of the music, he said, was "obscene and of lewd intonation, and certainly not fit for radio broadcast."[14]

Meanwhile, *Billboard* noted that the sudden popularity of syndicated R&B shows (such as those hosted by Hunter Hancock in Los Angeles, Zena Sears in Atlanta, and Alan Freed, who had just moved to New York) "could mean much to the r.&b. business, and perhaps eventually to the entire record business."[15] Obviously, the editors recognized the enormous implications inherent in the power to introduce a new record over a wide area in a short period of time. Moreover, *Billboard* also observed that the major record firms, which had previously regarded R&B as "regional or limited sellers," were now "jumping on the 'trends' initiated by the indie [independent] record labels more quickly today than ever before." The large companies were "pained" when independent labels racked up pop hits, and chagrined that "the backbone of the pop record business [young people] appear to want r.&b. music so much that they search it out in stores and on juke boxes."[16]

Peter Potter's on-air warning that some R&B songs were obscene and lewd underscored a serious vulnerability for rhythm and blues that made the entire music business nervous. "Control the Dim-Wits!" *Billboard* editorialized, acknowledging that some R&B records had been guilty of "overstepping propriety and good taste" and had already "precipitated legislative intervention." In California, the Long Beach sheriff's office had "banned the performance of one of the spicier r.&b. disks on juke boxes." Four West Coast radio stations had banned "one of the cruder" titles, and California newspapers had mounted campaigns against "the rash of double entendre recordings." Other parts of the country were said to be concerned as well, with police not only issuing fifty dollar fines in Memphis but actually confiscating juke boxes. *Billboard* found "cause for alarm." It was regrettable, it said, that law enforcement groups "found it necessary to apply restraining measures at a time when the r.&b. field [was] enjoying a tremendous measure of acceptance."[17]

A week later, the editors persisted. Fearing "pressure of sufficient force to precipitate action" by the FCC, *Billboard* appealed to manufacturers to "exercise taste and propriety lest a small band undo in a brief, greedy moment the progress made by the field as a whole, with its great artists, creative artists and repertoire men and writers." Disk jockeys and radio stations also had to assume moral responsibility; the "occasional distasteful disks must be weeded out." In this regard, the editors felt the specific need to caution its readers that the best-selling charts printed in every issue merely reflected sales figures and were not "a carte blanche programing recommendation."[18] In a related story, R&B record executives from the Apollo, Savoy, and Atlantic labels promised their support and endorsed the "movement against offensive content." They were joined by the president of the Music Operators of New York, who wanted *Billboard* to furnish him "with the titles of objectional records." Assorted distributors, dealers, and one-stop owners were less certain as to how to proceed.[19]

Though never mentioned by name, *Billboard* readers understood the most offensive titles to be three chart-topping, best-selling records by Hank Ballard & the Midnighters. The first record to catch on was "Work With Me, Annie" ("Let's get it while the gettin' is good / Annie please don't cheat / Give me all my meat"), followed by "Sexy Ways" and "Annie Had a Baby," all on the Federal label. Actually, the euphemism "work with me" originated with Johnny Otis, who thought that Ballard's proposed "sock it to me" was "too strong." According to Otis, the controversy over the song was started by a "phony politician" running for office. "The problem was that white kids were listening to these things for the first time," he told Arnold Shaw. "It was all right so long as blacks were listening, but as soon as the whites started listening it was no good. Then it became a big, political thing."[20] "Work With Me, Annie" was, according to *Billboard*'s annual tabulation, the number one R&B record in sales and number two in juke box plays for the year. ("Sexy Ways" was number ten and nine and "Annie Had a Baby" eight and ten.)[21] Johnny Otis blamed the controversy over the "Annie" songs on the white establishment. "They pointed to the effect of degenerate black lyrics on white youth. It was racism at heart," he told John Broven.[22]

Certainly there were aspects of racism inherent in many of the challenges to rhythm and blues music at the time, but the matter of what the black press frequently called "smutty records" did not divide exclusively along racial lines. "Dirt is dirt cheap," George F. Brown wrote in a 1951 column for the (black) *Pittsburgh Courier.* "I hate to harp on a subject [Brown had begun his attack on unsuitable music in 1948], but smutty records simply have no place in radio."[23] Brown went on a concerted campaign against "smut" in May and June 1953, attacking disk jockeys who played records that were "downright dirty." "Dirty discs must go or pretty soon we'll all have to listen to the radio in a sewer so we'll feel at home," he said.[24]

A week later Brown reported that "right" disk jockeys agreed with the campaign "to clean up the airwaves" and cut out the "purple platters." Radio stations should monitor their programs more closely, he advised, and the FCC "should police the air more thoroughly."[25] By the third week Brown was linking Havelock Ellis and *The Kinsey Report* with the "dirty wax craze." "Sex, sin and salaciousness are the order of the day," he complained, "and some disc jockeys vie with each other to see who can get on the air first with the dirtiest new record." Like a preacher at his pulpit, Brown pounded his point home: "Dirty records add nothing to a program. Dirty records run away responsible sponsors. Dirty records corrupt the minds of young people and old people who never grew up. Dirty records hurt the recording industry. Dirty records are just plain dirty."[26]

After that, Brown's efforts took on characteristics of a crusade. The FCC was doing "a fine job in keeping the networks and big stations in line," he said, but he urged the agency to monitor the smaller local stations and "revoke licenses if the culprits do not fly right." The newspaper's readers were urged to write the FCC directly regarding off-color disk jockeys and their "venal" station owners.[27] In a final installment, the columnist applauded the many readers who had praised the *Courier*'s "Smutty Record Drive" and positioned black disk jockeys as public figures who could become "sources for good" like Joe Louis and Jackie Robinson, black heroes who "did not gain fame and respect by catering to the smutty instincts of kids. Or grown kids."[28] "We mentioned [in 1948] that colored disc jockeys are the major offenders and we still say so," Brown reminded his readers a few months later. "The idea that we must always cater to the baser instincts of our people for success is heart-breaking to acknowledge."[29]

Almost a year later, the issue erupted again in the black press, this time over a white disk jockey. The *New York Age Defender* reported in July 1954 that radio station WINS was negotiating for the services, beginning in September, of Cleveland-based Alan "Moondog" Freed. Hundreds of radio fans and "at least 50 entertainers in the New York area have expressed indignation over the recent rumor," the paper said: "The protest stems chiefly from the fact that Freed 'apes' the Negro, making him a clown in the eyes of the public and refers to his juvenile followers as 'moondog puppies.' His manner of broadcasting is in bad taste and shows a degree of contempt for the intelligence of the Negro public." One unnamed "top variety star" claimed that "Freed is worse than Amos and Andy ever dared to be and if WINS brings him into New York it will be a disgrace to the entire Negro race."[30]

Age Defender columnist Alan McMillan vowed in August "to continue telling the truth about 'Moondog' Freed. He is not a champion of the Negro, never has been," McMillan said. He noted that a group of housewives was planning to boycott Freed's show "if and when it is presented on WINS. This is the first time to my knowledge that this particular radio station has attempted to go into the 'rhythm and blues' field," he said, "and it appears to this observer that they might have found at least one Negro disk jockey suitable for the show."[31]

While the New York black press positioned itself against the inevitable arrival of Alan Freed, Freed himself continued to exploit his popularity in Cleveland. On Friday, 6 August 1954, Freed served as the master of ceremonies at "The Biggest Rhythm and Blues Show," billed in the Cleveland Call & Post as the "Greatest Show and Dance Event of the Year," to be held at Cleveland Public Auditorium. Roy Hamilton was to be on the bill, along with the Drifters, Faye Adams, LaVern Baker, the Spaniels, the Counts, Big Maybelle, and Erskine Hawkins. Freed, the "King of the Moondoggers," was to be accompanied by "Mrs. Moondog and the 'Moon Puppies.'"[32] The show was an unqualified success, drawing some 9,600 music and dance fans to an event that was "strictly an inter-racial affair."[33]

WINS did bring Freed to New York in September, but not without further public criticism, or, as the Pittsburgh Courier called it, "the unwelcome mat which was laid down for [Freed] when he moved into the Gotham territory."[34] Age Defender columnist Sonny Murrain could see nothing particularly unique in the "crimes" of Alan Freed, "the glib ofay with the 'colored way,'" and estimated that "70 percent of the Negro disk jockeys aired in this baliwick" were guilty of playing the same examples of "phonographic pornography."[35] This argument did not impress George F. Brown of the Pittsburgh Courier. "Last year this writer raised a lot of sand about smutty records on the air," he said. "In recent months, rhythm and blues have been discovered to be a mint. So white disc jockeys are getting in the act and they, too, are spinning smutty records, in the belief that colored people desire this crippled attempt at entertainment."[36]

As it turned out, Freed took New York by storm. Though his primary audience consisted of white teenagers, by playing the R&B records that young Americans wanted to hear he eventually won over black youth as well.[37] Black performers, publishers, and businessmen began defending Freed in October 1954, since his success in promoting black music among white youth was in the interests of the entire rhythm and blues industry. In response to charges by New York disk jockey Willie ("The Mayor of Harlem") Bryant that Freed's shows were "not clean," Al Sears, composer, publisher, and former tenor sax player with Duke Ellington, advised his peers to "stop this childish nonsense about 'you can't sell papers on any corner in this town because we were here first.'"[38] *Billboard* picked up this local story and shared the "hassle" with the entire music trade, interviewing Freed himself, who claimed that he had never played smutty records on his program and pointed out that the *Courier* had praised him "only two years ago for showcasing Negro talent."[39]

The argument over sexual subject matter in rhythm and blues raged on for the rest of the year. The *Pittsburgh Courier* was praised by one industry spokesman for its "militant crusade" and its "pioneering policy in guiding the progressive pathways of American Negroes." Chris Forde, head of Tuxedo Records in Harlem, "marveled" at how the paper "stood fast in its editorial policy of pride-in-race." It is clear that for the *Courier*, at least, the subject of R&B lyrical content was about "contaminating the minds of Negro children" and solely an African American matter: "[Rhythm and blues records] are manufactured solely for the Negro market," Forde said, "and the manufacturer and his singer show no awareness of their responsibility to the young black minds who will listen to this trash."[40] Actually, of course, the whole matter was less about race than it was about age and social class. Older and more affluent members of the African American community, less likely to purchase or even listen to R&B, had little understanding or respect for this emerging popular music. When George F. Brown praised black recording artists who did not get famous "off a dirty record" he listed big band leaders (black and white), jazz instrumentalists, and performers of theater music, with no mention whatsoever of any blues performer or rhythm and blues artist.[41]

For other critics, the problem with song lyrics went far beyond sexuality.

Marty Richardson, writing in the *Cleveland Call & Post*, indexed the themes of current R&B songs that represented an "unadulterated filth campaign" that was "spilling over" Negro teenagers like "malignant diseases," glorifying "looseness, lewdness, laziness and licentiousness": getting drunk, owning cars or other "economically-unsound" luxuries, speaking poor English, and calling "for the use of knives and other violent aids in settling problems, especially the domestic." Richardson blamed the problem on "a more vicious possible reason as to why so many of the filth-records are made." The "back-yard, one-room record pressing companies, who don't [even] need $500 to go into business and saturate the market with obscenity, got sick and tired of having to face the truth that the only real contribution to American culture is the music of the Negro."

"If they keep up the present rate at which they are paying Negro artists to debase and putrify the Negro taste in music," Richardson concluded, "very soon they will never again have to face this fact. Nobody, but NOBODY, will claim that the Negro is making any contribution to music."[42] The last word in the black press for 1954 belonged to Larry Douglas, writing in the *New York Age Defender*, who saw some permanent good coming from the rising popularity of R&B. Freed was setting "New York and the entire Eastern Seaboard on fire by constantly airing rhythm and blues records," he said, and "doing a fine race relations job." Freed was "forcing" white disk jockeys who had never played R&B records on the air to play them and white record shops who never ordered R&B records to stock them. "This will eventually force the trade to release all records in the popular field under one heading — 'Pop,'" Douglas prophesied.[43]

Billboard's "campaign against off-color and double entendre r.&b. disks" was conducted in an entirely different vein from the black weekly newspapers. The trade magazine had no bone to pick with the broadcast media, no shared audience to attempt to win over, and no moral highground it needed to claim. *Billboard* was concerned not so much with the idea that a single record could prove offensive to the standards of a given community but that "all phases of the business" agreed that a real problem existed and needed to be solved. It was time, Bob Rolontz said, "for the few companies involved to stop releasing blue records." Artists and booking agents "should be most interested in seeing [off-color recordings] stopped," he said, because the singer or group that "hits the top with a dirty record" can never sell "clean ones" thereafter. In addition, the act is "marked from then on," booked only in certain clubs and sure to lose its value "after the first flurry" of popularity. According to the manager of "a top singing group," performers ought to remember that "when you use dirty material, you are on your way down, not up."[44]

Though sexually explicit recordings like the "Annie" songs were capturing most of the headlines, the real rhythm and blues story was less sensational but more significant. The number of disk jockeys playing R&B was increasing every month, Bob Rolontz observed, along with the variety of R&B material. Southern male blues singers were "selling," and so were "femme singers" and vocal groups. "Roy Hamilton and Johnny Ace, ballad singers extraordinary, are always right on top," he said. All that was missing was "a good instrumental hit."[45] Rolontz estimated that the "rhythm and blues beat, sound or arrangement" accounted for almost 20 percent of all records made by pop artists—an astounding figure driven by demand. "The kids," he explained, "have indicated that they want the music with a beat."[46] The "kids," moreover, were turning out to be increasingly important to the recording industry because, unlike their parents, they bought so many records. Record companies could not rely on adult customers. According to a 1954 survey made for Columbia Records, only 50 percent of U.S. families owned a phonograph, and only 13 percent bought even one record a year.[47]

The controversy over acceptable R&B lyrics brought David James Mattis, now production manager of Memphis station WDIA, back in the news in October 1954. "WDIA's Got a Broom," Billboard editorialized over the station's new, public procedure for "screening and banning rhythm and blues records which violate accepted standards of good taste" due to "its respect for—and devotion to—the rhythm and blues field."[48] WDIA had banned fifteen records, including all of the "Annie" songs. When listeners called in to request suggestive titles, WDIA disk jockeys read a prepared statement over the air: "WDIA, your good-will station, in the interest of good citizenship, for the protection of morals and our American way of life does not consider this record (blank) fit for broadcast on WDIA. We are sure all you listeners will agree with us and continue to enjoy our programs and the music you hear every day."[49]

Considerations of taste, race, and class aside, the controversy over R&B lyrics was also the source of intense industry rivalry, an inevitable part of the ongoing BMI-ASCAP feud. BMI, Broadcast Music Incorporated, the organization controlled by the broadcasting industry that licensed almost all R&B material, was a rival group to ASCAP, the American Society of Composers, Authors, and Publishers. ASCAP had been organized before World War I for the purpose of collecting royalties for the public performance of music its members had written or published. At the time, writers and publishers were able to profit from the "mechanical rights" income produced by royalties from the sales of sound recordings or sheet music, but they had no way to collect "performance rights" income for what the Copyright Act of 1909 referred to as "public performance [of music] for profit." ASCAP sued Shanley's Broadway Restaurant in 1915 for the unlicensed use of Victor Herbert's operetta *Sweethearts*, a landmark case eventually won in the Supreme Court. In the 1920s ASCAP successfully sued the radio industry, forcing individual radio stations to pay an annual fee for the performance rights of ASCAP licensed songs, and the movie industry.

By the end of the 1930s ASCAP had a virtual monopoly on the performance rights of American songs, but lost this control when it attempted to double its fees from radio in 1940. Radio executives considered the ASCAP demand "so outrageous," David Ewen says, "that they refused to discuss an agreement." Instead, six hundred radio stations founded their own licensing society, BMI, and beginning after Christmas 1940 refused to play any ASCAP licensed tune. Older Americans still remember the "musical wasteland" of radio during this ASCAP lockout. Except for a handful of tunes never heard before or never copyrighted in the first place, virtually no popular song written after 1884 was being played on the radio. There were no current tunes, no Tin Pan Alley products, no songs from Broadway musicals or the movies. Instead, radio stations played "I Dream of Jeanie with the Light Brown Hair" and other Stephen Foster compositions, since they were so old they were no longer protected by copyright and were in the public domain. ASCAP settled the dispute within a year, finding it could not survive without revenues from the radio industry, which had been providing more than 60 percent of its income.

By the time ASCAP gave in to the radio industry's terms, BMI had a stable of several hundred writers and publishers of its own. By design, the new organization had an open membership policy, did not restrict itself to New York or Hollywood writers, and actually encouraged membership from professionals engaged in "hillbilly" and "race" music. While ASCAP was busy pursuing what David Ewen calls the "traditional ways" of Broadway and

Hollywood, BMI was courting an emerging new audience. By recognizing the new audience and meeting the new demands, "BMI was able to grow prodigiously," Ewen says. "By [1955], 80 percent of all the music played over the radio was licensed by BMI."[50]

The people at BMI knew perfectly well that ASCAP interests were being served by public controversy over R&B "smutty records" and that the real object of the attack was conceivably BMI as a licensing entity. Certainly the organization had to defend itself. While it could not condone the lyrics to "Work With Me, Annie," a best-selling BMI licensed song, it had no way of preventing such material from being played on radio stations or juke boxes around the country. People who knew how the music industry worked understood how impossible it was to attempt to enforce any kind of censorship over song lyrics. For one thing, songs licensed by BMI *had already been recorded.* The recording itself was the reason for the license; indeed, a record had to exist before a license could be issued. The licensing society had nothing to do with the lyrical content of the song, or with the melody, arrangement, or chord progression.

Like ASCAP, BMI merely registered publishers, writers, and titles of songs at the beginning of the licensing process and then logged instances of the public performance for profit, primarily radio airplay, of these songs to calculate performance rights payments at the other end of the process. When an individual radio station chose to play a BMI song with off-color lyrics instead of another BMI song with acceptable lyrics, there was not much that BMI could do except to endure the unfavorable publicity or attempt through public relations to position itself as a take-charge organization committed to clamping down on writers and publishers determined to exploit off-color material.

Billboard reported in early November that BMI "had tightened up its inspection of new material," and while it had "no intention of imposing any formal censorship on song material" it was adding "new persons to its 'screening board,' including a young lady who might place a different interpretation on suggestive lyrics than her male confreres." According to the president of BMI, however, the real responsibility for insuring that "public programming follows the dictates of good taste" belonged to radio stations and other "users of music."[51] In a public relations coup, ASCAP revealed that it would soon "take a definite stand discouraging collaboration" between ASCAP writers and BMI writers—presumably to protect itself from charges of shared responsibility for off-color material. Though this kind of collaboration was legal under a court-ordered Consent Decree, *Billboard* reported that a potential ASCAP strategy might be to "refuse to claim an equity in the song. Adherents of this view claim that ASCAP would then be under no obligation to collect performance fees for such an ASCAP writer."[52]

While the controversy waged over song lyrics (*Variety* called them "leerics") and the suitability of rhythm and blues in the mainstream, the dispute had nothing to do directly with the sophisticated image of Duke Records or the heart ballads of Johnny Ace: Ace's records were virtual models of decorum. In early October, *Billboard* made "Never Let Me Go" one of "This Week's Best Buys," comparing Ace with Atlantic's Joe Turner: "Another artist who appears to be maintaining his high batting average, Ace in two weeks time has established his latest release as a strong seller in Philadelphia, Upstate New York, Atlanta, Nashville, Durham, Dallas, St. Louis, Richmond, Detroit and Chicago."[53] In addition, *Billboard* reviewed Duke 132 as a new record, citing its earlier review for the "A" side, and commenting for the first time on the "B" side. "Burlie Cutie" was said to be a "rocking instrumental that features a groovy tenor sax and a strong rhythm section. While the flip side is stronger, this strengthens its juke box appeal."[54] As it turned out, Cincinnati was the only territory in which the record flourished; "Never Let Me Go" did not penetrate the national R&B sales charts and only barely made those for juke box plays (number nine).

The momentum of Ace's career had clearly stalled in the fall of 1954. For the first time, an Ace release was not automatically an Ace hit. The debate over language, generational in character, with older Americans insisting that records be cleaned up, would not disappear despite the best efforts of industry spokesmen and black leaders alike. The emerging new white teenage audience was having none of it. Precisely at the time that a Memphis-based black crooner like Johnny Ace was singing perfectly acceptable lyrics, he was being eclipsed by an outrageous, hip-shaking phenomenon from his hometown. By then, Nick Tosches points out about the time period, "Elvis Presley, who had listened to the Beale Streeters during his high school years, was on his way to becoming the new rage."[55]

Billboard reported in November 1954 that pop music acts were experiencing tough times on the road. Three shows had "bombed," it said, one of them folding after playing only half its twenty-eight dates. The "Biggest Show of 1954," an integrated show starring Billy Eckstein, Peggy Lee, and the Pete

Rugolo Orchestra, canceled its remaining dates after encountering the weakest box office in the three-year history of "Biggest Shows."[56] At the same time, but with an altogether different scenario, the biggest rhythm and blues package in history was being assembled by Shaw Artists. "The Top Ten R&B Show," featuring ten headline R&B acts and an emcee still to be selected, was sixty days from its opening performance, but it already had forty-two confirmed bookings in arenas and auditoria in every section of the country except the far West.[57] While it may have been news to the industry that R&B was alive and well on the road, it certainly was not news to Johnny Ace.

While *Billboard* editorialized, Johnny Ace slept in hotel rooms and traveled around the country, living the nomadic life of an R&B recording star on an independent label. He had no permanent home or routine beyond the long string of hotel addresses and rumored whereabouts. He was known to stay at the Crystal Hotel in Houston, for example, at the Majestic in Cleveland, and, of course, at the Mitchell in hometown Memphis. But for all practical purposes, Ace was a kind of at-large and on-the-move extension of Duke Records and the Buffalo Booking Agency. In the preceding two years Ace had spent virtually every night on the road and in a different bed, leading the same kind of gypsy life experienced by B.B. King, whom Charles Sawyer estimates played 342 one-nighters in calendar year 1956.[58] Evelyn Johnson, who arranged both King's and Ace's personal performance schedules, does not doubt the figure, and she points out that Ace was a more popular performer in 1954 than King was in 1956 and could have played even more dates. "They almost worked nightly in those small towns and all," she says about King and Ace. "They did a lot. And then when they would go North many times they would have a five-day stop in a club."[59]

For the road-weary musician, the opportunity to sleep five nights in the same place must have seemed a heavenly reprieve. The chitlin circuit was "a ruthless pacemaker," Charles Sawyer says. "Successive one-night stands were often 800 miles apart. Days might pass before the pace allowed a night's rest in a hotel: play five hours, dismantle the bandstand, load the bus, ride fifteen hours on the nod, set up the bandstand, play five hours, dismantle the bandstand, and so on."[60] B.B. King told John Broven a similar story about life on the road as arranged by Buffalo Booking: "At Buffalo, Evelyn Johnson was in charge and she would say, 'Tomorrow you gotta go just right up the street, so be on time for the gig.' And like that would be 700 miles! And we used to complain among the band, we used to complain how we'd jump.

When we got a job say, 300/400 miles, that was nothing. Man you name it, we played it, we played so many places."[61]

The pace of road performances was only in part determined by business considerations. "Like so many times you could only get Friday, Saturday, and Sunday in the small towns," Evelyn Johnson recalls: "Now and again, when we reached a point where we were getting into the bigger places, there were times when in order to get there we had to work our way. Maybe we hit a town that would only play a Thursday, and yet [B.B.] had to open up in that particular club. That was a very rare thing, because it was against the union regulations."[62] Presumably, the rules were broken with the long distance drives.

For a black performer in the 1950s traveling through and playing hundreds of dates a year in the Deep South, the only problems weren't the hours and the miles. The humiliation and inconvenience of Jim Crow segregation laws and practices were hard on people. Black musicians traveling as a group to Birmingham, Alabama, had no trouble respecting the local ordinance that prohibited blacks and whites from playing checkers or dominoes together,[63] but laws regulating food service and bathroom facilities wore people down on a daily basis. B.B. King learned to use the 150-gallon gas tank on his bus as leverage to negotiate food service with the purchase of fuel, but even that tactic could not protect a band member's sense of dignity as he watched a restaurant worker "ceremoniously" break a coffee cup he had just drunk from, "as if to declare that some breach of the law of racial kosher had defiled it."[64]

Overnight accommodations were severely limited for African American musicians in the postwar era, not just in the more rural South but in other regions and larger cities as well, and not just for rhythm and blues performers. Las Vegas may have developed as an entertainment capital after World War II, but its traditions were inherited from an earlier era. No Negroes, Alan Pomerance points out, were permitted to stay in any Strip hotel, to enter a casino, or to gamble "in even the shoddiest joints downtown": "The 3,000 full-time local black residents could only get an apartment in the ghetto called 'Westside,' and black stars, in those days including Pearl Bailey, Billy Eckstein, the Delta Rhythm Boys, Harold Nicholas and Hazel Scott, were not welcome in the hotels where they were features, but were set up in housing for black entertainers in Westside."[65]

Sammy Davis Jr. remembered those days. He and his uncle and father were Las Vegas regulars as the Will Mastin Trio. "The other acts could gamble or sit in the lounge and have a drink," he says, "but we had to leave through the kitchen with the garbage. I was dying to grab a look into the casino, just to see what it was like, but I was damned if I'd let anyone see me with my nose against the candy-store window."[66] Later, when the Trio refused to sleep in Westside, one hotel offered a compromise: "three first-class trailers parked on the hotel grounds."[67] In fact, the first time that Davis was permitted to sleep in a hotel and enter a casino was in November 1954, when he was booked as a solo act at the New Frontier. He was not, however, welcome in any other hotel or casino during this engagement, nor were his personal guests accorded the same privileges as he: the only place he was permitted to entertain his friends was in his hotel suite.[68]

For African American performers like Sammy Davis Jr., the situation was even worse in Miami. Davis could provide the entertainment at the Beachcomber Hotel in Miami Beach, but he had to sleep on the other side of the bridge at the Lord Calvert, a hotel in the Negro section of Miami. The Beachcomber casino boss had a new Corvette for him to use during his engagement and special identification cards to show police. He specifically remembers the instructions: "'[The Corvette's] yours while you're here. Only white cabs can cross the bridge from Miami onto the Beach and they aren't allowed to ride colored guys.' He was telling it to me fast, like a man jumping into cold water. 'Here, I got you these cards from the Police Department. There's a curfew on the Beach for all colored people and they can arrest you unless you show 'em this, which explains you're working there.'"[69] Finally, Davis would only perform in places in which customers of color were permitted to see his shows, but that kind of decision could not fully protect him from racial humiliation on the road. Even in Chicago, once the desk clerk saw that he was a black man he could be denied hotel room reservations made and confirmed weeks before.[70]

Besides fatigue and racism, there were other "routine dangers" to be faced on the road—"personal hazards," Charles Sawyer calls them, "that threatened life and body." B.B. King, for example, by 1980 had already survived sixteen auto wrecks in addition to the dance hall fires, shootings, fights, and other forms of personal violence.[71] Some of the dangers were inherent to the business of live music. Liquor was an essential part of the music scene, of course, and the use of drugs was not uncommon. Some members of the audience invariably got high, lost inhibitions, became sexually provocative or demanding or jealous, and on occasion turned reckless. Violent deaths

Dirty Talk and One-Night Stands /// 123

in black music include Robert Johnson (poisoned), Little Walter Jacobs and Sonny Boy [John Lee] Williamson (beaten), and Sam Cooke (shot). Other dangers were less dramatic. It was easy on the road to suffer from time-structure hunger: there was too much sitting around, too much waiting to go on stage, entirely too much time to kill. Boredom wore many musicians down, drove some to drink, and others to drug addiction. As Charles Sawyer points out, "the ways in which life on the road can claim an entertainer are subtle and unforgiving."[72]

At least for B.B. King, there were other challenges on the road besides the evening performance. King was in charge of his show and responsible for more than a dozen people who traveled with him. He rode in a bus he controlled, and when it broke down he improvised transportation to meet his booking obligations, even if it cost him money. He made rules and enforced them, hired and fired musicians for his road band, and advanced money for sidemen experiencing family emergencies. King was like an "Old South patriarch," Sawyer says, with "ultimate responsibility for 'The Company.'"[73] Unlike King, Johnny Ace assumed no responsibility for the show or the troupe; he was merely the headliner of his road show. "He was like a puppet," Evelyn Johnson says. "He was estranged from things. He was only happy when he was [performing]. He didn't talk much. Life was just like a routine for him, but that was what kept him going."[74] Actually, what kept Ace going was the Duke/Peacock/Lion Music/Buffalo Booking Agency system.

By November 1954 the system established by Robey and Johnson for the promotion of both Duke and Peacock records and the personal appearances of their recording stars was clearly making inroads into the national R&B music scene. In other cities the success of this operation might have been acclaimed and rewarded with local status and prestige, but neither white Houston nor black Houston seemed impressed. "The people in this city pegged [Robey] as a flamboyant, playboy gambler," Evelyn Johnson says. "They never ever, until this day, understood the magnitude of that operation. The sad part is they didn't even know what *Billboard* was, or *Cash Box*. I remember we had a joke about it. I can't remember the details, but when [the Houston paper] reported it they called it *Billbox* and *Cash Board*."[75]

The lack of musical knowledge about how the industry worked did not make Houston a musically inactive city, however. Lightnin' Hopkins, Sippie Wallace, Eddie "Cleanhead" Vinson, Gatemouth Brown, Big Mama Thornton, Ivory Joe Hunter, and Charles Brown were all considered Houston blues acts, even though many of them had migrated to the West Coast at the end of the Depression or during the war years. Later, Houston claimed Percy Mayfield, Albert Collins, and ZZ Top.[76] Robey apparently forgave Houston for not recognizing the true measure of his achievement, remaining especially loyal to the city's annual "Juneteenth" commemoration of the end of slavery in Texas. As the manager of the Buffalo Booking Agency, "Juneteenth" presented a particular challenge for Evelyn Johnson. Many club owners in the South and the Southwest wanted her bands in mid-June, but she had to give Robey, who insisted that Duke and Peacock artists participate in the local celebration, "first call."[77]

Robey's influence over Evelyn Johnson's independent judgment in regard to booking talent signed to Buffalo typified the unique, and special, partnership they had. Certainly the relationship between Robey's record companies on one hand, and Johnson's booking agency on the other, was synergistic, and when recording stars of regional or national stature came out of Houston it was precisely because of the total package of support and promotion that the Robey/Johnson partnership made possible. But such a relationship was forbidden by industry guidelines. Ordinarily, a musician's agent or manager or representative was in partnership with the musician, not the owner of the record company. The American Federation of Musicians, under the leadership of James C. Petrillo, had fought the "communications-industry owners" for almost twenty-five years by 1954, holding, according to Russell Sanjek, "the power of economic life or death over any business that employed live musicians."[78] The Petrillo organization empowered Evelyn Johnson, License #652, to "act as agent, manager, or representative for members of the association."

In the historical, adversarial relationship between the musician's union and management, Johnson's role was to represent the union musicians she booked and managed. With B.B. King's band and the Ike and Tina Turner Revue, the service she provided as head of Buffalo Booking was perfectly legitimate and proper: King was signed to a label owned by the Bihari brothers, and the Turners were not affiliated with a label. She never bothered to sign the Turners to a record contract because she "didn't need another unknown," but she did make money on their bookings: "Those were money-making things for me because so far as the rest of [the Duke and Peacock acts] were concerned, I usually used what I was making bailing them from town to town, fixing flats, and sending Western Union, that sort of thing. But with Ike it was straight, clear money. And I still split the commission with him and made money. Whereas I wasn't making money on my own."[79]

The acts she considered her own, of course, were the Duke and Peacock artists she controlled as Robey's chief administrator. In a legal sense Johnson's personal handling of traveling union musician Johnny Ace was completely compromised. The financing for the Ace/Thornton unit had been arranged in Houston, with Don Robey putting up the front money necessary to establish the act as a road show. The road band itself was put together by Robey, and other personnel, including road managers responsible for making decisions on a daily basis, were selected in Houston by Robey and Johnson. While she was theoretically watching out for the personal interests of Ace and Thornton, she was also, in practical terms, necessarily watching out for Robey's interests and what was best for the entire spectrum of Robey-owned businesses: Duke Records, Peacock Records, and Lion Publishing, plus the needs of her own Buffalo Booking Agency. "I feel like Jane Pittman, sitting on a porch in a rocking chair when I start talking about this kind of thing," she says, "because it's so complicated and intermingled. You see, I operated in a conflict of interest."[80]

Johnson's compromised position kept her deep in the background publicly, though everyone on the inside knew of her contributions. "I never could stand up and be counted," she explains. "And I was fighting too many battles to fight the industry to let them know that somebody besides Don Robey was doing something. And then women weren't accepted in the first place, young women certainly weren't accepted, and black women were unheard of. So you see I was a triple minority."[81] She was also, she told Alan Govenar, "mother, confessor, lawyer, doctor, sister, financier, mother superior, the whole nine yards" for the musicians she represented. "What they needed they asked for, and what they asked for they got."

According to B.B. King, whom she booked for almost a decade, Evelyn Johnson "was one of the great women of her time. I don't think she gets enough recognition, because to me she was one of the pioneers."[82] The "Booking Queen," the *Pittsburgh Courier* called her: "An astute business woman, Miss Johnson's combination of beauty and brains has captured a gigantic hold on the nation's rhythm and blues range from deep in the heart of Texas."[83] Gatemouth Brown agrees, considering her the intellectual power of the whole Peacock operation. "She was very important," he says. "She *made* Robey if you want to know the truth."[84] This was more than in-house gossip. It was widely known that Evelyn Johnson was central to the success of all of Robey's businesses, and she was frequently suspected of being the "brains" behind them. Though she will not comment on that directly, she does not deny it. "Don Robey," she says, "had two things: guts and money."[85]

Johnson asserts that her business relationship with B.B. King and Ike Turner—legitimate and aboveboard clients—was more profitable for her agency than the business relationship with the Duke and Peacock Records clients with whom she was linked through Robey. "So far as Buffalo Agency's concerned," she contends, "everybody owed me money but B.B. King and Ike Turner."[86] How exactly did the details of this Robey-Johnson partnership work? What accounts of Johnny Ace were cross-collateralized between Duke Records and Buffalo Booking to keep up with revenues earned by Ace and expenditures made on his behalf? Presumably, all of Ace's records earned artist royalties, and many of the "B" sides generated additional money—mechanical income—owed to Ace as songwriter. These revenue accounts were standard record company fare. Against this income, the record company could charge production costs of Ace's records, promotion expenses, and any money paid to the artist in advance. All of these transactions represented standard record company agreements.

In addition, Ace would have earned income for his personal appearances and incurred expenses on the road. His Western Union advances would have been posted to an account to be recouped, along with expenses associated with the late-model car that Robey provided, and other overhead costs. How all of this worked between Duke Records and the Buffalo Booking Agency is impossible to know. According to Johnson, the front money advanced to the "special" clients represented by Buffalo Booking (performers like Ace who were signed to Robey's record labels) was "deducted from what they earned": "I sent as much out as came in. What happened was in the booking you get a deposit with a returned signed contract. It was supposed to have been 50 percent. That came in. However, I wound up giving back to [the performers] because they collected the balance on the spot. You see, it was always a breakdown in transportation, getting out of the hotel, and there were those who were users in the first place—they would get the money in order to keep me from having it." Some of Robey's artists "bled" her agency, she says, since "they always got so much money in advance." But money never flowed from Buffalo Booking to Robey, she insists: money earned on the road went "only back to the artist."[87]

> *I said, "Johnny, don't you point that*
> *gun at me. Point it on your own fool self."*
> *—Clarence "Gatemouth" Brown*

Silent Night,

Deadly Night

Around Thanksgiving, as a way of describing industry preparations for the 1954 Christmas buying season, *Billboard* chose a gun metaphor. In "Diskers Aim Guns on Christmas Wax," Bob Rolontz explained that this was the time of year for record companies to "let go with their heaviest ammunition." In addition, a story titled "In a Tavern Hot Gun Play" noted that coin-operated gun games featuring "a new .22 type rifle unit" had attracted "enthusiastic players" in taverns all over the country.[1] Johnny Ace was an enthusiastic player of his own gun games by that time. According to Evelyn Johnson, he had purchased a .22 pistol at a pawn shop in Florida from a man musicians in the band called Boss Lewis. The gun, a Harrington & Richardson Model 6 double action revolver, built between 1906 and 1942 in Worcester, Massachusetts, cost Ace an estimated fifty dollars. The seven-shot H&R Model 6 was a "suicide special," collector and historian Larry Moody says, the kind of gun people today call a "Saturday night special."[2] Ace's pistol, as seen in the published photographs, was nickel finished with a 2½-inch barrel.[3] Charles Sawyer notes that Ace once wanted to have the plastic grip replaced with pearl, but Don Robey could not arrange to have the work done quickly enough to suit him.[4] Evelyn Johnson believes it was the only gun he ever owned.

Ace treated the pistol carelessly. "He always acted like a kid," bandleader Johnny Board says. "He bought a gun in Florida and treated it like a toy. He and I were the only ones who could drive his car and when we stopped on the road sometimes to relieve ourselves in a field, he would take out the gun and shoot in the air like a child with a cap pistol."[5] Guitarist Milton Hopkins describes life on the road with Ace as if it were child's play. Ace was a "jokester," he says. "He loved to wrestle and horse-ass, and play around, and play the dozens, and all this kind of stuff, which I thought was good. And he was always jolly and full of pep and energy. And he loved to drink gin, and he liked women." In addition, "he was as strong as a goddamn mule. He would wrestle four or five of us down, anytime. He loved to play. That's the kind of guy he was." The gun and the wrestling, he believes, were just Ace's ways of "horse-assing around—that was what that was. He was real playful."[6]

Hopkins told Charles Sawyer that "Johnny's idea of fun was driving his Oldsmobile 90 miles per hour, his pistol in his hand, shooting out the zeros on the roadside speed-limit signs."[7] Other people close to Ace also knew about his recklessness. Johnny Otis remembers a tour of Florida dates when Ace's roadie and right hand man, "so frustrated he was crying," came to Otis's hotel room to complain. "Man, he's doing that shit again," he told him. "He's got that goddamn gun and he spins the barrel and he points it at me and it just scares the shit out of me. He does it while we're riding along on the highway."[8]

Other indications suggest that Johnny Ace was not a happy man in late 1954. Galen Gart notes that Ace's "heavy drinking and eating had added forty pounds to his once-lithe frame. He also sported a new process hairdo and mustache," which completely destroyed the young and innocent look featured in his Duke Records publicity stills.[9] B.B. King, who saw Ace during this period, told Charles Sawyer that he thought the pressure of being famous and living on the road was getting to Ace:

> You can't imagine how it is, out here. You spend three nights in one hotel and learn that the door to the right goes to the toilet and the one on the left goes out into the corridor. Then you change cities, and the first

night in the new hotel, you wake up standing in the corridor, not sure where you are or how you got there. As it turns out, you turned right heading for the toilet, more asleep than awake, and the directions in this hotel are reversed. . . . People come at you all the time: people with propositions, people asking favors, people telling you that you promised to do this or pay them such and such, and you don't remember any such thing.[10]

During the Thanksgiving holidays, a rumor reached Ace's friends at the Mitchell Hotel in Memphis that Ace had been killed in a car accident. Of course this was not true, but it served as a kind of inoculation for the bad news to come at Christmas time. There were other signs of trouble between Thanksgiving and Christmas. Gart reports a "hair-raising, 90 miles-per-hour ride along the Gulf Coast from Houston to Beaumont in Ace's new Oldsmobile" and "numerous incidents" of Ace shooting his pistol out of his hotel room window.[11] Charles Sawyer also alludes to reports that Ace "repeatedly fired the gun out a window, thus provoking several complaints about the noise."[12]

Then, in a December incident at Don Robey's office, Ace, Gatemouth Brown, and others were picking up contracts when Ace, as a joke, pulled out his pistol and pointed it at Brown. "And he was playing with me in the office and this is the truth," says Brown. "I said, 'Johnny, don't you point that gun at me. Point it on your fool self.' That's exactly. Now Evelyn [Johnson] didn't like what I said because he was making them a lot of money at that time. Okay, well it made no difference to me." Some reports have Brown pulling a knife to defend himself that day in Robey's office, though Brown denies that he did. And while it is difficult to get Gatemouth Brown to criticize anybody, he is willing to make an exception for Ace. "Now, the man to me was very ignorant," he says. "I have to say it because it's the truth." Later, when Evelyn Johnson called him with the news "Johnny Ace has killed hisself," Brown's response was, "Well, better him than me."[13]

In addition, Sawyer claims that in the last days of his life Ace seemed to exhibit "an emotionally charged attraction/repulsion toward the pistol." When he wasn't playing with the gun, Sawyer says, he was turning it over to friends for safe keeping—"at least four times" in the days before his death. Sawyer also reports what he calls "another marginal episode," one that suggested "a self-consciously self-destructive mood" much different than the image Ace projected of "an unreflective and carefree person": "It happened on the road to Houston a day or two before Christmas Eve, with Johnny Ace and his band in his Olds. Johnny was at the wheel. According to bandleader Johnny Board, Ace ran through a red light and sideswiped a curb. Then he pulled over and stopped the car. Turning to Board, he said, 'I don't know what's wrong with me. I shouldn't be driving. Take over the wheel, will you?'"[14]

On Christmas Eve the Ace/Thornton unit performed in Port Arthur, Texas. Ace drove to Houston after the show, arriving at his girl friend's apartment at 1814 Alabama Street around 9 A.M. on Christmas Day and sleeping until 2:30 P.M. Olivia Gibbs, a twenty-two year-old waitress at the Club Matinee, had been seeing Ace for a year and a half and considered herself engaged to be married to him, though she knew that he had a wife and two children in Memphis. As a Christmas present, she had given him a yellow-gold three-stone diamond ring. Johnny had invited the band over to her place for Christmas dinner, she told authorities, at which time "he started playing with a small .22 caliber pistol." He played Russian roulette, she said, with an unloaded gun.[15] *Ebony* reported that on the day of his death he "had been playing with the gun all day and earlier had given two girls bullets with the flamboyant boast, 'If I fool around and kill myself, here's a souvenir.'"[16]

In an issue dated the same day, *Billboard* advertised Ace's next hit record. Don Robey had purchased two quarter-page holiday ads wishing deejays and (juke box) operators a Merry Christmas and Happy New Year and promoting the latest Peacock and Duke Records, among them Ace's "Pledging My Love" b/w "No Money" (Duke 136).[17] The "A" side had been recorded back in January with the Johnny Otis Band; the "B" side was cut in July with the Ace road band. The timing of the new release was rather routine. Ace's last hit, "Never Let Me Go," something of a disappointment, had fallen off the national charts in late November and by 25 December did not appear on any of the territorial charts. Robey generally waited for such a time to begin the promotion of Ace's next record.

Christmas was always just another work day for Ace, and while the Johnny Ace/Willie Mae Thornton unit did not sell out City Auditorium in Houston for a "Negro Christmas dance" on 25 December 1954, it did draw a respectable crowd of approximately 3,500. Ace and Thornton had finished the first set, as they always did, with a duet of the Ace hit "Yes, Baby." "Big Mama would open the show," Evelyn Johnson remembers, "and Johnny was the feature. Then finally they did the duet, and they would close together and that was very fascinating and people went wild over it."[18] During intermission, between 11:00 and 11:15 P.M., Ace was backstage in the North side dressing room, playing with his gun and drinking vodka. When he complained to Olivia Gibbs of such a painful toothache that he didn't think he could go back on stage after intermission, she got an aspirin from Evelyn Johnson, and Ace held it to his tooth.

Depositions given by three witnesses indicate at least five people were in the dressing room, including Gibbs and her friend Mary Carter, who had a pint of vodka she was sharing with people as they came into the room. The most complete account of what followed is the deposition, presented here in its exact words, given to authorities by Willie Mae Thornton at 12:40 A.M. on 26 December 1954.

> We arrived at the City Auditorium at around 7:20 p.m. and the dance started about eight o'clock. I did not sing until about nine o'clock when I sing five numbers. The band played several numbers before Johnny Ace came on to sing. He sing several numbers and he and I sing the duet "Yes Baby." The band played two more numbers. I then went to the dressing room to change clothes, but I got busy signing autographs and I did not get to change clothes. Johnny Ace came to the dressing room and he signed some autographs. He started to leave out the door when some people stopped to talk to him. About that time, Olivia, Johnny Ace's girl friend walked up and Johnny and Olivia came into the dressing room. Johnny sit on a dresser in the dressing room and Olivia sit on his lap. Shortly after he sit down, two more people who were in the dressing room, Mary Carter and Joe Hamilton, began running around. I looked over at Johnny and noticed he had a pistol in his hand. It was a pistol that he bought somewhere in Florida. It was a .22 cal. revolver. Johnny was pointing this pistol at Mary Carter and Joe Hamilton. He was kind of waving it around. I asked Johnny to let me see the gun. He gave it to me and when I turned the chamber a .22 cal. bullet fell out in my hand. Johnny told me to put it back in w[h]ere it wouldn't fall out. I put it back and gave it to him. I told him not to snap it at nobody. After he got the pistol back, Johnny pointed the pistol at Mary Carter and pulled the trigger. It snapped. Olivia was still sitting on his lap. I told Johnny again not to snap the pistol at anybody. Johnny then put the pistol to Olivia's head and pulled the trigger. It snapped. Johnny said "I'll show you that it won't shoot." He held the pistol up and looked at it first and then put it to his head. I started toward the door and I heard the pistol go off. I turned

around and saw Johnny falling to the floor. I saw that he was shot and I run on stage and told the people in the band about it. I stayed there until the officers arrived.[19]

Olivia Gibbs told police she didn't think the gun was loaded when "Johnny started fooling with this little pistol again" because when Ace was playing with it that afternoon at her apartment it was *not* loaded. As she described the scene, "Johnny was sitting on the [dressing room] table and I was by him and he had his arm around me":

> I saw Johnny look at the gun and then he put it up to my head and pulled the trigger and it snapped. I saw him look at the gun again and then he put it up to his head and pulled the trigger and the gun fired. He then fell off of the table and on to the floor. Everybody ran out of the room except Mary Carter, Willie Mae Thornton and me. I thought he was just playing and I picked up his head and then I saw the blood. I then ran to the box office and told Evelyn Johnson that Johnny had shot himself.[20]

Mary Carter's deposition also corroborated Thornton's account of the shooting:

> After I had been in the dressing room a few minutes Johnny had a small pistol and he was pointing it at some of the people and he would pull the trigger and we could hear it "click," after awhile he put the gun to Olivia's ear and pulled the trigger and I could hear it "click." Johnny then reared back in his chair and told us he "was going to show us how it worked," he then put the gun to his right ear and pulled the trigger. I then heard a "pop" and Johnny fell over in the floor and I saw blood start to running out of his head on the left side.[21]

Versions of the shooting by witnesses vary only in superficial ways. One widely circulated unofficial report had Willie Mae Thornton noticing the expression on Ace's face at the moment he realized he was going to die. She told Nick Tosches, "that kinky hair of his shot straight out."[22] Johnny Otis heard this story too and says he believes Thornton. "She was with me for a couple years, and she was always a straightforward, nice person. Also, I think—I don't know if it was her—somebody told me that he realized what he had done and his hair stood straight up."[23] According to Evelyn Johnson, "Shock did that to his hair."

Evelyn Johnson will never forget 25 December 1954. "[Johnny] was so handsome that night," she says. "He came and spent, which he never did, all of his time in the ticket booth, joking and going on. Then, when it was time for him to go, he went onstage. That's something he had never done."[24] She also remembers the horror at intermission, beginning with Gibbs running to the box office screaming "Johnny has shot his brains out!" As Johnson told Alan Govenar: "And that little bullet made a small opening right there and his hair stood on end like horror movies. His brain oozed out of that little hole. He bled so immediately and so profusely until it was like a river. And it coagulated just that fast. He had a little smirky grin on his face and his expression was, 'What'd I say?'"[25]

Charles Sawyer claims that when Houston disk jockey Clifton "King Bee" Smith, the emcee of the show the night Ace killed himself, stopped the band and informed the audience of the tragedy backstage some of the patrons "threw debris on the stage in disgust and disbelief."[26] Evelyn Johnson never saw any of that:

> Oh you're kidding me. Those people went into instant mourning. The only problem was, [Ace] was scheduled to have appeared on a number of engagements through New Year's. When I called those people, one person tried to tell me to send the band! Here's this man just taken off to the mortuary, and he wants to send the band! Now the band — they were comatose. There was one member who never drank, and I think he drank about a half a bottle of whiskey. They were just totally out of it. They were zombies. Finally, after the fourth or fifth call, I went bezerk on [the man who wanted to book the band] and cursed him out to the point where somebody took the phone. That was the only thing that came up. The man wanted me to send Big Mama and the band to play that engagement. How cruel could you be?[27]

According to the "Inquest Proceedings," homicide detectives found Ace's body, fully clothed in a gray suit, lying on a dressing room floor cluttered with whiskey and vodka bottles. (The whole auditorium was described as cluttered with half-pint bottles.) Justice of the Peace Walter Reagan, whose precinct included City Auditorium at 600 Louisiana Street, was called to the scene and determined the cause of death to be "Playing Russian Roulette — Bullet wound in right temple — self inflicted," with entrance of the bullet "about 1 [inch] above & 2 [inches] to right of right eye. No exit." The inventory of "personal effects" included a three-stone diamond ring, a Lucerne watch, a tie clip, a key chain with five keys, a lighter, and $23 in currency. In parentheses detectives noted "no billfold or credentials."[28]

Ace's death was the logical result of a bad case of "pistolitis," according to retired Houston homicide detective Drayton M. "Doc" Fults, one of the officers called to City Auditorium that night and "probably the only one left alive on that [Johnny Ace investigation] deal": "You see, when a guy has a gun — it's called pistolitis — it's no fun unless he shows it to people — shows he's got a gun. That's the trouble with people that carry guns, they want to show it to somebody because it ain't no fun if they don't show it. And then that's what gets them in trouble. And he got ahold of this little gun, and he was just playing with it."[29] Johnny Otis had seen it all before. Ace, he said, "was obsessed with that shit."[30]

The press story of Ace's death hit Memphis black radio immediately. Most adult Americans remember where they were when they heard about Charles Lindbergh's flight across the Atlantic, or the Japanese bombing of Pearl Harbor, or the assassination of John F. Kennedy, but Ernest Withers will never forget the early morning of 26 December 1954, when he heard about Johnny Ace. "I had gone to West Memphis mostly on a social junket to the Plantation Inn," he says: "I was with a party of four, and we heard the news on the car radio the very night that it happened. It was a tragic feeling, but I thought with a sense of hope that he wouldn't be dead. We came all the way back then to the Club Handy to be with the mourners, with the people who were most concerned — Earl Forest, Rosco Gordon — actually they were prodigies of Beale Street like Johnny Ace."[31]

No one disputes that Ace was playing with the gun at intermission, but it remains ambiguous whether or not he was playing Russian roulette. Russian roulette is a game with rules: each player spins the cylinder of a gun loaded with a single bullet, points it at his head, and snaps the trigger. Despite the name, the technology that made possible such a ritual was American, as was ingenious salesmanship that brought the weapon to Russian notice.

Samuel Colt invented the revolving-breech pistol, commonly called the six-shooter, in the mid-1830s and found a way to mass produce the guns using interchangeable parts. A quarter-century later, in 1856, Colt went to considerable trouble and expense to introduce his brain child to Russian society, when he personally presented a pair of revolvers to Czar Alexander II as a coronation gift. The matched guns were smaller and lighter than any Colt had ever manufactured, complete with the Czar's imperial arms and monogram inlaid in gold. The case that held them ("a superb example of the jeweler's art") was made of expensive woods with gold and silver trimmings. Loading tools were included, along with a bullet mold and a set of spare parts. Altogether, the gift cost Colt $5,000, but it was even more expensive to arrange the opportunity to present it.

Colt was shocked to find out that protocol prohibited his attendance at the actual coronation—he was not of royal blood, not a member of a reigning house or the Czar's household, nor was he an accredited representative of a friendly nation. Alexander II "personally regretted" that Colt could not attend the ceremony, but he was "welcome to drop in at a rehearsal." The Czar also offered to meet privately with him to receive his gift. Colt, however, "could not envision any pecuniary profit or social prestige in that arrangement." So the American industrialist, employing true Yankee ingenuity, pulled strings to get himself appointed as a special, one-time, non-salaried attaché to the American embassy in Russia, making him eligible for the real event. He paid his own travel expenses; he even made a honeymoon trip out of the adventure. According to his biographer, Colt considered the listing of the Colt six-shooters among the gifts the Czar received to be "international advertising of incalculable value."[32]

By the time Colt got his valuable international advertising, however, and well before his gun with revolving chambers was widely available to the Russian army, one kind of life and death gambling with single-shot pistols had already been popularized by Russian army officer Mikhail Lermontov's story "The Fatalist," the last chapter of his novel *A Hero of Our Time* (1840). The fictional setting is a Cossack infantry battalion where soldiers are arguing over "the Moslem belief in a man's fate being written in heaven." Lieutenant Vulich, an officer of Serbian origin with a "gaming passion," picks up a pistol, and without knowing whether it is loaded or not puts it against his temple. "Mr. Pechorin," he says, "take a card and throw it up in the air."

> I took from the table what I vividly remember turned out to be the ace of hearts and threw it upwards. Everyone held his breath; all eyes, expressing fear and a kind of vague curiosity, switched back and forth from the pistol to the fateful ace which quivered in the air and slowly came down.

The moment it touched the table, Vulich pulled the trigger . . . the pistol snapped!

"Thank God!" many cried. "It was not loaded . . ."

"Let's take a look, anyway," said Vulich. He cocked the pistol again, took aim at a cap that was hanging above the window. A shot resounded—smoke filled the room. When it dispersed, the cap was taken down. It had been shot clean through the middle, and the bullet had lodged deep in the wall.[33]

More than one hundred years later, a *New York Times* reader named Albert Parry corrected editors of the newspaper for crediting the Russians with *inventing* Russian roulette. "It's possibly the only invention they don't claim," he wrote. He acknowledged that Russian army officers had liked Lermontov's story and that they adopted this "dangerous trick" into a popular deadly competition named after them (Russian roulette is also known as "Cossack Poker" or the "Cuckoo Game"). "But the story was not of pure Russian origin," he said; it came from England. Parry argued that Mikhail Lermontov admired the English poet Lord Byron, translated his poems, wrote Byronic prose, and probably got the idea for "The Fatalist" from a story Byron told about his roommate at Cambridge—Edward Noel Long.[34]

Indeed, in the "Ravenna Journal" Byron related an anecdote about his friend that could well have been the inspiration for Lermontov's dramatic scene in "The Fatalist." Long "was such a good, amiable being as rarely remains long in this world," Byron wrote in his journal on 12 January 1821. "Yet, although a cheerful companion, he had strange melancholy thoughts sometimes." On one occasion, "he told me that, the night before, he 'had taken up a pistol—not knowing or examining whether it was loaded or no—and had snapped it at his head, leaving it to chance whether it might not be charged.'"[35]

Johnny Ace certainly shared with Byron's friend Long a cheerful amiability mixed with "strange melancholy." In addition, Ace was the kind of romantic hero in postwar America that Byron himself was in late Romantic England: handsome, pleasure-loving, a hearty male companion, a love object for women, unsuitable for marriage, and, as Byron's biographer describes the poet during his Cambridge years, "full of animal spirits and still boyish a great deal of the time."[36] In many ways it can be said of Ace what has been often said of Byron—that he woke up one morning and found himself successful. As for the fictional adaptation of Byron's account of Long's gamble with death, Lermontov's use of the "fateful" ace of hearts as the starting signal for pulling the trigger of a gun that may or may not be loaded was apparently of pure Russian fabrication. It is, however, the perfect symbol for Johnny Ace, the singer famous for his heart ballads. Indeed, the ace of hearts is prominently displayed on the cover of his only long-playing record, the posthumously released *Johnny Ace: Memorial Album*.

With a gun in his hand, Johnny Ace played a game less ritualistic and personal than conventional Russian roulette and a good bit more menacing and social. Ordinarily, Ace liked to point the gun at *other* people's heads. All three depositions taken the night of his death report him aiming the gun at other people. No witness who gave a deposition mentioned Ace spinning the cylinder before pulling the trigger, but the "Inquest Proceedings" ruled that he had, concluding that he had been playing Russian roulette: "Deceased had been drinking & playing with small 22 calibre H&R revolver & according to officers had also snapped the pistol after spinning the cylinder at his girl friend seated on his lap at the time." Detective Fults clearly remembers witnesses telling him that Ace "spun" the cylinder and that "it didn't go off the first time."

Two of the three eyewitnesses specifically remember Ace looking at the gun before snapping the trigger. Olivia Gibbs "saw Johnny look at the gun" before he snapped it at her, and in her words, "I saw him look at the gun again and then he put it up to his head and pulled the trigger and the gun fired." Big Mama Thornton also remembered him looking at it before he "put it to his head." What was this about? What could Ace see from the gun? The way the seven-shot H&R Model 6 is built the only thing he could have possibly seen was if either chamber number two or chamber number three had a bullet. Chambers one, four, five, six, and seven would have been invisible to him. It is possible, of course, to know how many "safe" snaps you have—snaps that will come up empty—if you have one bullet and have been able to see it in one of the two open chambers. Not to see the bullet represents real danger, one in five, and only a suicidal or drunk or desperate man would gamble with his life against those odds.

Certainly Ace was reckless with his handgun, and evidence suggests that he may have been self-destructive in the final months of his life, but was he suicidal? Did he intend to kill himself? In the literature of self-inflicted gunshot deaths like Ace's, "exhibitionistic 'Russian roulette' cases" are frequently ruled by authorities to be accidents, especially when there is evidence that the victims "did not consider themselves to be gambling with death."

In a study of one hundred such "equivocal" deaths in Los Angeles in 1959–60, for example, researchers concluded that all of the Russian roulette deaths were actually accidents rather than suicides since each victim "thought that he knew where the bullet was located (and was in fatal error)." One victim was a man who demonstrated Russian roulette "whenever a new, impressionable woman was invited to his house." A second victim was a gang bully who used the game "to frighten a new initiate to the gang and prove the youth a coward," and the third victim was a police officer attempting "to convince a young woman acquaintance that the gun he carried was not dangerous." All of the deceased used "tricks" to determine that a bullet was not in firing position.[37] Ace's behavior seems to be consistent with these case studies. Indeed, some of the coverage of Ace's death in the black press described the tricks employed by Russian roulette players. "The secret of this trick," Ralph Matthews wrote in the *Cleveland Call and Post*, "is that if the gun is in perfect working order and precision perfect, the [chamber] containing the bullet being heavier will drop to the bottom away from the firing pin. The uninitiate, not being familiar with this secret of balances and counterbalances are [*sic*] terrified and enthralled by the daredeviltry of the gunman which makes him a bigshot."[38]

At the time, there was no evidence to suggest that any of the other people in the room had willingly participated in Ace's dangerous gun game. Detective Fults, who remembers Russian roulette as "something that kind of was going around at the time" believed during the initial investigation that Ace was the only person playing, and he still does. Ace's friends and intimates agree. Johnny Otis's understanding about the shooting, for example, is that aiming the gun at somebody else's girl friend prompted the behavior that led to the final tragedy. Johnny Ace was sitting in the dressing room waving a gun around in the direction of a young man sitting with his girl friend on his lap. "Wait a minute, man," the guy said to the singer, "don't wave that gun at my girl. You might be Johnny Ace, but I don't appreciate that shit. You want to wave it, point it at somebody, point it at yourself." An embarrassed Johnny Ace then put the gun to his temple and pulled the trigger.[39]

Johnny Board, the bandleader who was on stage at the time of the shooting, told a similar story to Dempsey J. Travis. There was, he said, "a piano player who worked at a tavern across the street. He was running back and forth during intermissions to talk to Johnny in his dressing room, which was full of people drinking and having a good time. Suddenly this fellow said to Johnny, 'Man, you've been clicking that gun on everybody. Why don't you click it on yourself?' Johnny took the gun out and clicked it, and the bullet blew his brains out."[40] Ace had "guts," B.B. King says. "But don't ever dare Johnny to do something dangerous 'cause the boy would up and do it. Finally that did him in."[41]

For all the subsequent speculations that could connect Ace to Russian army officers and Lord Byron's friends, it all came down to one final and dramatic moment. A policeman at the scene said, "That's all she wrote," as he rolled Ace over, *Ebony* reported, but he "could not have been more wrong. Johnny Ace, the man, was dead—but Johnny Ace, the legend, had just been born."[42]

Don Robey and Evelyn Johnson, owner of the Buffalo Booking Agency and Robey's right hand, celebrating success. According to insiders, Ms. Johnson was central to the success of all of Robey's businesses and was frequently suspected of being the "brains" behind them. (Photograph by Benny Joseph. Courtesy of Rice University Press)

Don Robey fulfilling his promise to Cash Box *that "If It's Not a Hit I'll Eat My Hat" (1957). The gold record above his shoulder is Johnny Ace's "Pledging My Love." (Photograph by Benny Joseph. Courtesy of Rice University Press)*

Left: *A scene from inside Robey's Bronze Peacock Dinner Club, ca. 1950. Robey parlayed the Bronze Peacock into a series of entertainment-amusement businesses that made him a Houston "Horatio Alger." (Courtesy of Galen Gart, Big Nickel Publications)*

Below: *Bill Holford, owner of Audio Corporation of America (ACA) and engineer of most of Ace's recorded sides. (Photograph by Roy C. Ames. Courtesy of Galen Gart, Big Nickel Publications)*

Johnny Otis, bandleader, songwriter, and producer of Johnny Ace and Big Mama Thornton hits. Otis's Rhythm & Blues Caravan was known in black communities all over the country. (Courtesy of Galen Gart, Big Nickel Publications)

Johnny Board, saxophone player and musical director of Johnny Ace's road band, sometimes called the Johnny Board Orchestra. Board had performed with Coleman Hawkins, Lionel Hampton, and been a member of the Count Basie band after World War II before joining a house band that backed vocalists signed to Robey's Peacock label. (Courtesy of Galen Gart, Big Nickel Publications).

Paul Monday, piano player with the Johnny Ace road band. Monday played during Big Mama Thornton's set but was usually replaced by Ace when the star came on stage for his part of the show. He may also have played on recording sessions when the material involved difficult chord changes or progressions. (Photograph by Benny Joseph. Courtesy of Rice University Press)

Facing page: Willie Mae "Big Mama" Thornton, who opened Ace's shows. (Courtesy of Galen Gart, Big Nickel Publications)

Duke Records star Buddy Ace, promoted by Don Robey as the brother of the deceased Johnny Ace but actually a Texas musician named Jimmy Lee Land. In 1956 Robey advertised Johnny's last record and Buddy's first record as a matched set. (Photograph by Benny Joseph. Courtesy of Rice University Press)

B.B. King at Houston's City Auditorium—the site of Ace's death. Though King was not signed to a Don Robey record label, Evelyn Johnson arranged his personal appearances. At the peak of Ace's success, club owners had to book both King and Bobby Bland in order to get the Ace/Thornton show. (Photograph by Benny Joseph. Courtesy of Rice University Press)

Facing page: Clarence "Gatemouth" Brown. Don Robey launched his career and established Peacock Records specifically to record him. (Photograph by Benny Joseph. Courtesy of Rice University Press)

C.C. Pinkston, drummer and vibes player for the Johnny Ace road band, often billed in the Alabama and Georgia territories as the C.C. Pinkston Orchestra. (Courtesy of Galen Gart, Big Nickel Publications)

He was living a fast life. He had too much money at one time, too many womens, and it was just too much for him. Eventually, I imagine, he might would have come around. I heard he was planning on coming home before he got killed.
—Jean Alexander

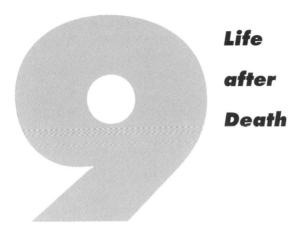

Life after Death

Legends took longer to create in the 1950s than they do today. No one was online. There was no CNN, no *USA Today*, no MTV or TV tabloids, not even a daily thirty-minute news program on ABC, CBS, or NBC. In 1954 television had not yet become the instrument that penetrated every household; nor had it yet brought disparate sectors of American society—much less the world—together as part of what Marshall McLuhan called the Global Village. Johnny Ace was merely a rhythm and blues star at the end of 1954. Unlike African American performers who recorded for major labels, aiming single records at a general audience and succeeding or failing in the basically white field of pop music (black *white* stars), Ace was a black *black* star, virtually unknown outside the African American community.

Even if the white policeman who rolled Ace over had known about "Pledging My Love," the new single record released in Houston three days before Ace died, and even if he were part of the small minority of whites who admired rhythm and blues, he could not have conceived of a record by a solo, black, male rhythm and blues performer being purchased in mass quantities by white teens or being played in heavy rotation by white radio stations. There was no precedent for such a phenomenon: American popular music in 1954 was almost as segregated as southern lunch counters. At the time of Ace's death rhythm and blues was still primarily a minor market and a small operator's game, since most of the major record companies had given up "race music" during World War II, when the government required consumers to trade in an old record in order to buy a new one. Charlie Gillett points out that the six major labels of the period (RCA, Columbia, Decca, Mercury, Capitol, and MGM) so dominated the American popular music scene in the early postwar era that they accounted for 97 percent of the million-selling records issued between 1946 and 1952. As for the smaller field of rhythm and blues, even by the end of 1953 "the Negro market," as it was called, accounted for less than 6 percent of total American record sales.[1] It is small wonder that Johnny Ace was not widely known outside of the black community.

In addition, the white press (especially the southern white press) did not ordinarily cover "Negro" news in 1954, since African American culture was not yet a part of mainstream American daily life. Outside of a handful of black major league baseball players, professional boxers, Olympic athletes, and entertainers, white America knew very little about black America. It was only after the success of the bus boycott in Montgomery, Alabama, in 1956 that a leader in the black community gained what Nelson George calls the "attention and admiration of white America" and became a celebrity in the national sense.[2] Before that time, the exploits of black Americans rarely made the white newspapers.

One is reminded of how little progress in this regard the nation had made in a quarter of a century by recalling the blatant racism in the opening scene of Ben Hecht and Charles MacArthur's play *The Front Page* (1928), set in the press room of the Chicago Criminal Courts Building. While most of the news-hound reporters play poker to pass the time, McCue is "calling all the police stations, hospitals, etc. on behalf of his companions, in a never-ending quest for news": "McCue (into phone). Hello, Sarge? McCue. Anything doing? . . . Yeah? That's swell. . . . (The players pause) A love triangle, huh? . . . Did he kill her? . . . Killed em both! Ah! . . . Was she good looking? . . . (A pause. With vast disgust) What? Oh, Niggers! (The players relax.)."[3] In the politically charged environment of a postwar America threatened not only by the actions but also the public relations initiatives of cold war adversaries, such artistic and public displays of racism were no longer considered politic. The standard of newsworthiness that drove the joke in *The Front Page*, however, remained unchanged. When he became a reporter for the *Washington Post* on Christmas Eve in 1948, Ben Bradlee remembers "listening to the police radio describe a crime soon after I came to work and asking the night city editor if he wanted me to go out on it. 'Naw,' he answered, 'that's black.'"[4]

It was pure sensationalism that caused Johnny Ace to receive coverage in the major white press when the *New York Times* buried on page twenty-one the wire story report of the unusual circumstances of his death: "HOUSTON, Tex., Dec. 26 (UP)—A Memphis, Tenn. bandleader was shot to death playing Russian roulette last night while holding a pretty girl on his lap during a dressing room party. The police said John Alexander, 26 years old, leader and featured singer of Johnny Ace's band, died at the height of a big Christmas night dance in the city auditorium."[5] The *Times* story had the place of death correctly identified, and the date, and the singer's age and birthplace. It was impossible to tell, however, that Johnny Ace and John Alexander were, in fact, the same person, but it soon became apparent that there was negligible interest in either name. The compilers of the 1954 *New York Times Annual Index* revealed what was most important about this story to mainstream Americans: they indexed it under neither "Alexander, John" nor "Ace, Johnny," but only under "Russian roulette."

While the white press missed the personal dimension of the Johnny Ace story, the black press certainly did not. What was incidental to white readers of the *New York Times* was front-page news across black America: "Russian Roulette Pays With Death for Johnny Ace" reported the *Cleveland Call and Post*. "Juke Star Johnny Ace Kills Self" announced the *Chicago Defender*. "Gun Game Fatal to 'Wax' Star" declared the *Pittsburgh Courier*. "Cards Stacked against Johnny Ace in Suicide," the *New York Age Defender* explained.

Ace had performed in black clubs in both major and secondary markets all over the country. Black America *knew* Ace, not in the abstract but in person, and part of the power necessary to establish Ace as a legend in the black community turned out to be his previous accessibility. In some locations newspapers found local angles to exploit. On the West Coast, the *Los Angeles Sentinel* noted that Ace had visited the city in November and was due to return in February. "It was in Los Angeles where his rendition of his first hit, 'My Song,' started him on the road to success," the paper claimed.[6]

Ace "skyrocketed to fame in Chicago," argued the *Defender*, since "My Song" sold 55,000 advance copies in the city "before even the first pressing."[7]

The *Cleveland Call and Post* published the most personal and dramatic coverage of Ace's death, and presented it in the context of his known behavior in that city. "The memories which cause shudders here among the play girls who were his guests during his recent sojourn in Cleveland," Ralph Matthews reported, "stem from his wild champagne and liquor parties in which he insisted on proving his skill with a revolver." Ace was an "incurable egotist and showoff," Matthews said, who "took delight in sending chills down the backs of his friends." The singer "died as he lived amid a riot of gals, guns and gaiety and a number of Cleveland girls are trembling in their boots at the terrifying thought that they barely missed being a party to and possible victim of his penchant for playing 'Russian Roulette.'"[8]

While rhythm and blues fans mourned Ace's passing, his body lay in state in Houston at Pruitt and Pruitt Funeral Home for one day—from Monday morning, 27 December, until Tuesday the twenty-eighth—when it was shipped by rail to the Southern Funeral Home in Memphis.[9] The funeral was not held until Sunday, 2 January, more than a week after Ace's death. "Eight days in an economically broad family is not long, not for black people," Beale Street photographer Ernest Withers says. "It's how much time it takes to bring loose ends together."[10]

The length of time between the death and the funeral was certainly beneficial to Don Robey, who took special care to manage the death of his most commercially popular artist in a way that would impact the most favorably on the sales of Duke Records. Robey hired Andrew "Sunbeam" Mitchell ("the local man between Johnny Ace and Don Robey," according to Ernest Withers), and Mitchell then recruited Withers to help document the event and put a spin on the story favorable to Robey's interests. Withers remembers that Robey wanted to emphasize the size of the funeral crowd, his own personal involvement in the funeral plans, and the possible replacement for Ace in his touring show. "I even went to the church and got Reverend Bell to agree to let us have the funeral at the church. He was pastor of Clayborn Temple—and [I] met Robey. I got a picture of Robey and Evelyn Johnson getting off the plane, coming to the funeral, and met by Sunbeam," Withers says. Though Withers was not part of the Robey inner circle (he "never went past the door"), in January 1955 he was Robey's man in Memphis. "I supervised and over-the-shoulder dictated the story," he remembers. "I think I had a fellow working with me who was more literate as a writer."

In his business files Withers still has a carbon copy of the "cutline story" that was accompanied by photographs of Ace's funeral and sent airmail the night of 3 January 1955 to twelve of the most important black newspapers:

News Release

Cutline Story

RELEASE IMMEDIATELY

FINAL NOTE in the spiraling entertainment career of singer-bandleader John M. (Johnny Ace) Alexander, Jr., was sounded last Sunday at Clayborn Temple AME church in Memphis, Tenn. — hometown of the Peacock [*sic*] Recording artist — with abount [*sic*] 4,500 relatives, friends, fans and others of the entertainment world present. Out of towners in Memphis for the funeral of the 26-year-old singer who lost to "Russian Roulette" in a dressing room while playing a Christmas Day dance in the City Auditorium, Houston, Texas, included Don D. Robey, owner Peacock records, and Evelyn Johnson, owner of Buffalo Booking agency. Mr. Robey and associates worked closely with Ace's family in arrangements for the funeral which, excluding the one in October for political leader E. H. Crump, was probably Memphis' biggest in recent years. The well-known Rev. Dwight (Gatemouth) Moore of Birmingham, Ala., appeared on the formal services program. Clayborn Temple, which seats 2,000, could not hold the overflow crowd. UPPER RIGHT, Evelyn Johnson and Don Robey arrive at municipal airport where they were met by Andrew Mitchell, Memphis promoter. LOWER LEFT, members of the Johnny Ace band leave the church with body. Included among pallbearers was Harold Conner who reportedly is being groomed to front the Johnny Ace aggregation. (Ernest Withers Photo).

Many of the black newspapers used Withers's photographs, though not all gave him photo credit, and most published accounts of the funeral relied on information from the Withers news release, often under a local reporter's byline. Withers billed Robey sixty dollars for his services, and Robey sent a letter and check promptly: "We Thank You very Kindly for the wonderful cooperation that you offered," he wrote. "I must say that the welcome, the complete coverage, and the cooperation, cannot be beaten, and again, we Thank You."[11]

In a page-one story, the *Houston Informer* reported that five thousand people jammed the 2,000-seat Clayborn Temple AME Church on the day of the funeral, though the estimate of the crowd size was likely taken from the Withers news release.[12] The (Memphis) *Tri-State Defender* and *Memphis World*, representing not only the local black press but their respective chains of newspapers as well, were less concerned with the number of mourners than with documenting the number of participants in the hour-long funeral service and naming the out-of-town guests, the presence of whom enhanced the reputation of the deceased. The Reverend R. McRae, pastor of Bethel AME Church (this was the Alexander family's church, where Johnny had once sung in the choir) delivered the eulogy, and Rev. Dwight (Gatemouth) Moore of Birmingham, Alabama, contributed "remarks." In addition, there was "prayer by Rev. Louis Williams, scripture by Rev. W. L. Bell, acknowledgements by Robert Duncan, [J]r., and solos by Harold Conner and Mrs. Myrtle Sorrell."[13]

Pallbearers, according to the *Memphis World*, "were such theatrical personalities" as Little Jr. Parker, Fred Ford, Hosea Sapp, Rosco Gordon, Norman Matthews, William Saunders, Harold Conner, Phineas ("Finas") Newborn, and Robert Duncan Jr. Among honorary pallbearers were Don D. Robey, Evelyn Johnson, staff members of Duke Records, Andrew Mitchell, B.B. King and members of his band, Willie Mae Thornton, and members of the Johnny Ace band.[14] The turnout for the funeral represented "one of the largest crowds in the history of this historic city of song" the *Pittsburgh Courier* reported, which "crowded every nook of Clayborn Temple AME Church and flowed into the streets."[15]

Interestingly, both of the white Houston daily newspapers, the *Post* and the *Chronicle*, printed accounts of Ace's death, but neither of the white dailies in Memphis, not the *Press-Scimitar* nor the *Commercial Appeal*, published a word, as if to deny the fact that a local boy had made good, lived hard, died young, and come home to be buried and mourned by thousands of fans. Within the black press generally, coverage of the funeral and Ace's interment at New Park Cemetery was respectful if unsentimental.[16]

As for black radio, Memphis station WDIA intended to honor the memory of Johnny Ace after the funeral by playing his records on the air. Like many black radio stations of the time, WDIA alternated secular and gospel programming. "The conventional wisdom in the trade," Louis Cantor says, "was that WDIA's audience also logically divided itself into two general categories, each frequently to the exclusion of the other." Gospel listeners tuned in their favorite shows, then turned the radio off when the rhythm and blues programs began.[17] On the day that WDIA began to pay homage to Johnny Ace, his mother called the station to demand that it desist. "She stopped it," Jean Alexander says. "She didn't want him in it [secular music] and she didn't want them to be playing it." Cantor, who worked at WDIA at the time, does not doubt that a gospel-music-only listener as well placed in the community as Mrs. Leslie Alexander could have been so powerful in early 1955.[18]

According to family accounts, Don Robey found Mrs. Alexander to be a formidable figure as well. Robey visited the Alexander household shortly after arriving in Memphis from Houston, bringing with him, Johnny's sister Norma remembers, "all of his suggestions." Robey wanted the funeral held in a large Memphis church that was also used as a convention center. "But he didn't come up with any money," Norma says, "and we would have to pay for the use of the facility. It's a large place. Dr. King spoke there one night." Mrs. Alexander was firm. "I have the insurance policy on the children and I also have a burial policy with Southern [Funeral Home]," she told him. "And that's what I'm going to have to rely on unless you're going to be responsible for a part of the funeral expenses." Norma says her mother told Robey "she was going to have everything at the funeral home. She was going to have his body to lie in state the day before, and the next day just go on through with the funeral." Robey, naturally, did not approve of such modest arrangements. As Norma tells the story,

> But he didn't think that would be a good idea, that it wouldn't be the wise thing, with her son being a celebrity in the public eye. It wouldn't be a large enough place, and she said, "But do you have any of his funds?" "As I told you, he didn't have any money," he said. He went on talking about the X number of dollars he would advance John, Jr. to go on these engagements, and that he just didn't have anything. So she said, "He didn't have anything with you, and he didn't have, and didn't send, funds to me, and I'm going to bury him with what I have, and then I'll be the one to make all the arrangements—the place it's going to be and just everything."

Norma is convinced that when Robey left the house that day he knew that he had lost the argument with her mother and that, against his wishes, the funeral "would be done at Southern Funeral Home." Mrs. Alexander was not deliberately trying to be difficult. The family church, Bethel AME, where Johnny was "still on the roll," was not large enough for his funeral, was not even as large as the Southern Funeral Home. Robey had big plans when it came to burying her son, but for his own reasons he apparently did not want the Alexander family to know he could help finance it.

If money changed hands, and there is good reason to believe it did, the family probably did not see any of it. As it turned out, of course, the funeral was held at Clayborn Temple, not the largest possible venue in Memphis, but the largest denominational AME church in town. Ernest Withers, working for Robey, may have secured permission to hold the funeral at Clayborn Temple, but it was the pastor of Bethel AME who convinced the family to change its plans. "Rev. McRae came to the house," Norma says, "and he talked with my parents and he listened to my mother. He really was the one who talked them into changing it from the funeral home."

The Reverend John Alexander, Johnny's father, was especially important in the final funeral site determination. Norma remembers that it was after the preacher talked with her father that the new deal was struck. Rev. McRae explained to Rev. Alexander: "[Johnny] grew up as a child in [Bethel AME] and he just drifted, but being in the public eye like this I would really like to go on and have it at the church. And we use Clayborn Temple to have our annual conferences, and I would really like for you to have it at the church." "I will get with her and we'll talk it over," Mr. Alexander told him.[19] Norma does not believe that the family had to pay for the use of Clayborn Temple. She did, however, believe that Don Robey, the person she considered her brother's "manager" who "came out to the house and told us he was doing wonders with this child because whenever he wanted something he advanced him," was a white man until B.B. King told her differently.

It is not known if Mrs. Alexander thought Robey was a white man, nor, indeed, if it would have made any difference to her at all. As for Robey, he was routinely mistaken for white, especially by white people, just as Johnny Otis was almost always mistaken for black. In *Black Culture and Black Consciousness*, Lawrence W. Levine explores "color pride" within the black community, identifying twenty-seven "distinct shades" of African American complexion. According to photographs, Robey was probably perceived the most accurately between the range of "bronze" and "brightskin."[20] Ernest Withers understood perfectly well that Robey was a black man and further assumed that his color worked to his advantage. "I never knew he *had* to pass for white," Withers says. "People with light skin in those days always got a little more of the courtesies whether they passed or not. That's the old caste system."

Don Robey was not the only visitor from Houston who called on the Alexander family before the funeral. Evelyn Johnson, "the booking agent," and Olivia Gibbs, "the girl friend," also came to pay their respects. Of the two women, Norma has the clearest recollection of meeting Gibbs and hearing the first-hand account of her brother's death. "She said she was on his lap at the time of that incident, and she wished he had taken her along," Norma remembers Olivia saying. When she revealed to the family that she had planned to marry Johnny, Mrs. Alexander reminded her that he was already "very much married and had the two children." Given the chance, she would also have reminded her celebrity son. "It wouldn't have been nothing for John Jr. to have married two or three women," according to St. Clair Alexander, who also believes that "some woman connected with Johnny" had to be institutionalized and never came to the funeral.

The funeral presented the women most central to Johnny Ace's life in sharp contrast—from the enduring strength of his mother to the fleeting celebrity of his girl friend. Of the two, Olivia Gibbs's suffering was more accessible, and she consequently became a celebrity in the black press for several weeks after Ace's funeral. Not only had this lovely young lady witnessed the actual shooting, but she made good copy. She was, after all, the "woman in pain," heartbroken and abandoned not because of anything she did or did not do but because she had been victimized by male posturing, self-destruction, sheer carelessness, or just plain bad luck. She was also convenient and available, granting "exclusive interviews" to several papers and earning at least one by-line. "The only person who can partly clear up the mystery [of Ace's death]," the *Defender* chain reported, "is attractive Olivia Gibbs, a waitress in a local club in Houston's Fifth Ward. Unfortunately, Ace's happy-go-lucky and strange, unhappy periods were short-lived, and we doubt from such a brief courtship [with the singer] that Olivia really knew the innermost thought of her boyfriend."

According to Olivia, her relationship with Ace began one day when "a total stranger scurried up to her and asked, 'Will you marry me—Now?' Being a cautious woman, Olivia says she asked, 'And just who are you that I should marry?' 'I'm Frank,' he replied." Many days later, when her "Frank" took the stage to sing as Johnny Ace and she discovered who he really was, she had already fallen in love with him. He had pursued her, she said, and she finally gave in "to find out what made this blues singer tick." The experience was painful. "Today, the loneliest woman in the world is Olivia Gibbs," the *Defender* concluded. "She hears 'Pledging My Love' and her heart breaks."[21]

Somewhat awkwardly, the *Pittsburgh Courier* described Gibbs as the "fiancee of Ace (who at the time of his death was still married)." She had attended Wisconsin University [*sic*], the paper reported, and she could give the "eye-witness story of Johnny Ace's 'winner take all' bout with Russian roulette." "Olivia Gibbs is lucky to be alive because her head was against that of Johnny Ace when he pulled the trigger," said the *Courier*, "but the fact that the revolver was of small caliber saved her life. The slug stayed in Ace's brain." In an accompanying photograph she is featured in a bathing suit, holding a 78 rpm copy of (presumably) Ace's "Pledging My Love" in front of her. "I'll miss those nightly phone calls," she told the paper. "He called me every night when he was on the road, as if he wanted to hear me for inspiration before he went on the stage." Although she was not "involved in the separation of Ace and his wife," she "hoped for a divorce clearance by June" so they could be married. "I loved Johnny and he loved me," she said. The *Courier* reported that Ace's latest hit, "Pledging My Love," was dedicated to her, and the last photograph taken of him was with her. His inscription had been, "Love you always." "But always is not forever," the *Courier* commented grimly.[22]

In a by-line story for the *Houston Informer*, Gibbs attempted to answer the question "Did Johnny Ace Commit Suicide?" The answer was "No," she said. "Johnny's death was an accident. The world didn't owe him anything. He had everything to live for. All he wanted was to be liked by everyone and that's why he tried so awfully hard to please everyone. The *Informer*'s account of his death was true." She had received a diamond wristwatch from Ace for Christmas, she said, and had given him a three-stone diamond ring. He had always been affectionate to her, but "he was unusually attentive on this, his last day alive. He told me if I ever doubted him, to play his 'Pledging My Love' and 'Cross My Heart.'" After one more rendering of the eyewitness account of Ace's death, Gibbs sought refuge: "And now that I have told my story—maybe I can get some rest and if I can rest, maybe I can ease the pain, and if I can ease the pain, maybe I can begin to live again."[23]

Black newspaper stories and summaries of Ace's career refused to romanticize or glamorize his death. In the mid-1950s black leaders did not refer to themselves as "race" leaders as they had in the 1920s, but the black press maintained a strong sense of race consciousness in its mission, news policy, and editorial opinions. This was a crucial time in African American history—after the historic *Brown vs. Board of Education* decision by the Supreme Court but before its implementation had been attempted or subverted. It is not surprising that the black press, standard bearer for middle-class black respectability, could find little to praise or dignify in a foolish and self-destructive act of Russian roulette by a nationally known blues singer. "Blues singer" was the description invariably applied to Ace, a kind of categorical imperative denoting not only that he represented nonstandard culture but probably iniquitous culture as well. Ace once sang hymns and spirituals with his family, the *Cleveland Call and Post* reported, but according to his father, he "forsook religious music for the low-down jazz type."[24]

But even in the blues culture itself, Ace's death was neither romantic nor glamorous. As Albert Murray says about "The Blues as Music": "With all its preoccupation with the most disturbing aspects of life, it is something contrived specifically to be performed as entertainment. Not only is its express purpose to make people feel good, which is to say in high spirits, but in the process of doing so it is actually expected to generate a disposition that is both elegantly playful and heroic in its nonchalance."[25]

Murray acknowledges that the blues may serve as an aphrodisiac and that the music has been connected to violence, but he argues that in the "blues-idiom merriment is not marked" by "sensual abandon" or "ecstatic trance": "One of its most distinctive features, conversely, is its unique combination of spontaneity, improvisation, and control. Sensual abandon is, like overindulgence in alcohol and drugs, only another kind of disintegration. Blues-idiom dance movement being always a matter of elegance is necessarily a matter of getting oneself together."[26]

No one in the black press ever perceived Johnny Ace as a person capable of getting himself together. "He trumped his own ace," the *Pittsburgh Courier* began "The Johnny Ace Story," "and drew a bigger crowd to his funeral than he ever did to his dances." Further, the paper dignified in print the gossip and hearsay that accompanied the news of Ace's fatal accident. "Hard on the heels of Ace's death came rumors," the paper reported. "Some people said that Johnny Ace was a user of dope. Others said that he hit the bottle pretty hard. Still others said that he was despondent and did not want to live." Olivia Gibbs told the paper that "none of these rumors had any basis of fact, except that he did drink pretty hard." The *Courier* ended the story with the same gambling metaphor it began with. "Johnny Ace trumped his own ace in a dangerous game," it said, "and they carried his body back to the Cradle of the Blues from whence it sprang. He played well but not wisely. That's when the blues walked in and they carried Johnny out."[27]

The hometown *Tri-State Defender* was equally tough-minded, reprinting an article that appeared in the *Louisville Defender* that questioned the reasons behind Ace's death (it "will long be a controversial and whispered conversation"). Once, when the singer was in "one of his strange, unhappy moods, he fondled and played with a pistol in the presence of Olivia [Gibbs]. It is not on record that Johnny was a performer covered with vanity," the paper admitted, "but was it egotism that made him ask his girl friend: 'I think I'll make a good corpse, don't you?'" According to the story, Ace was manic-depressive. "Whether [Gibbs] was thoroughly in accord with his despondent and down-hearted moods—then suddenly soaring to the saturation point of a happy-go-lucky fellow, is not known," the paper admitted. "But that's what made Johnny tick."[28]

Ralph J. Matthews, in the *Cleveland Call and Post*, attempted some reconstruction of Ace's character ("he came home every five or six months" to see his wife and children, he reported incorrectly), but in a sidebar to the writer's editorial cartoon of Ace gambling with Death and losing, Matthews explained Ace's death in the most unsentimental and unromantic terms: "Sitting in his dressing room in a Houston Dance Hall on Christmas Day Johnnie Ace, popular band leader singer, was showing off his skill at 'Russian Roulette' when he blew out his own brains."[29]

The story on the streets of Memphis was similarly harsh and earthy. "I think Johnny Ace's thing was just the child, the kiddish in him," Ernest Withers says, "plus I don't know whether it was a prank or whether he had gotten high off of marijuana. You know, how accelerated does a guy get? Well, you live by the sword, they say you die by the sword." Solomon Hardy, a drummer who played with Ace in one of the early manifestations of the Beale Streeters, believed it was the "sudden, easy money" that ruined Ace, making him "lose his common sense so he became a dope-smoking limelight fanatic."[30] If there was a poignant voice in Memphis outside of the immediate family, at least one with a deeper understanding of Ace as a person, it belonged to David James Mattis. Though Mattis was still resentful that Don Robey squeezed him out of the business he had founded, he never blamed Ace, for whom he retained great regard: "Johnny Ace was the nicest, sweetest, quietest little guy and when he died, I went down to the funeral parlor. I was the only white one there. They brought his body back to Memphis and I was ready to cry. And I saw this great big fat bloated elephant. It was just terrible what had happened and I thought, 'God, you really copped out on me. You wouldn't have been that' and then I thought, 'Ah, I couldn't have changed anything. That's the way it would've been if you were in that business.' That's why I was glad to have gotten out of it."[31]

*["Pledging My Love"] is
spiraling upwards at dazzling
speed, and is almost as popular
with pop customers, as with R&B.*
—Billboard, 15 January 1955

"Pledging My Love"

It was ironic that on 1 January 1955—the day before Ace's funeral—
the rhythm and blues columnist for *Billboard* happened to use
Johnny Ace as an example of the "good things" that the R&B business had "to be thankful for" during the previous year. Duke
Records was grateful for Ace's "eight hits in a row," Bob Rolontz
claimed, suggesting not so much that news traveled slowly in 1954
but that deadline pressures for copy in the print media have always
been advanced during the holiday season.[1] It was not until 8 January that *Billboard* reported Ace's death ("Johnny Ace Is Victim of
Russ Roulette"), and then it incorrectly identified the date as 27 December and Ace's age as twenty-three.[2] Coincidentally, the lead
story in that issue of *Billboard* was titled "Music-Record Year Ends
Up With Bang." Sheet music sales were down, network radio "took
it on the chin," and the band business merely held its own, the trade
magazine said, but local radio was prospering, record sales were
profitable, and recording artists "continued to dominate the talent
picture."[3]

On 15 January *Billboard* mourned the loss of both Johnny Ace and sheet music sales. Bob Rolontz called Ace's death "the saddest note of the old year." He extended condolences to Ace's family, Duke Records, Don Robey, and sales manager Irv Marcus. "In Ace's short career he came up with a remarkable string of hits," Rolontz said, "all notable for their sincerity and quality."[4] The lead story, however, dealt with the emerging problem faced by pop music publishers. Kitty Kallen's "Little Things Mean a Lot" had been a hit for an impressive twenty-six weeks in 1954 yet was not able to generate even 300,000 units of sheet music sales. At a time when mechanical income (royalties generated by the sale of records) was considered "only sufficient to help the over-all promotional endeavor," it appeared that without sheet music sales music publishers could count only on performance income (royalties based primarily on radio airplay) as "predictable income."

Billboard speculated that the performance money picture for the future was "dubious," since it did not appear that independent radio "could continue to maintain its current state of health."[5] Yet even as *Billboard*'s headlines bemoaned the way the present marketplace fell short of the past, stories elsewhere in the magazine forecasted the future. On the strength of pop record sales featuring rhythm and blues material ("Sh-Boom" [Crewcuts], "Shake, Rattle and Roll" [Bill Haley & the Comets], "Hearts of Stone" [Fontane Sisters], "Tweedlee Dee" [Georgia Gibbs], and "Sincerely" [McGuire Sisters]) even such conventional performers as Perry Como and Tony Bennett were recording R&B material in early 1955.[6] Less noticed, in the rhythm and blues section, was a "This Week's Best Buy" notice for Johnny Ace's "Pledging My Love." "The recent death of Ace gave added impetus to what would probably have been heavy first week sales in any case," *Billboard* speculated. "It is spiraling upwards at dazzling speed, and is almost as popular with pop customers, as with R&B."[7]

On one level, "Pledging My Love" was just another slow "heart" ballad like Ace's other hits, but the legacy of this song and the popular musical trend it set in motion suggests that there were additional forces at work. The song begins with rolling piano chords and chime-like vibraphone notes. "Forever my darling, my love will be true," Ace sings, with a natural and perfectly controlled vibrato in his mellow baritone voice. "Always and forever, I'll love just you." He is unpretentious and believable. "Just promise me darling your love in return. Make this fire in my soul, dear, forever burn." The last demand may be excessive, but the warmth and sincerity he communicates softens the meaning to that of a reasonable request. The saxophone sustains the chords; the bass and bass drum together accentuate the first and third beats of every measure. The drummer plays brushes, providing back beat with the snare drum and hi-hat cymbals.

"My heart's at your command, dear, to keep love and to hold," the bridge begins. Ace's voice is high in the mix and out in front of Johnny Otis's vibraphone fills, the notes sustaining and overlapping. "Making you happy is my desire dear, keeping you is my goal." By then, James Von Streeter's soft, breathy, and distant tenor saxophone provides most of the melodic fill. While Ace's voice retains its vibrato, there is little vibrato in the saxophone, reflective of the "cool" jazz style then in vogue. Both the sax and the vibes are most active in the bridge, and the combination of vocal vibrato, vibes, and breathy saxophone in the bridge raises the emotional intensity of the lyrics before reaching the last verse. "I'll forever love you the rest of my days," Ace promises. "I'll never part from you and your loving ways." The tone, mood, and sentiment represent not only a standard Johnny Ace performance but the quintessential Ace performance.

Initially, the consumer demand for the record may have been accelerated by Don Robey's public relations efforts. Since confused contemporary accounts in the press set the date of Ace's death as 24, 25, 27, or 31 December, it is alleged that Robey deliberately moved the Christmas night death back twenty-four hours to the more sentimental setting of Christmas Eve for the purpose of selling records. "By moving the date back by one day," Galen Gart observes, "one could further romanticize the event by linking it to the normally happy expectations that most people experience on the night before Christmas. And time has proven Robey correct: the 'official' Duke version of the Ace shooting has been repeated so often through the years that December 24th is almost always the date cited in music histories dealing with the incident."[8] For almost forty-five years the consensus date of Ace's death has been Christmas Eve — even his family remembers it that way. It is likely, however, that the date of death was merely remembered incorrectly and that no one deliberately changed anything. "Christmas Eve is what everybody said," Evelyn Johnson explains. "[Robey] had no reason to say it was *any* certain date."[9] Indeed, Robey seems to have promoted both Christmas Eve and Christmas night as the "fatal night."

On 22 January, *Billboard* acknowledged the emerging popularity of rhythm and blues by adding a radio airplay chart to its regular charts measuring record sales and juke box plays. "We have held off running a deejay chart for a long time," Bob Rolontz explained, "simply because we wanted a chart which would be representative of the actual records being played [throughout] the country. With the growth of r.&b. shows and the great expansion of r.&b. jocks, we are now satisfied that our new r.&b. deejay chart is both representative and legitimate."[10] Ace's "Pledging My Love" appeared on this first airplay chart as the number nine song (it was number ten in sales) and was given an impressive review score of 95 out of 100. The "B" side, "No Money," was rated 77: "Routine blues effort is sung with feeling by Ace over a strong beat by the ork. Flip [the "A" side] has the power."[11] The record appeared on the local charts of almost half of the R&B territories: Atlanta, Charlotte, Cincinnati, Philadelphia, and St. Louis. In a large display ad for "Pledging My Love," a photograph of "The Late Johnny Ace" introduced readers to a listing of his "eight national hits in a row." Ace was "Duke's Greatest Recording Artist," the ad maintained. "His Songs Will Always Live."[12]

Billboard paid unprecedented respect to rhythm and blues in general and Johnny Ace in particular in its 29 January 1955 issue. In a special section called "Spotlight on Rhythm & Blues," *Billboard* estimated the current gross of the "aggregate rhythm and blues field" at $25,000,000 a year, with record sales doubling in 1954 to approximately 10 percent of the total industry gross.[13] Especially noteworthy were R&B "one-nighter packages" that were succeeding "in the face of falling road income" for the industry as a whole.[14] Primarily, R&B groups were generating excitement over individual singers and bands, with some new groups like the Chords and the Charms accounting for the biggest records of the year.[15] The trend for this new music was "sparked" originally by independent R&B labels, but soon the major labels "got into the act." In a reversal of how the music business had previously worked, the R&B independents "showed up with increasing frequency on the pop returns [throughout] 1954," but "most of the majors failed to crack the r.&b. market to any extent." This was the main story of the year, followed by the successful "drive against smutty disks," in which *Billboard* "helped spearhead a clean-up campaign" and could now "report that today most of the r.&b. disks are comparatively dirt-free."[16]

Still, for all its growing appeal, *Billboard* acknowledged a continuing resistance to this emerging new field of black music. "Despite all the bold talk of some months ago—that about the 'poor taste' or 'passing fancy' aspects of rhythm and blues music—the record customers continued to make their choices known." The important lesson to be learned from it all was "not a musicological or ethnological lesson" but a basic business one: the consumer, not the supplier, dictates the fashion. "It's as simple as this," *Billboard* said, "the public usually needs what it wants."[17] As if to emphasize the point, the magazine ran a piece by Al Jarvis, whose "Make Believe Ballroom" in 1932 made him, arguably, the first radio disk jockey. Jarvis believed that "youngsters have taken to rhythm and blues in much the same manner that youngsters of a generation ago took to swing." He played R&B, he said, because his audience wanted to hear it, and he warned broadcasters who donned "the cloak of judge and jury" and refused to program R&B that they did a "disservice" to their audiences. As for the charge of obscenity in the music, Jarvis could "safely say" that young people didn't get a "lewd connotation" from the music. "Paradoxically," he said, "it is the adult conception of the teen-ager that is obscene."[18]

Bob Rolontz, *Billboard*'s regular R&B columnist, could not keep the swagger out of his "Rhythm & Blues Notes" on 29 January. "This is an especially felicitous time to spotlight the r.&b. field," he said. "Not even when country tunes were dominating Tin Pan Alley was there the same air of excitement and commotion as there are today about r.&b. tunes and r.&b. artists." Rhythm and blues records were the "pop records of the day," he said, and what was especially "heartwarming" was that original R&B hits were also selling in the pop field. "This means," he said, "that many r.&b. artists, limited a short while ago to a small circle of fans, are now known to all record buyers."[19] As a measure of this new popularity and respect, *Billboard* featured a long tribute to Johnny Ace prominently placed not in the R&B section of the magazine but in the popular music section, next to the respected "Honor Roll of Hits":

> The music world lost a remarkable talent with the recent tragic death of Johnny Ace. The singer had a hit with his first record on the Duke label, "My Song," and came thru with hits consistently thereafter. Ace's simple and unaffected style of singing, his evident sincerity and heart, actually started the r.&b. field on a type of song that has come to be known as a "heart ballad."

> The singer had more of talent than most; he could also write a song.

And he did this well time and time again, getting into the lyrics a direct and personal appeal.

The death of Ace created one of the biggest demands for a record that has occurred since the death of Hank Williams just over two years ago. Orders for his new recording, "Pledging My Love," began to pour into the Duke-Peacock diskery in the same amounts as the large diskeries usually receive for a new record by a big pop artist.

The diskery went into full scale production on the record, and had its plants in Houston work on extra shifts, and now has records being made in the East and on the West Coast.

In addition, at the request of his many, many followers, the label is bringing out an LP of all of Ace's previous hits, which will soon be available to the public. There are more Ace records in the can, and the firm intends to bring them out from time to time.

In the short space of three weeks since the record was released, Ace's "Pledging My Love" has jumped to the No. 4 position on The Billboard's best-selling rhythm and blues chart. With its current sales in pop markets, many observers expect it soon to jump into the pop charts. And the cover recordings of the tune are now beginning to happen as well, with the first released this week by M-G-M Records, with Tommy Mara on the vocal. Many more are expected. Some deejays are already touting the Ace disk as possibly one of the biggest r.&b. records of the year.

The appeal of Johnny Ace [throughout] his sadly short career is epitomized in his last recording. It has the tenderness that marked all of his records. The demand for Ace's record is a tribute to him both as an artist and a writer, and it shows that he will not be soon forgotten by his many, many fans.[20]

Billboard charts for the week affirmed that Ace was not being forgotten. In one week "Pledging My Love" had moved up to the number four position in both R&B sales and airplay and had penetrated additional territorial markets: Baltimore/D.C., New Orleans, and New York. "Across the nation from the loudspeakers of record stores on Harlem's 125th Street to the cafe juke boxes of Memphis, Houston and the West Coast," Galen Gart contends, "'Pledging My Love' was causing grown women to weep and write suicidal poems to newspapers and magazines."[21]

On 5 February "Pledging My Love" showed up on all three R&B charts, as the number two song in sales, number four in airplay, and number seven in juke boxes. The pace of the record's popularity as a juke box hit had been slowed only by the manufacturer's inability to satisfy the demand for 45 rpm copies of the record. Bill Holford cut masters for both 45 and 78 rpm versions of Duke 136 early in December, but "Pledging My Love" was the first Duke record to attract a large pop audience (primarily teens) and therefore from the beginning sold more 45s than 78s. Bob Rolontz declared in his column that the record had broken through to pop, creating "a flurry of excitement," though *Billboard*'s pop charts would not reflect this crossover for another two weeks. Cover records were being made by pop artists, Rolontz said, and tribute records were being released in the R&B field "to further enhance the growing Johnny Ace legend."[22] Indeed, one of the tribute records, Varetta Dillard's "Johnny Has Gone," earned a "Review Spotlight" as a potential R&B hit: "Here's the first in what may well turn out to be a series of wax tributes to the late Johnny Ace. The canary warmly sings the clever special lyrics written to include the titles of Ace's old hits. The melody is familiar. A great performance by Miss Dillard, plus the sales-sentiment inspired by the recent Ace tragedy should put this one over big."[23] In addition, a display ad for Johnny Moore's Blazers promised a "double barreled scoop!" "Johnny Ace's Last Letter" b/w "Why, Johnny, Why" constituted "Two Sensational Songs in Tribute to the Great Johnny Ace."[24]

Early 1955, it must be remembered, was still a time in which the power of local radio was misunderstood and underappreciated in the popular music business. In one general audience survey, for example, *Billboard* was surprised to learn that the top rated disk jockeys in New York City were not "always the best record plug." Local high school students ("generally conceded to be the biggest segment of pop record buyers") had their own preferences in deejays. "The rhythm and blues craze undoubtedly is responsible for Alan Freed's popularity with the teen age set," *Billboard* speculated, since Freed was the number two deejay among youth but not even in the top sixteen in terms of the general audience.[25] A national poll conducted by the Teen-Age Survey Service had determined that teenagers were the radio disk jockey's "best friend." Almost 100 percent of teenagers owned a radio, it was discovered, and 83 percent favored "deejay and pop music programs" over any other type. A Starch survey commissioned by NBC revealed that almost half of all youth over ten years old in America listened to the radio at night; two-thirds of that group watched no television at all.[26]

By 12 February "Pledging My Love" was the number one R&B record with disk jockeys, number two in sales, and number three in juke box play. All territories except Chicago reported the record a hit. In addition, *Billboard* reviewed three pop covers of the song for that week alone. The version by the Four Lads "should get a healthy share of the loot certain to accure [*sic*] to the material," the pop reviewer predicted, and Louis Armstrong's reading was also "sure to get a share." The most favorable review, however, was reserved for Teresa Brewer: "The hefty Johnny Ace click is traced in a knowing performance by the canary. This will please many, many listeners. Coupling of these two big tunes ['How Important Can It Be' was the 'B' side] should make this disk figure strongly in juke boxes during the next few months."[27]

There is a certain "business as usual" quality in the pop reviews that is both understandable in the context of the historical relationship between R&B and popular music yet undeniably simpleminded in its obliviousness to the changes in the pop audience that were rapidly taking place. In R&B itself there seems to have been a higher consciousness, though not necessarily a more noble intentionality. As Dave Clark, the record promotion man who sometimes worked for Don Robey, admitted later: "We paid a lot of money on Johnny Ace's 'Pledging My Love.' We paid black payola and we paid white payola. Only difference is that white payola cost more money."[28]

"Pledging My Love" made its first appearance on the pop "Best Sellers in Stores" chart on 19 February, one of the pop "Territorial Best Sellers" in New Orleans (number nine) and Cleveland (number three). Though it was the first record out of Duke or Peacock to cross over to pop, it was part of a discernible trend in the music business. Up until a few months before, *Billboard* pointed out, the most popular songs in America had always been licensed by ASCAP at a rate of seven or eight to one over songs licensed by BMI. By early 1955 the popularity of R&B had reversed the monopoly: seven of the top ten tunes comprising *Billboard*'s "Honor Roll of Hits" for 19 February were BMI-licensed songs.[29] The popular music environment in early 1955 was ripe for infiltration by BMI publishers like Don Robey's Lion Music, independent labels like Don Robey's Duke Records, and R&B artists like Johnny Ace. Unfortunately for Robey, by the time he hit it big he had lost his artist with the greatest crossover appeal. It is not coincidental that on 19 February 1955—the week that "Pledging My Love" broke pop—

Robey announced that he had signed the brother of Johnny Ace to a Duke Records contract.

Two major crossover achievements were documented on 26 February: "Pledging My Love" was included in *Billboard*'s prestigious "Honor Roll of Hits" list ("the nation's top tunes according to record and sheet sales, disk jockey and jukebox performances"), and the first "Pledging My Love" cover version became a pop "Best Buy." Teresa Brewer's "pop-styled version of Johnny Ace's great r.&b. hit" was doing extremely well, reported *Billboard*, with "the exception of those territories where the Ace record is firmly entrenched and pop customers will have no substitute."[30] It was also reported that for the first time in pop music 45 rpm records were outselling 78 rpm records, or, as *Billboard* put it, "For First Time Click Tunes Sell Faster On Donuts."[31] On 5 March "Pledging My Love" won *Billboard*'s Triple Crown by charting as the number one R&B hit in sales, in radio airplay, and in juke box play. It was the number one song in all of the R&B territories except Cincinnati (number two) and Chicago (absent), and overall the number twenty-one best selling pop record in America.

Not since Cecil Gant's "I Wonder" from 1945 had a ballad by a single black, male performer signed to an independent R&B label enjoyed such popular success in America.[32] "While the scattered success of a few left-field novelties could be written off as 'musical-acts-of-God,'" Al Pavlow observes, "ballads like 'Earth Angel' [the Penguins] and 'Pledging My Love' could not, and as the barrage increased, one fact became startlingly clear: *the rhythm and blues field itself was breaking pop!*"[33]

Two years earlier, when Hank Williams died in Oak Hill, West Virginia, in the back seat of a car taking him to a New Year's performance in Canton, Ohio, songs "describing the event or commemorating his career" turned up almost immediately on country radio and juke boxes.[34] The same pattern of eulogies accompanied the death of Johnny Ace. In the world of R&B, the romantic legend of Ace was so central to the marketing of "Pledging My Love" that no R&B label dared to make a cover of the song. The only way to capture some of the Ace mystique was to release musical tributes to the deceased singer. More than half a dozen tribute records were released, and at least two of them were covered by other R&B labels.

"Johnny Ace's Last Letter" had already charted as an R&B juke box hit by 5 March, by Johnny Moore's Three Blazers (vocal credit: Frankie Erwin).

In this sad representation of Ace's death, the singer is a lonely figure apologizing to his audience for his inability to function any longer:

> Goodbye everybody, had to be this way
> I'm tired of living — misery every day
> Please forgive me
> Too late to be sorry, I'm doing wrong.

The record succeeded in spite of *Billboard*'s warning that "the lyricist has taken a lot of license with facts of Ace's death, and the Ace fans might even object to this version of their idol's ill-fated demise."

The flip side of "Johnny Ace's Last Letter" was another Ace tribute. Linda Hayes's performance of "Why, Johnny, Why," was said to be "a good reading of okay material."[35] In a theme that was repeated by other tribute songs, the vocalist thanks Johnny Ace for his gift of song and promises to join him soon in heaven:

> You gave the world your heart in song
> To love and remember
> To have when you're gone
> We'll meet again soon
> It won't be long
> In heaven, I'll be with you.

The Rovers' "Salute to Johnny Ace" was another attempt to eulogize the fatal night in Houston: "Can't you remember last December when Johnny said goodbye? / No one pretended that they were happy, 'cause everybody wanted to cry." The Five Wings' "Johnny's Still Singing," a "sincere reading," *Billboard* said, with "appealing sentiment,"[36] suggests that Ace has continued his singing career in heaven: "I know he'll teach all the angels the songs he wrote and sang to me / And I know all the angels in the choir will sing each song so heavenly."

The most heavily, as opposed to heavenly, promoted Ace tribute was Varetta Dillard's "Johnny Has Gone," which charted as an R&B hit from late February through the middle of April and enjoyed special success in the urban Northeast.[37] The singer suggests in the song that Ace's "Pledging My Love" was so tender a rendition that an angel could not help but bring Ace into heaven on the spot:

When he sang *my song, pledging his love*
An *angel* was listening, and called him above
The clock is standing still since he has gone away
I'll *cross my heart* until I hear his voice some day.

Five of Ace's hits are mentioned in this relatively small section of lyric, serving virtually as an advertisement for Ace's old records. The technique was not lost on Don Robey, who put out a tribute of his own, "In Memory." Singing with the Johnny Otis Band, Marie Adams catalogs Ace's Duke Records:

Johnny, Johnny, Johnny I miss you so
I *cross my heart, never let you go*
I'll *follow the rule*
I'm *saving my love for you.*

The competition to promote Ace homages grew so fierce by early February that R&B labels lobbied Bob Rolontz for credit as "the first diskery to make a record in tribute to the late Johnny Ace."[38] Not surprisingly, labels took whatever advantage they could find. Fred Mendelsohn told Arnold Shaw that in order to help the sales of "Johnny Has Gone," Savoy Records spread the story that the singer, Varetta Dillard, "was Johnny's girlfriend, which she wasn't." While the record companies may have resorted to trickery, there is evidence that the R&B audience was authentically moved by the sentiments expressed in the Ace tributes. Johnny Fuller, who claimed to have sold a million copies of his version of "Johnny Ace's Last Letter," told Shaw that in 1955 R&B club owners "asked him not to perform the song because of the tears and hysterical reactions it brought from female customers. There was a Johnny Ace cult," Shaw concludes, "as there was a James Dean cult."[39] Clearly, a new phenomenon was at work. Indeed, by April the national R&B charts would include not only "Pledging My Love" but Varetta Dillard's tribute to Ace, and the territorial charts would reveal the popularity of Johnny Fuller's version of "Johnny Ace's Last Letter," which *Billboard* had previously noted as generating "intense excitement."[40]

The extraordinary reception of Johnny Ace as not only a great balladeer but a symbol of accomplishment in a field of music previously marginalized thrilled Don Robey. On 26 March, Duke Records purchased a half-page ad in *Billboard* designed after a thank you note. Personalized from Robey and sales manager Irving Marcus, there was a specific thank you to the trade papers, trade magazines, Duke Record distributors, R&B disk jockeys, pop disk jockeys, and juke box operators "for making 'Pledging My Love' The Biggest Combination Record R&B and Pop." Naturally, Robey's reference was to "the original version by the Late Johnny Ace."[41] Though most white radio stations played the Teresa Brewer cover, the Ace original was still Top 20 in pop retail sales and Triple Crown R&B for the fourth straight week.

The song would chart pop for another four weeks and R&B for an additional six. In Detroit, the record was strong enough to be "battling it out with 'The Ballad of Davy Crockett' for number one pop position."[42] *Billboard* noted that the extraordinary strength of R&B material in the pop field despite the "scarcely-veiled antagonism of many pop publishers and artist and repertoire men" had caused popular music not only to lose "the initiative it enjoyed for years" but forced it to spend "much of its activity in covering."[43] Though pop radio stations were slow to respond to the demand for R&B material, *Billboard*'s survey of the juke box industry revealed that 59 percent of the operators were using more R&B records than they had the year before, an "astounding increase."[44]

The overwhelming success of "Pledging My Love" in retail sales, in juke box and radio airplay, as a hit on the R&B charts and on the pop charts as well, meant that the song would earn big money for its writer and publisher. It also provided a copyright history as complicated as it is revealing. The original copyright, sought by Lion Publishing on 15 March 1954, for an unpublished song, credited Don Deadric Robey as the author of both words and music. It is generally believed that Ferdinand "Fats" Washington, known primarily as a lyricist, wrote the words to "Pledging My Love," but Robey left him off of the copyright application altogether while giving him half of the credit on the record label itself and on the licensing society paperwork for BMI (on 21 January BMI indexed the song as an even split between Robey and Washington for purposes of paying out performance rights money). For reasons no one can explain, Robey filed two additional copyright claims on successive days. On the first, filed 26 January, he listed himself as the sole author of the unpublished song "Pledging My Love" (words and music by Don Deadric Robey, Lion Publishing Company). Then on the very next day he filed a second application for a copyright on a *published* song, assigned jointly to Wemar Music Corporation and Lion Publishing, crediting Robey with words, and F. Washington with the melody. (It is more likely that Washington wrote the words, as he did to many B.B. King compositions, that Johnny Ace was actually the composer, and that Robey merely took the credit.)

One week later, according to *Billboard*, the publishing firm of E. H. Morris took over "selling rights" to the song, with industry rumors that a legal hassle might result, since publisher George Weiner had been "acting in the capacity of selling agent."[45] Actually, George Weiner, who owned Wemar Music, had already completed his work, arranging on Robey's behalf the first wave of cover versions of "Pledging My Love" by Teresa Brewer (Coral), the Four Lads (Columbia), and Tommy Mara (MGM) *before* the record broke nationally. In other words, Don Robey had sought the cover versions himself, giving up action in the property for a percentage of the larger volume sales the covers would bring, acting not as the manufacturer of a Duke Records release but as the owner of Lion Publishing, the publisher of "Pledging My Love." This dimension of the "covering process" is not widely known. Especially in the season of 1954–55, when the whole music business was in transition, white pop covers of R&B hits are commonly described as ruthless and racist business practices—a kind of legal stealing permitted by the 1909 copyright statutes—consciously designed by the large white record labels to exploit the smaller, black-owned companies.

Covering—recording a song previously recorded—had been a regular part of the music business since the sales of phonograph records replaced sheet music as the industry's cash cow in the early 1920s. According to Russell Sanjek, the legal basis for covering goes back almost a half-century, to the Aeolian Company's attempt to monopolize piano rolls of popular songs by entering into secret agreements of exclusivity with major music publishers. When competing piano roll manufacturers and executives of the infant phonograph industry learned that they had been frozen out of almost 400,000 compositions owned by eighty-seven major publishers, they petitioned the Congress and the White House. The result, part of Theodore Roosevelt's trust-busting tendency, added a compulsory licensing provision to the Copyright Act of 1909 that not only stopped that monopoly but any future attempt to manipulate access to popular musical properties. A royalty of two cents for each mechanical reproduction of a song was established (piano roll, record, or cylinder, the fee was the same) with the copyright owner possessing the *right of first exploitation only*, after which others were free to exploit it for the same rate of two cents per song.

The decision opened up the popular music business and saved Aeolian a fortune (its secret agreement called for a 10 percent royalty); it also led to some new aggressive music business "songplugging" practices in the promotion of potential hit songs: free "artists' copies," complimentary orchestra/band arrangements in various keys, and "subsidies" for performers. In 1917, when the Keith-Orpheum circuit (187 theaters) attempted to stop an elaborate "payment system" for vaudeville singers, a new "gratuity system" was invented that distributed pieces of song ownership.[46]

By the 1950s virtually all hit songs existed in multiple versions; indeed, some of the music trade magazines, notably *Cash Box*, employed a single system of calculating the week's top hits by lumping together *all* recorded versions of a song. So did *Your Hit Parade*, "a Saturday-night fixture on NBC," initially on radio and later a successful television show that used its own "nation-wide survey" to determine the Top 10 hits of the week. These were then performed in lavish production numbers by Dorothy Collins, Eileen Wilson, or Snooky Lanson (*Your Hit Parade*'s own regular vocalists), singing in their own styles with unique musical arrangements and imaginative choreography.[47] Since most popular songs of the period came from the theater or the movies anyway, and since it was quite rare for original Broadway musical voices or Hollywood film stars to have pop record hits of the songs they performed, such covering seemed the normal order of things. The major labels generally covered one another and sometimes even covered themselves. A pop song could be released first with a male vocalist, for example, and later with a female singer, an instrumental version for dancing, or a novelty arrangement.

In addition, by the early 1950s it was routine for major labels to issue country and western covers of pop songs, since C&W was a distinct and entirely different market controlled by the same major interests. The genius of Hank Williams, the "Hillbilly Shakespeare" signed to giant MGM, had even made it routine to reverse the covering process — to release pop versions of C&W records. In this kind of covering, however, big companies with white artists covered other big companies with other white artists. Rhythm and blues changed everything, and when R&B records began to penetrate the pop charts in their original R&B versions, white cover versions "were viewed not as an effort to popularize a fringe music, but an attempt to wipe out a small competitor," Al Pavlow points out. "And, since the victims were black, it began to look like racial prejudice, which it wasn't. It was *show-biz*."[48]

The scene that began in 1954 and continued into 1955 appeared to take on a new intentionality with a fixed pattern. An original R&B performance by a black artist was released by a small, independent (sometimes black-owned) record company. Then it was covered by a white performer's version of the song, released by a large, white-owned major record company with the capability for national distribution and promotion. The white version was not so much a cover of the song as a *copy*, an attempted *duplication* of not only the melody of the song but the musical voicings and rhythmic quality of the arrangement, plus the singer's distinctive vocal style as well in many cases.

While the law establishing the legality of this duplication may have been enacted in a pure and color-blind manner, it certainly seemed discriminatory to the African American community. Langston Hughes editorialized against what he called "Highway Robbery Across the Color Line in Rhythm and Blues" in the *New York Age Defender*, observing that the roots of such imitation went back more than one hundred years, when blackface minstrelsy "swept the nation" in the 1840s. It may be a compliment to Negro performers to be copied "note for note and slur for slur," he said: "But it just happens that the white performers can carry copies of Negro material into the best night clubs, the biggest theaters, and onto the movie screens of Hollywood where poor Negroes hardly ever get a look in—not to [speak] of the fields of radio and television where colored performers with regular jobs are few and very, very far between."[49]

Hughes's point was understandable. In 1955, radio music programming was still segregated, just like network television that, editorialized the *Chicago Defender*, had erected a "glass curtain" to keep black performers off the screen and out of the big money. "TV will not be a truly American 'thing' until it integrates all people, regardless of color," the paper argued.[50] The most dramatic and widely publicized example of this kind of exploitation was LaVern Baker's Atlantic R&B hit "Tweedlee Dee," covered by Mercury's Georgia Gibbs. Baker's original hit the *Billboard* R&B charts on 15 January 1955, and both the Baker and Gibbs versions made the pop "Best Seller in Stores" charts on 29 January. But in the following six weeks Gibbs's cover climbed to number three while the Baker original fell out of the Top 30 altogether.

It was generally acknowledged that the success of Gibbs's version, played on white radio stations and promoted, pressed, and distributed by a major label, had to do with how closely the "sound" of the song approximated Baker's. Indeed, few could dispute the resemblance, nor was it accidental. According to Arnold Shaw, before Gibbs even went into the studio the Mercury arranger "carefully studied" the Baker recording: "Since the copyright law does not protect arrangements as such, he was free to copy the bass line, the drum rhythms, and whatever else gave the Baker disk its marvelous drive, vitality, and danceability. In short, the Gibbs version was a copy of the Baker platter."[51]

Baker went public with her complaint in February, telling the black press that she "was investigating the possibilities of filing a $250,000 suit" against two white singers who "used her entire arrangement" in their covers. "Why don't they hire their own arrangers to fit my song to their styles, instead of fitting their styles to my arrangement for which I paid $1,500?" she asked.[52] A week later she knew what the A&R men at Mercury, the other major labels, and even her own Atlantic Records already knew: the legal basis for copying an arrangement had been clearly decided by "A Little Bird Told Me."

"A Little Bird Told Me," sung by Paula Watson on Supreme Records, had been covered by Decca's Evelyn Knight even before the original hit the R&B charts in November 1948. The cover version, an immediate pop hit expected to reach sales of 1,500,000 by early 1949,[53] was a "duplicate," Supreme alleged in a $400,000 damage suit against Decca, and had attained its success only because it had "stolen" the Watson arrangement, which had been copyrighted separately. After a three-day trial in May 1950, Los Angeles Federal Court Judge Leon Yankwich ruled that nothing in the original record's arrangement constituted property ownership and that only copyright owners could hold rights to original music. Both records were played in court, *Billboard* reported, and because of its "importance as a precedent-setting suit Decca put its big legal guns to work to prepare an ironclad defense."[54] The Decca executives testified "as to the musical fine points" so effectively that the judge not only heard "differences" in the two arrangements but found "a much better product" in the Decca version.

Variety reported that the music industry had "long understood" that arrangements were not protected by copyright. "Technically, making an arrangement that differs from the published stock is not permissible without the consent of the publisher as holder of the copyright," it noted, though it is to the publisher's advantage to waive this right "to have his material played and sung by bands and artists who want their own individual versions."[55]

Indeed, warning deejays not to jump to conclusions about which version of a song was "original" and which a "cover," Coral Records pop A&R chief Bob Thiele argued that "ideas for arrangements" often came from a publisher's demonstration record. "It's the publisher's demo," he maintained, "that's really being covered."[56]

Clearly the problem created by covering was not so much legal as political. Independent R&B record companies like Atlantic, whose publishing subsidiaries copyrighted virtually every song they recorded, did very well when their material was covered by a major or pop label, as did the writers of the songs. In fact, many R&B labels went to extraordinary lengths to secure covers of original material. Most owners of R&B material were so anxious to cooperate with the pop exploitation of their copyrights that they initiated deals with pop publishers and willingly offered percentages of songs in exchange for cover versions. Randy Wood, owner of the notorious cover-label Dot Records, is reported to have demanded (and received) from the owners of copyrights whose songs he covered "up to 70,000 royalty-free records for disk-jockey promotion."[57] Everyone, in fact, seemed to prosper from covering. Only the front men and women, performers like LaVern Baker and Etta James who did not generate their own material, were the ones left out of the profits, and they were the ones who made the loudest noise in 1955.

LaVern Baker pursued the matter of Georgia Gibbs's cover of "Tweedlee Dee" as both an economic and a political matter, appealing publicly to Rep. Charles Diggs Jr., the newly elected black Democratic congressman from Michigan. Insisting that the note-for-note duplication of her arrangement cost her $15,000 in lost royalties ("purchasers bought other versions of the tune, thinking it was hers"), she asked Diggs to investigate the current "outmoded" law with the possibility that he "might see some wisdom in introducing a law to make it illegal for one singer to duplicate another's work."[58] Baker's lobbying worked. On 2 April 1955 Diggs introduced a bill proposing the creation of a federal copyright fact-finding commission.[59] The negative publicity was an embarrassment to the major labels. The day the Baker story ran in *Billboard*, Mercury Records eastern A&R men (known professionally as Hugo and Luigi) issued a statement in which they claimed that R&B had hit its peak, was fading, and "consequently" no R&B material would be scheduled for future Georgia Gibbs recording dates.[60] What they didn't say at the time was that another Gibbs cover, this one of Etta James's

"Wallflower" ("Roll with Me Henry") had already been recorded and was on its way to surpassing the success of even the Baker cover.

The new Gibbs record, titled "Dance with Me Henry," entered the pop "Best Seller in Stores" chart at number twenty-one on 26 March, eventually peaking at number three in late May.[61] Etta James reacted much as LaVern Baker had, and in early June she aired her grievance through the black press. The *Chicago Defender* described the nineteen-year-old R&B star as "mad, very mad" and maintained that Mercury's Georgia Gibbs "must again deny charges of plagiarism." James would file a $10,000 lawsuit in New York during her upcoming appearance at the Apollo, the *Defender* said, noting that this time Gibbs had "taken the candy right out of [the] Little Lady's mouth."[62]

Imitation is said to be the sincerest form of flattery, and in the music business it might even have been within the law, but substituting white copies for black originals soon became a public relations nightmare. New York's WINS, the new home of deejay Alan Freed, decreed in August 1955 that it would no longer play "copy" records of hit songs, "disks which copy — often note for note — the arrangement and stylistic phrasing of the singer." Among the fourteen titles mentioned by program director Bob Smith as verifiable originals was LaVern Baker's "Tweedlee Dee" on Atlantic, the only version of the song the station would henceforth play: "The new policy is being enacted in the interest of fairness to the original artist and label. It will be recalled that some months back, Atlantic's LaVern Baker had protested to her congressman that she was being financially damaged as a result of copy records issued on top of her hits."[63]

By that time some of the majors had discontinued the practice of covering for their own reasons. RCA, for example, began to toughen its publishing policy in the spring of 1955, demanding "guarantees of exclusivity" for the songs it released. Noting that the media in general and the disk jockey in particular "often show strong loyalty to the original waxing," RCA concluded that covering had become counterproductive: "the added hype stimulated by a major jumping on the indie's back frequently [rebounds] to the indie's benefit."[64]

Johnny Ace, of course, had never been in a position to be "financially damaged" by white covers of his records. There were no white Ace covers at all until after his death, and then, it turned out, none that could compete successfully with the original. As it happened, for the first time in the postwar era record buyers chose a ballad by a solo black male singer signed to an independent label as *the definitive performance* — making Ace's "Pledging My Love" an important transition point in the diffusion and transformation of minority culture to mainstream America. Indeed, the death of Ace and the subsequent crossover success of his posthumous hit was a harbinger of change that was beginning to revolutionize popular music in America. The emerging new audience for popular records differed from the previous audience in two significant ways: demography and taste. This was an adolescent audience, demanding a specific musical performance of a song — a unique and distinctive performance against which all subsequent performances would ruthlessly be judged.

The major record companies had hoped all along that the pop audience would be satisfied with the black songs without the black singers, but, as Charlie Gillett points out, by the end of 1954 the "audience was determined to have the real thing, not a synthetic version of the original."[65] To the chagrin of the traditional music industry, white teens in 1955 seemed to associate the performance of "Pledging My Love" with the personality of Johnny Ace the singer. Cover artists Teresa Brewer, the Four Lads, and Tommy Mara may have performed the same song, but they had not killed themselves playing Russian roulette, validated the myth of black primitivism, or dared to explore the ultimate in rebellious behavior. Only Johnny Ace had lived the fast and dangerous lifestyle to its fullest. Moreover, according to Galen Gart, "Pledging My Love" was the kind of sentimental ballad that provided deejays "the ideal vehicle with which to mourn the baby-faced balladeer." It was, he said, "as if an entire generation of teenagers and young adults was for the first time sharing a strange, profound and communicable sadness."[66]

Royalties earned by Lion Publishing Company for "Pledging My Love" helped establish the staying power of Robey's record labels. In fact, independent record companies that survived the transition from rhythm and blues to rock 'n' roll in the 1950s (Atlantic is even a better example than Duke/Peacock) invariably did so on the strength of their publishing subsidiaries. Though covering worked to the disadvantage of R&B performers who did not generate their own material — the practice denied them the artist royalties their R&B records might otherwise have earned — for the R&B writer/performer, however, covering meant additional, and larger, royalties. Pop records sold in huge quantities (writers and publishers shared two cents a song), and pop versions of R&B songs were played on the radio to huge audiences (writers and publishers shared equally in performance rights money). Fats Domino, for example, had the R&B hit on "Ain't That a Shame," but it was Pat Boone's cover version that brought Domino and writing partner Dave Bartholomew the big money.

Clearly, Don Robey was ahead of the curve in acting more like a publisher than a manufacturer in January 1955, though it would take another year for the industry to observe and discuss any conflict of interest. In February 1956, after "Pledging My Love" and fifteen other R&B derived tunes had constituted most of BMI's total awards for 1955 heavy radio airplay, *Billboard* acknowledged that "the indie diskery with a hot tune is sometimes more eager to promote the ditty than the platter," essentially cutting the independent R&B record distributor out of the action.[67]

Don Robey would have seen nothing wrong with exploiting musical properties rather than R&B records. In fact, since he had almost never recorded any material he did not own, he was in an ideal position to take advantage of the business opportunities provided by the demand for R&B material. He was also in position to exploit the legend of the man who was becoming "the late, great Johnny Ace" (according to disk jockeys everywhere), "the coloured James Dean" (Mike Leadbitter), "the Ace of Duke" (Peter Grendsya), "the first fallen angel" (Nick Tosches), and "the first rock 'n' roll casualty" (Colin Escott).[68] The question was Robey's ability to grasp firmly what he saw so clearly. When Ace died, he left only six unreleased tracks, and Don Robey had writer credit on only one song. The timing may have been right to launch Ace to the next level and the market may have seemed infinite, but the available product was slim. Robey attempted to meet the challenge by repackaging Ace's single records and spreading out releases of the previously unreleased sides over the next eighteen months — a period nearly as long as Ace's entire career.

[The photo] came all the way from
Texas, with a sad and simple face
And they signed it on the bottom
"From the late great Johnny Ace."
—Paul Simon,
"The Late Great Johnny Ace"

Imitations

of Love

For Don Robey, whose Duke Records company was not yet three years old, March 1955 must have seemed like the promised land. Johnny Ace's "Pledging My Love" was number one on all R&B charts (even Varetta Dillard's tribute to Ace was on all charts). It was at or near the top in all R&B territories, strong in several pop territories, a Top 20 record in pop sales (Teresa Brewer's cover was number seventeen in radio airplay), and the number eleven song in *Billboard*'s prestigious Honor Roll of Hits. It didn't get any better than that for an independent R&B record company, and for Robey, it never would again.

The extraordinary posthumous reception of Ace by the pop audience even led Robey into the long-play album business. Throughout March, Duke Records released several albums of Ace's previously recorded material, including the first Duke 33⅓ rpm product—a ten-inch LP titled *Memorial Album for Johnny Ace* (LP 70) with lush liner notes written by a Duke employee under the pseudonym of "Dzondria LaIsac":

A single adjective is not sufficient, in itself, to describe the greatness of [Johnny Ace's] style. And, rhetoric, generally, because it is surrounded by invisible bars of fragile superfluity, cannot clearly picture the sentimental suavity and exhuberant richness, the nostalgic warmth, the blue-note and the slight but perceptible "tear"-beat that pervaded his effervescent style. He knew where a song should go, where he wanted it to go . . . and his artistic energies were spent in making "His Song" reach its destination. And so, the songs he sang became part of him, he a part of them. His was a message of love and he gave it to the people! His personality and versality were projected into and mirrored in every quatrain, paired couplet and poetic and emotional metaphor of every song he sang. And there was always that strong "blue" undercurrent, infectiously permeating his performances, whether on record or during a one night stand at a nightclub. A notable achievement that only a few of the great artists have been able to duplicate.[1]

When Ace's new, white teenage fans demanded 45 rpm versions of his previous records, Robey released two 45 extended-play albums, EP 80 and EP 81, *Memorial Album: Johnny Ace* and *A Tribute to Johnny Ace*—which together covered the eight songs that Robey insisted were Ace's hits.[2] Meanwhile, the staff at Duke found itself "swamped with requests of photos of Johnny Ace. Letters have come in from all over the country," *Cash Box* reported, "and the Peacock staff has been busy for weeks mailing pics to the teeners."[3] Presumably, one of these requests came from singer/songwriter Paul Simon of Queens, New York, who at the time was fourteen years old. Almost thirty years later, in Simon's song "The Late Great Johnny Ace," a young musician is listening to the radio in 1954, hears of Ace's death, and sends away for his photograph: "It came all the way from Texas, with a sad and simple face / And they signed it on the bottom 'From the late great Johnny Ace.'"[4]

It was not until mid-July that Robey released the first posthumous single, "Anymore" b/w "How Can You Be So Mean?" The "A" side, "Anymore," featured Ace on his standard sad and mournful ballad—this time with virtually the same arrangement as "Pledging My Love" (the songs were cut at the same session in January 1954). As the "B" side, Robey chose an up-tempo blues-rocker written by Ace called "How Can You Be So Mean?" with the big band sound of the Ace road band (Robey credited the "Johnny Board Orchestra" on the record label) and some exciting guitar work by Milton

Hopkins. This cut was recorded in Houston at Bill Holford's ACA studio in July 1954—the last Ace session.[5]

While it is clear that Robey considered all of the Ace blues contributions as "B" side/throwaway material, it is also evident that he had high expectations for "Anymore," another Fats Washington sad ballad like "Pledging My Love." Robey, who had copyrighted "Anymore" as an unpublished song for Lion Publishing Company on 7 June 1954 (words and music by himself), took out another copyright on 18 February 1955, crediting words and music to Don Deadric Robey *and* Ferdinand Washington. "It is a real sad one," Robey told *Ebony* immediately before this first posthumous Ace release. "He sings it like a man who knows he's going to die." Writers at *Ebony* decided that Ace's voice recalled "a dim cafe and a bent man crying in his beer."[6]

It took *Ebony* more than six months after Ace's death to cover the phenomenon of Ace's popularity—a long time in the journalism business—and even then the magazine seemed to do so reluctantly. *Jet,* its gossipy sister publication, published a matter-of-fact one-paragraph story in an early January issue,[7] but as the most important general-circulation black periodical in America, *Ebony* took itself, and the rigid morality of its editorial policy, quite seriously, and was known to exclude from its pages African American personalities whose lifestyles it deemed unworthy of emulation. Still, occasionally, the magazine was compelled to address stories it did not approve of such as "The Strange Case of Paul Robeson" in 1951 and "The Strange Case of Johnny Ace" in 1955. *Ebony* could not validate Paul Robeson's communism any more than it could sanction the high-flying life and self-inflicted death of Johnny Ace. But the popularity of Robeson and Ace within the black community could not be denied.[8] The death of Ace, for example, was simply "illogical." According to *Ebony,* "Johnny Ace had the world on a string. He had just bought a brand new car. He was making more money than he had ever dreamed of and women adored him. At 25, he was the hottest rhythm and blues singer in America. So he killed himself."[9]

Ace quit school in the tenth grade, the magazine erroneously reported, fell in with the wrong crowd, served time in a Mississippi jail, and was estranged from both his parents and his wife and children. In his climb to the top of the R&B charts, *Ebony* observed, "Johnny picked up some 40 pounds, a process hairdo, goatee, mustache. Friends said he drank heavily in [the] months before [his] death." The story quoted his girl friend ("He could be all alone in a crowd"), his personal manager ("He had known great sadness somewhere"), and Memphis radio executive David Mattis, the man who discovered him ("Too many women, too much money, too much food"). Nevertheless, *Ebony* acknowledged that Ace had become nationally known *after* his death and that the Duke recording star had "begun to symbolize the ultimate in love" to bobby-soxers, college girls, and even mature women. The magazine positioned Ace as a kind of spokesman for the losers of the world, the down and out. "Giving of himself, singing it seems from some hurt recess in his soul," *Ebony* said, "Johnny sang the blues of the have-nots and the seekers who lost too soon," coverage more notable for its moralizing than for its accuracy.[10]

Within the music trade, however, it was business as usual. "This is the first Ace record issued since the top artist's recent death," *Billboard* said in its review of "Anymore." "It's a potent ballad similar in mood to his last, long-enduring smash, 'Pledging My Love,' and it could be the one his tremendous following has been waiting for." The magazine's prejudice against Ace's up-tempo material, however, is revealed in the description of "How Can You Be So Mean?" ("The flip is a rhythm opus from farther down the barrel").[11]

The next week, the record was a "Best Buy" on the strength of "enthusiastic sales reports" from Philadelphia, New York, Buffalo, Pittsburgh, Cincinnati, Cleveland, Nashville, Durham, Atlanta, and St. Louis. "The late Johnny Ace," proclaimed *Billboard*, "still exerts a powerful hold on the imagination of the national r.&b. market, considering the widespread acceptance of this disk within its first week of sale."[12] The half-page ad in the R&B section of *Billboard* for 23 July features Johnny Ace's hits in a stairway to heaven motif, beginning with "My Song" and in progressively larger print "Cross My Heart," "Angel," "The Clock," "Please Forgive Me," "Saving My Love for You," "Never Let Me Go," "Pledging My Love," and "ANYMORE!" which "is destined to be the greatest," and accompanied by Robey's claim that the new record had sold 300,000 copies before its release date.[13]

There is little external evidence that the market was so hungry, however. "Anymore" turned up on the first R&B territorial chart on 30 July (Philadelphia) and on the first national R&B charts on 6 August (number nine in retail sales and number thirteen in radio airplay). The record peaked the week of 20 August, when it made the juke box play chart for the first time (number eight) and kept its other ratings as well. On 27 August, Robey advertised "Anymore" as "going pop," urging the industry not to overlook "How Can You Be So Mean?" the flip side that was "going strong."[14]

It never happened in the real world, however, and by mid-September the record fell off all R&B charts. Technically a hit (Ace's last), "Anymore" behaved on the charts more like "Never Let Me Go" than "Pledging My Love," even though Robey claimed in a small display ad in the 8 October *Billboard* that the record was Ace's "biggest one" and a "Triple Crown Award Winner."[15] From this point on, in fact, the marketing of Johnny Ace would not only prove to be an uphill struggle but a losing proposition, a reality temporarily delayed by all of the publicity generated by the industry's November and December "roundup" articles. All stories on the breakthrough and success of R&B in 1955 would highlight Ace in general and "Pledging My Love" (the most played R&B song of the year) in particular.

At the beginning of 1956 Robey tried again. An ad in *Billboard* for 7 January 1956 claimed that before "that fatal Christmas night in 1954 JOHNNY ACE had just finished a record session. From that session came this record release": "So Lonely" b/w "I'm Crazy, Baby".[16] Of course there was no such dramatic last session. "So Lonely" had been recorded in January 1954, along with "Pledging My Love." "I'm Crazy, Baby" did come from Ace's last recording session, but that was in July—hardly a date Ace had "just finished" before killing himself. One thing the songs had in common was that Robey could claim no writer credit in either property. As it turned out, "So Lonely," an Ace blues composition about depression (Ace's voice even has a vulnerable lisp to it) with a mournful Johnny Otis arrangement, was not the "A" side of Duke 148 after all. Robey may have changed his mind or, as he had done early in Ace's career, he may have let the industry trade magazines decide. At any rate, *Billboard* chose "I'm Crazy, Baby" as the song to watch: "The late great Johnny Ace lives on as the label brings out two fine sides cut shortly before his death. On top is an exciting emotion-packed love ballad. The flip contains some wonderful blues sounds in the typical Johnny Ace style. These are two classy efforts with loads of commercial appeal."[17]

"I'm Crazy, Baby" is unlike any other Ace cut in that it seems to showcase Ace as a big band singer. His vocal phrasing is in the style of Sammy Davis Jr, and Ace employs (for the first time) the lower register of his voice. The Count Basie-like arrangement emphasizes horns, with a tinkling piano high in the mix. The AABA song is more musically sophisticated than any other Ace side, with its standard I–vi–ii–V progression serving merely as the turnaround between verses. Ace's road band did the backing, and Christopher Columbus Pinkston, the drummer and vibes player, got full writer credit on the copyright. But for all its innovation and sophistication, the record never caught on. Since the song did not successfully penetrate any of the R&B territories, it never became a *Billboard* "Best Buy," nor did it ever register as a hit on the R&B charts. Duke Records bought a quarter-page ad in the 4 February *Billboard* to reprint the flattering "Spotlight" review from two weeks before, but no one paid attention.[18] The Ace momentum had unmistakably stalled.

The *style* of music represented by Ace's hit records, however, continued to do well in the marketplace. *Billboard* noted in early 1956 that the category of music previously called rhythm and blues "barely begins to describe the myriad material" being released today. Though recent evidence indicated that a cleaned up and "funky" flavored blues might be coming back, the old style blues numbers, concerned with losing or lacking money or love and spiced with "double or even single entendre," could not compete in "these days of disk jockeys, speedy distribution and multi-competitive recording activity." Mostly, the trend had favored a "'refined' type of ballad," like Johnny Ace's "Pledging My Love," resulting in a "noticeable widening of the range of r.&b. subject matter." The recent "acceptance of so-called rock and roll music—a popularized form of r.&b.—in the pop and country markets has encouraged old-time r.&b. cleffers to concentrate on this hybrid form," *Billboard* reported. It also noted that "the major diskeries, which have been notably unsuccessful in crashing the pure r.&b. field, have virtually given up trying and have turned instead to rock and roll." The success of Bill Haley and the Comets for Decca was a good example of the majors' new strategy.[19]

An additional change in the field of rhythm and blues was the extent to which the ownership of hit songs had "upset the more traditional elements within the publishing fraternity." Invariably, in the field of R&B the music publisher and record manufacturer were the same person, *Billboard* observed, and increasingly this publisher/manufacturer was acting more like a music publisher—making deals for a pop cover of an R&B tune before the record even took off in the R&B market.[20]

In a blatant attempt to cash in on his deceased star, Robey notified *Billboard* in February that he had signed "another Ace for the label, the brother of Johnny." "His name is Buddy Ace," Bob Rolontz told his readers, "and he has just finished a stint in the Armed Forces. From what we hear his voice bears a close resemblance to his brother's."[21] Johnny did not have a brother named Buddy, but he did have a brother in the service, St. Clair Alexander, who was a singer. In April Robey informed *Billboard* that he was planning another Johnny Ace release, to "be followed by some sides by Buddy Ace," though he waited until July to actually do it. Then, in an announcement/ advertisement to "Dealers, Distributors, Jockeys, and The Trade," Duke Records presented the Ace brothers as a kind of matched set. The "LAST RECORD ON THE IMMORTAL JOHNNY ACE" was now available to "complete your collection" ("Still Love You So" b/w "Don't You Know," Duke 154) along with the "FIRST RECORD ON THE VERSATILE BUDDY ACE" to "start your collection" ("Back Home" b/w "What Can I Do," Duke 155). The Johnny Ace record, the ad promised, would even surpass "Pledging My Love."[22]

Don Robey planned to promote the release himself at an industry convention in New York in early August 1956, as *Billboard* put it, to make the "scene personally to lay down the jive."[23] This was the same National Association of Music Merchandisers gathering Robey had attended four years earlier, when he had first showcased Duke 102 and the charm of "My Song" by newly discovered Johnny Ace. Indeed, he had promoted the side so heavily then that he claimed he created a hit even before he went into production with the record. As the *Pittsburgh Courier* put it, the song "sold 53,000 copies before it was released."[24]

At this point, however, even *Billboard* resisted buying into the marketing of Johnny Ace. When the magazine reviewed ten new R&B records on 18 August, it gave the Johnny Ace songs the lowest ratings of any of the twenty sides evaluated. "Another blues job by the late great Johnny Ace comes out of the can," the magazine said of "Don't You Know," and though "the loyal fraternity may want the disk, it's not up to the previous top efforts." "Still Loves You So" was equally disappointing, "a very slow, melancholy, minor-key heartbreak-type blues." *Billboard* even found the sides by Ace's "brother" stronger than Johnny's: "[Buddy Ace] sings with feeling and warmth on a moving ballad with a solid beat."[25]

Launching the career of a musician said to be Johnny Ace's younger brother by connecting his first record to Johnny Ace's last record shows something of the desperation that Robey must have felt over his inability to continue to exploit the legend that Johnny Ace had become. His problem was simple: he had now run out of Ace recorded material. Back in March 1955, when he was down to four unreleased Ace songs, Robey had tried to maintain some semblance of truth in his advertising when he persuaded Johnny's brother, St. Clair Alexander, to travel from Fort Riley, Kansas, to Houston for a "try-out." "Robey wrote me a letter saying he wanted me to come down there," St. Clair says, but only sent the amount of money necessary to pay his fare. This typified a widely known frugality. Bobby Bland recalls getting out of the service and learning that all Duke recording sessions had been moved from Memphis to Houston. "I remember the bus fare to Houston was $13.80," he says. "They sent me $15."[26] St. Clair had plenty of time—he was boxing for Special Services and had no Army duties except for his training—but he felt that he needed more money to finance the trip: "So I got my mother to send me whatever it was to take a train to Houston and back. I told her I was in jail. I had another guy to call her, and he said I was in jail, so she sent me the fare to get me out of jail. But that was enough money to go to Houston and back, so I went to Houston. I did some songs down there in their studio, but I don't know if they ever cut them or not. I went down there and did some numbers at the Matinee Club. I stayed there at the Matinee Hotel."[27]

Robey named him Buddy because he didn't think his actual name "fit right," St. Clair says. "He paid me for a whole month down there. I was staying in a hotel on his bill, and every day he'd come around and give me fifteen or twenty dollars spending money." For St. Clair, the worst part of the experience was that his mother found out not only that he lied to her about being in jail but had fooled her into financing an opportunity for yet another son to become involved in what she considered the wretched lifestyle of rhythm and blues. "She found out about it because she read it in the *Jet*, or somebody read it in *Jet Magazine* and told her about it," St. Clair recalls.

Apparently, Robey did not think St. Clair's voice was suitable for his purposes, so nothing ever came in the way of a recording contract, though later St. Clair moved to Chicago, where he performed Johnny's songs and recorded some of his own as "St. Clair Ace."[28] As it turned out, the "Buddy Ace" who sang "Back Home" and "What Can I Do," on Duke 155 was not related to Johnny Ace at all. When St. Clair did not work out, Robey signed Texas musician Jimmy Lee Land to a Duke Records contract and made him out to be Johnny's brother, "Buddy Ace."[29] St. Clair did not know about the invention of Buddy Ace then, but it does not surprise him now. "I heard [Robey] was a rotten catch when I was down there," he recalls.

There was no reason for *Billboard* to attempt to resuscitate the career of

Johnny Ace more than eighteen months after his death—especially when the Ace market was so flat and so small—so it cavalierly rejected both sides of Duke 154. In a different context, however, the "B" side of this record now appears noteworthy. On "Don't You Know," words and music credited to John Alexander, Ace is a blues shouter in the manner of Big Joe Turner. The big band arrangement by Johnny Board, complete with recurring "Night Train" quotes, is the perfect background to showcase Ace's best blues piano performance. Ace's gospel turnaround at the end of the instrumental break is straight out of church, representing an impressive and early appearance of gospel sounds in secular R&B.

"Still Love You So" is much less interesting. Written by or at least credited to Sherman Johnson, this ballad had been recorded at a session in Los Angeles with the Johnny Otis Band almost three years before. Though it was copyrighted with the other songs done at the Radio Recorders studio, Robey had apparently never considered putting it on a record. Bill Holford mastered this "outside tape" in Houston, assigning it an ACA number that was almost four hundred sides after Ace's last entry in the ACA logbook.[30] Clearly Robey had reached the absolute bottom of the Johnny Ace barrel.

Duke Records did not represent the direction R&B was taking in the early fall of 1956, and Johnny Ace did not appear on any charts. Indeed, in the fall of 1956 the only Memphis musician to chart consistently was Elvis Presley, whose pop songs were not only crossing over to country and western but to R&B as well. Ace is mentioned in *Billboard* only once more in 1956, in connection with the death of James Dean. Varetta Dillard, whose tribute to Ace "Johnny Has Gone" was her last R&B hit, became the first artist to celebrate Dean ("I Miss You, Jimmy"), with "other dirges to Dean" reportedly underway on various labels. "Any a.&r. men currently seen in a state of acute melancholia," observed *Billboard*'s R&B columnist, "can be safely predicted to have a Dean disk under wraps."[31] Since none of the tributes to Dean succeeded in the R&B market, it is clear that while some of the world may have considered Johnny Ace the "coloured James Dean," devotees of rhythm and blues did not consider Dean to be the white Johnny Ace.

By early 1957 Don Robey began to focus on launching a new artist to the level previously attained by Johnny Ace and maintaining his own reputation as a mover and shaker in the music business. For readers of *Billboard*, he not only predicted the end of the calypso trend in pop music ("It will kill itself by excess," he said) but envisioned rock 'n' roll as the permanent force it would become: "Rock and roll will be around a long, long time. Rock and roll is like hot molten lavas that erupt when an angry volcano explodes. It's scorching hot, burns fast and completely, leaving an eternal scar. Even when the echoes of the explosion subside, the ecstatic flames burn with vehement continuity."

Robey's prose might be purple, *Billboard* explained, but he "is as hot as a $1 pistol right now" with his "biggest hit since 'Pledging My Love' by Johnny Ace."[32] The record of the moment was Little Junior Parker's "Next Time You See Me," but it barely made the R&B Top 10 lists, peaking at number seventy-four on the pop charts. A few months later Bobby (Blue) Bland's "Farther Up the Road" was "the hottest platter in the label's history and may exceed sales of Johnny Ace's 'Pledging My Love.'"[33] As it turned out, Bland's record topped the R&B airplay chart but peaked at number forty-three on the pop charts—a pattern repeated for the fifteen more years that Robey owned his label. A Duke or Peacock record would be released, promoted, hyped, compared favorably to Ace's "Pledging My Love," and then settle for a considerably more modest success.

It was during this time that Robey had to promise his contacts at *Cash Box* that he would "eat his hat" if the new record he was asking them to promote was not a hit. Eveyln Johnson does not remember which record he guaranteed the success of, "Next Time You See Me" or "Farther Up the Road," but she does recall the photograph by Benny Joseph that Robey sent to the magazine to keep his word. Robey is at his desk, a napkin tucked under his chin with a knife and fork in his hands, ready to cut into a stylish straw hat. Presumably, the salt, pepper, and large glass of water on one side of the hat and the catsup, Worcestershire sauce, vinegar, and pepper sauce on the other are designed to complement this main course.

Robey had not given up on the marketing of Johnny Ace, however, as he began to repackage previously released Ace songs. He told *Billboard* in July 1957 that *Johnny Ace Memorial Album Number II*, a conventional 12-inch LP, would contain "a number of never-before-released items along with some of the late singer's biggest hit sides."[34] There was no new material, though; all of the twelve songs included had been previously released. Most of the tunes were "A" sides, with every single represented except Duke 128 ("Please Forgive Me" b/w "You've Been Gone So Long").[35]

Finally, in December 1958—four years after Ace's death—Robey reissued "Pledging My Love" in a remastered form, recoupled with the only posthumous song he had writer credit on: "Anymore," making both sides Don Robey-Fats Washington collaborations. "Pledging My Love" b/w "Anymore" is especially challenging to the discographer since Robey cataloged it as Duke 136, the same number as the 1954 original ("Pledging My Love" b/w "No Money"). The half-page ad in *Billboard* promised:

> The same *voice*, the same *artist*, again sings the once-in-a-lifetime smashes. TWO powerhouses, destined to creat a new sensation in all markets, have been completely *re-mastered* and brought up-to-date via choral backdrop and modern instrumentation. But only this has been added . . . NOTHING taken away! It is JOHNNY who sings . . . and the strange "blue" undercurrent, the nostalgic warmth, the exhuberant richness that so infectiously permeated his performances and made him and his songs eternally *great* are still there! So it will be, always! The most sensational singer of our times . . . the immortal JOHNNY ACE And The World Famous JORDANAIRES.[36]

Bill Holford insists that he had nothing to do with the engineering of this infamous remastered version of Ace's hit ("I didn't put those strings on 'Pledging My Love,'" he says), and the presence of the Jordanaires still angers Johnny Otis almost forty years later. Robey had promised not to change any of the sides that Otis produced for him, Otis says, but then "he put those goddamn soprano eunuchs on there." Apparently, Robey thought that was going to cause Ace "to cross over and people would buy more."[37]

The other song, "Anymore," was not improved by adding a doo-wop chorus either, and while it may be less offensive, it is certainly sillier. "The original Johnny Ace recording gets an updated, souped-up backing to go with the vocal," said *Billboard*, which went on to review the original flipside of "Pledging" ("No Money") as the "B" side of the release—revealing that the actual product did not even exist at the time.[38] As it turned out, the record was a complete flop and the last attempt by Robey to resuscitate Ace as a recording artist.

Given the success of Duke and Peacock artists in the 1950s in the transitional period between rhythm and blues and rock 'n' roll, the 1960s were surely a disappointment to Don Robey. Willie Mae Thornton was long gone by that time. After "Hound Dog," she never had another record on the national R&B charts, and after the death of Johnny Ace her whole career unraveled. She left Peacock in 1957 and moved to the San Francisco Bay area. It is possible that Robey refused to renew her recording contract, but Thornton insisted she quit because the label cheated her.[39] Though Robey was able to exploit other Memphis musicians he had acquired in the Duke Records deal that brought him Johnny Ace, notably Junior Parker and Bobby "Blue" Bland, neither attained Ace's crossover success. As Galen Gart suggests, they were "too 'uptown' for white blues fans and too laid-back for white soul fans of the era" and therefore "relegated to a never-ending tour of the chitlin' circuit."[40]

To keep up with the times, Robey developed new talent, signing both black and white acts and creating subsidiary labels (Backbeat and Sure-Shot) aimed at the teenage market. One of Robey's new performers, a white Texas rocker named Roy Head, was able to accumulate three Top 40 hits, including "Treat Her Right," a number two song in America for a two-week period in 1965, but his entire career at the top lasted only three months. As R&B became more and more popular, Robey's importance as an independent entrepreneur in the field of black secular music began to diminish.[41] He could not, for example, equal the promotion and distribution efforts of relative newcomers like Stax, a Memphis label distributed by Atlantic Records, and Berry Gordy's Motown, a completely independent operation much like Robey's own.

For Robey, the final blow came early in the 1970s, when he lost a protracted court battle with Chess Records of Chicago, a company with whom he had long been at odds. The legal battle lasted eleven years, according to Evelyn Johnson, who had warned Robey not to "defy those people in Al Capone town," but Robey would not listen.[42] Chess and Duke/Peacock had been engaged in a turf war since the mid-1950s. It was believed in Houston, for example, that the Chess brothers had made a practice of paying Chicago disk jockeys *not* to play Johnny Ace records, or if they did play them, not to report the airplay to the trades. "They were being played in Chicago," Evelyn Johnson believes, "but they were never credited." The lawsuit, however, was over gospel music — specifically that Chess had illegally signed Peacock artists the Five Blind Boys and the Rev. Robert Ballinger. When the courts ruled against him, Robey sold his entire music business interests to ABC/Dunhill in 1973 for a reported $1,000,000. By this time Robey's publishing companies controlled 2,700 copyrights, and his various record labels had one hundred contracted artists who owed the various companies $250,000 in unrecouped advanced royalties. In addition, there was an inventory of approximately two thousand unreleased masters.[43]

Don D. Robey's contract with ABC/Dunhill called for him to remain active in the music business as consultant to the parent firm, which he did until his death on 16 June 1975, from a heart attack at age seventy-one. *Living Blues* praised him as an R&B pioneer "whose business ventures brought employment, popularity, and fame to many blacks," describing Duke/Peacock as "one of the last important independent record businesses."[44] *Rolling Stone* called him "a leading figure in rhythm and blues and gospel recordings in the Fifties and Sixties" but doubted that he had written the songs credited to him. "He ran his business with an iron fist," the obituary reported, and "exerted strong control over his artists." According to Walter Andrus, the audio engineer on many Little Junior Parker and Bobby Bland sessions: "[Robey] was just like a character out of *Guys and Dolls*. You had to see him to believe him. He'd have a bunch of heavy guys around him all the time, carrying pistols and that kind of stuff, like a czar of the Negro underworld."[45]

Though this characterization of Robey seems exaggerated to insiders, one fact remains true: the very thing that Robey consistently and prominently displayed as part of his personal, everyday life—guns—is what also killed his golden goose. Evelyn Johnson, who had been his business partner for more than twenty-five years and his wife from 1953 to 1960, believes that on balance Robey's contributions were positive. "Don Robey did everything *his* way, up to and including the Internal Revenue," she says. "He was a man that could get by. He could do whatever he wanted to do. And it might have skirted, but it was within the law. And he was. And he did far more good than he did bad."[46]

Members of the Alexander family in Memphis were more likely to accept the notion of Don Robey as a "czar of the Negro underworld" than a man who "did more good than he did bad." Immediately after Johnny's funeral early in 1955, Mrs. Leslie Alexander directed her daughter Norma to go to Houston, see Don Robey, and arrange for some kind of payment to Johnny's widow and children. The family believed that Johnny had made a fortune in the music business. They had seen him driving expensive cars, they knew for certain that he always carried large amounts of cash in his pocket, and they were led to believe that he always had everything he needed. Evelyn Johnson was considered Ace's manager, knew his itinerary, Norma was told, "and if he's at the Apollo theater in New York and he was out of funds they'd just wire him four or five hundred dollars—anything he needed." In addition, published accounts of his death by the black press in

Houston mentioned a new 1955 Oldsmobile he had just purchased and was about to pick up.[47]

But in Houston, when Norma met with both Don Robey and Evelyn Johnson, she was told that Johnny had no money coming and the Oldsmobile mentioned in the newspapers did not belong to him. In fact, the singer's high standard of living left him owing the company money in future royalties and expenses advanced to him before his death. Norma, who knew her brother received cash advances, did not believe that he was without assets or earning potential. Her employer, Universal Life of Memphis, helped the Alexanders engage the services of an attorney in Dallas, but the lawyer later advised the family that Robey was too powerful and had too many friends in Texas for them to launch a successful suit.

Jean Alexander's determination rivaled Don Robey's power, however, and twenty years later she filed a $50,000 suit in Federal Court on behalf of her and the children against ABC Records, ABC/Dunhill Music, Duke Records, Peacock Records, Buffalo Booking Agency, Lion Publishing Co., Evelyn Johnson, and Don D. Robey. "Johnny 'Ace' Alexander, in the year 1952," the complaint alleged, "being in his early twenties, uneducated, having no business experience, placed himself, as an entertainer, artist and composer, into the hands of Don D. Robey, an experienced, mature businessman of Houston, Texas, with long experience in the music field." He worked "night and day" for Robey and Evelyn Johnson, "his trusted managers and advisers," the suit charged, but "they gave him only spending money, furnished automobiles, transportation" and after his death "fraudently [sic] concealed their obligations to the lawful heirs of the deceased." Lois Jean Alexander, the widow of Johnny "Ace" Alexander, "was twenty years of age at his death, without funds, being the surviving parent of two small children."[48]

Robey was already dead by this time, and Buffalo Booking Agency had been dissolved in 1968, but Jean Alexander flatly refused to settle for an offer of $5,000. Finally, her lawyer advised her to accept the sum of $10,000 from Lion Publishing to keep the case from being removed to Houston, where the settlement might either be withdrawn or reduced. She took it in 1976 and shared it equally with her children, Glenn and Janet. The law firm received an additional $3,750.

Jean Alexander's husband waited nearly as long for justice of his own. The first serious consideration of Johnny Ace's contribution to rock 'n' roll came in 1970 when a reissue of *Memorial Album Number II* was reviewed enthusiastically in *Rolling Stone*. "This LP gives us not only an excellent portrait of the late Johnny Ace," Bob Kirsch, the reviewer, says, "but a perfect example of rock in its earliest stages." Ace was "enigmatic," and while he won "virtually every blues award available, his voice was much smoother and his delivery more sedate than that which we commonly associate with 'soul' music." Kirsch marveled at the control of the singer and the backup band, which reminded him of music released by the Platters and the Clovers. "It's almost a compromise music," he observed, "not black enough, yet not white enough. The answer may be that these artists were in a transitional stage, for it was the 'smooth' blacks who first appeared on the white charts." Ten of the twelve songs on the album are the "heart ballads" that Ace was famous for, in Kirsch's words, songs "on the 'Dreamy Side' of the Oldies But Goodies series." Even so, "Ace is always the blues. He's always the underdog, always begging, never dominating."

The reviewer was convinced that Ace was a major figure in the history of rock 'n' roll. "It's ridiculous to ask whether Johnny Ace was a great influence or was greatly influenced," Kirsch says. "The answer is both. One thing for sure; he was a master of early rock." Even the "certain degree of masochism" running throughout the album is characteristic of vintage rock, Kirsch says; "Ace is always on the bottom, ready for more." Furthermore, as an artist bridging rhythm and blues and rock 'n' roll he alone seems "caught in transition," since Clyde McPhatter and Sam Cooke, who "sang in the same manner," and Fats Domino, who used "similar backup," all "lived to move into the white market":

> We are left with Ace in transition, which is where he stopped. His kind of music is rarely heard these days. Our rock revival (Lewis, Haley, etc.) is actually a reactivation of rock's second wave. Johnny was the first.
>
> Everything here is typical; everything but Johnny Ace. And the album is a masterpiece for what it is: a first step in the evolution of rock.[49]

Kirsch's observation that Ace's style belonged more properly to rock 'n' roll's first wave is prescient. Ace was "more sedate" than traditional blues singers, he says, and his music was "almost a compromise" between black and white. Johnny Otis has a special sensitivity to this kind of compromise. Otis has respect for all styles of African American music, including "the raw Mississippi blues singers." "I love that too," he says. "Don't misunderstand."

But he has a special regard for "rhythm & blues people like Johnny Ace," who were "different."

Performers like Johnny Ace "were not blues," Otis explains, "they were *rhythm and blues.*" As club acts they were more sophisticated with "a little more musicality." These were the performers who were "really ignored and almost put down by the white writers." According to Otis, the treatment of artists like Ace indicates a form of "white arrogance," because it suggests that "black people are not the best judge of what was the best art to come out of the community, but the white writers are." Johnny's performances represent African American art, Otis says, "and to a great degree you have to take your cue from the people of the community. They know better than you what they like and what is black artistry." Johnny Ace was just "too smooth for the white critics and the white writers for a long time."[50]

For Evelyn Johnson, too, "smooth sailing" characterized Ace's style. "He was a natural and yet all day long you could find boys who could outsing him," she says. "But they didn't have that certain something that he had."[51] Arnold Shaw agrees. "Ace did not have a distinctive voice," he says, "and his songs and recordings were so starkly simple they seemed crude. But he had warmth and a tugging sense of youthful yearning, qualities that later contributed to the success of Johnny Mathis . . . and Sam Cooke."[52] Charles Sawyer believes it was his "boyish charm that women found irresistible" and maintains that "musicians who knew him still compare him with Nat 'King' Cole and Lou Rawls." Ace, he says, "was among the very first R&B artists to show a potential for 'crossover.'"[53]

Johnny Ace was also irresistible to a generation of future rock musicians still in high school in the late 1950s. "I just carry that other time around with me," Bob Dylan once admitted. "The music of the late Fifties . . . when music was at that root level—that for me is meaningful music. The singers and musicians I grew up with transcend nostalgia—Buddy Holly and Johnny Ace are just as valid to me today as then."[54]

Ace of
Hearts

By 1979, Johnny Ace was so forgotten a figure in the world of music that Sheldon Harris failed to include him in his giant, 775-page biographical dictionary of blues singers called *Blues Who's Who.* Though Harris references the "Johnny Ace Revue" in both the Bobby Bland and Junior Parker entries, and mentions Ace in connection with the Beale Streeters in the B.B. King entry, it is lamentable that Johnny Ace—the headline performer whom Buffalo Booking would agree to send club owners only after they had purchased shows featuring Bland, Parker, and King—was now seen as a marginal figure of negligible influence.[1]

Time would be kinder to Elvis Presley, considered by Leonard Bernstein to be "the greatest cultural force in the twentieth century."[2] By the late 1970s Elvis was the "American king," who had, after Mickey Mouse, the "second most commonly reproduced image in the world."[3] In the three years following his death in 1977, *dead* Elvis earned an estimated $20,000,000. He was everywhere, still promoted as "The World's Greatest Entertainer," setting personal records for big money years for his manager and estate without the nuisance of large operating expenses. "Nothing has changed," Col. Tom Parker had told one of the Memphis Mafia after his death. "This won't change anything."[4]

Indeed, the national obsession with Elvis persisted into the 1980s and spiraled out of control. Albert Goldman's 1981 biography, called simply *Elvis*, generated more than $2 million in subsidiary rights before its publication.[5] In 1982, Priscilla Presley took over management of Elvis's personal home, Graceland, and turned it into a tourist mecca and money machine that attracted, after the White House, the most visitors to any public home in America—earning the $500,000 preparation costs back in just thirty-eight days.[6] "No one," Greil Marcus observes in *Dead Elvis*, "could have predicted the ubiquity, the playfulness, the perversity, the terror, and the fun of this, of Elvis Presley's second life."[7] Johnny Ace, on the other hand, may have had a "second life" in the 1980s, but it clearly lacked the fan base and the profit sharing for his estate: he became a romantic figure for the new breed of rock writers who invariably projected, in the worst kind of presentism, their own post-Watergate conspiracy theories on his death.

In *Rock of Ages*, a history of rock 'n' roll from its beginnings to the present day, Ed Ward suggested that the new music "may have begun sometime during the night that changed 1954 to 1955, when Don Robey got a phone call from the great New Year's Eve extravaganza at Houston City Auditorium." Ward was almost a week off on his date, of course, but his point that Ace's death changed the musical culture was well taken, and he observed that "hysteria broke out, especially among the women. In the months to come, a cult would develop, an eerie, almost pathological devotion to the memory of the late singer. These teenagers almost celebrated death."

About Don Robey's professionalism and business astuteness, however, Ward seems to have known little. He reports "rumors" that Ace "was riding high and would never have committed suicide, or even taken such a risk," since "he had gone off, cocky, and signed a contract with another record company." Robey, he says, "was known to be less than meticulous when it came to contracts, and more than likely, Ace's would have been easy to break." The death itself, according to the author, was steeped in mystery:

> There was one particularly appalling story that had a hired assassin squeezing in through the bathroom window in the backstage area, walking out of the bathroom toward a group of people playing cards—a group

that included Willie Mae Thornton and Johnny Ace—grabbing Ace from behind, sticking a gun in his mouth, firing it, and wrapping the corpse's fingers around it, confident that although the other card players recognized him, they knew better than to squeal and that the irregular death of a black man would hardly warrant notice by Houston police.[8]

Other credible authorities implied conspiracies as well. Colin Escott, in "Johnny Ace: The First Rock 'n' Roll Casualty," positioned the singer as "bridging the gap between authentic black music and a white audience weaned on Make Believe Ballroom" and likened his death to that of Bessie Smith's, "clouded by intimations." Ace thought the gun he was playing with that night was not loaded, Escott insisted: "Either Ace had forgotten that he had loaded the gun, or he pulled the trigger by mistake. The third—and most sinister—explanation is that someone had loaded the gun during the show. And that is the root of the conspiracy theories that have sprouted up since his death."[9] Even Nick Tosches, who included Johnny Ace as one of his *Unsung Heroes of Rock 'n' Roll* ("Number One with a Bullet"), could not resist conspiracy. Noting that American popular culture "has always loved the self-killed," Tosches called Ace's Russian roulette death only the "accepted story." "There is another story," he said, "but lawyers will not let it be printed here, since it implicates living people who have lawyers of their own."[10]

Among the many voices advancing revisions or suggesting conspiracies in Ace's life and career, the nadir was reached by Robert Duncan. Duncan was able to achieve an even lower depth of falsification by adopting the no-one-really-knows-what-happened-that-night-but-maybe-it-went-something-like-this style of writing, where the "historian" invents outrageous dialogue for the events backstage at Houston's City Auditorium. In "Johnny Ace: The Games People Play," a chapter in his *Only the Good Die Young*, the backstage men's bathroom door flies open and half of Johnny Ace's band stumbles out "enveloped in a cloud of marijuana smoke." Spinning the chamber of his gun and pointing it at his temple, Ace calls out "through the haze" to his band: "Say! What do you got says I can?" "Shee-it," says Slugger, the bass player, who throws down a "Ben Franklin." (According to Duncan the band had won a bet like this on another occasion, when Ace chickened out. "I oughta just take your damn money for you being such a dumb buncha niggers thinkin' I'd do somethin' so stupid to a sweet young thing like me," Ace is reported to have said that night in "some raggedy-ass Dixie town.")

This time around Slugger says, "I'll take your hundred bucks. C'mon, Johnny Ace, let's play." When the gun goes off, everyone hits the floor except Slugger, who stands "frozen beside a card table with a piece of Johnny Ace's brain on his hand." All of this happens on Christmas Eve, Duncan says. "It makes a great story."[11]

In addition, Ace's musical career was distorted during the 1980s by extensive revisionism aimed clearly at the huge R&B record collectors market. He was a "tragic figure, plagued all his life by mishappenings," Dean Tudor wrote, who "finally did himself in by Russian roulette. The seriousness of his endeavors coupled with his personal failings, though, produced superb music from the early fifties." Ace was a "cult figure," whose "ballad style determined the development of soul and of reggae music."[12] In 1986 Colin Escott told readers of *Goldmine* that back in 1972 he and Martin Hawkins, while cataloging tapes recorded at Sun Studio in Memphis, had discovered two songs "probably recorded by Johnny Ace."

These songs ("Remember I Love You" and "I Cried [Last Night]") were in an unmarked box of tape that "disappeared" over the next ten years, he explained, before they could be given another listen for inclusion in the *Sun Blues Box*.[13] One of these songs, however, emerged in 1989 as "the last unreleased Johnny Ace title" in the Various Artists album *The Original Memphis Blues Brothers*. Ray Topping, who wrote the jacket notes, claimed to have found the master for "I Cried" by Johnny Ace. The song was on a small reel of tape, he said, stripped away of all the other masters and stored in an unmarked tape box "hidden away in a dusty corner" at the Modern Records tape archives. Topping provided no evidence at all that the vocalist of "I Cried" is Johnny Ace, and, indeed, no one familiar with Ace's voice could ever make so preposterous a claim. Worse, the album graphics created nonexistent documents to suggest that the annotator had done his research, among them a concocted telegram ("YOUR SON JOHNNY SHOT AND KILLED HIMSELF TONIGHT") from Evelyn Johnson to Mrs. Leslie Alexander, dated 12:43 A.M. on 25 December—reporting Ace's death *almost twenty-two hours before it happened*.[14]

Fraudulent documents are particularly despised by those whose names appear on them. Evelyn Johnson ran Don Robey's Bronze Peacock nightclub and helped him launch Peacock Records. She learned how to copyright songs, to put together tours, and to keep the business records of the hundreds of artists signed to Robey's labels. It was her Buffalo Booking

Agency that saw to it that all Robey's artists supported their own record sales by playing one-nighters she arranged, and if Johnny Ace ever had a personal manager, it was she. Evelyn Johnson was on the scene before Ace's contract was purchased from David James Mattis, and she was on the scene not only after Ace's death but after Robey's as well. Yet for all she knew then and all she knows now, almost forty years after Ace's death, when she was informed of the rumor that the singer had been murdered, she had to admit, "Now that one I have never heard." And of all the speculation and innuendo connected with Ace's death, the phony telegram enrages her the most. "I sent a telegram to tell his mother on a *telegram* that he had shot himself to death?" she asked, dumbfounded. "Like they don't have telephones? That's the most ridiculous thing! To me, that's an insult! It's degrading!"[15]

St. Clair Alexander, performing as "St. Clair Ace," tried as late as 1987 to sing Johnny's songs professionally. He sang in Chicago on Christmas Eve (he will "pay heartfelt homage to his older brother in four sets beginning at 9 tonight at Bob's Place," reported the *Sun-Times*)[16] and two months later in Memphis at Cadillac Bob's Showroom, where the show was called "Johnny Ace Lives" and connected to a celebration of Black History Month. "'ST. CLAIR ACE,'" the official poster promised, "Will Revive The Buried History of his Brother, The First R&B Cross-Over Artist." But the trouble with trying to sing like Johnny, St. Clair says, was that it was impossible to replicate his timing: "It was sort of like off-beat, you know. If you listen to his [records], where he should come in, he don't come in. He had an off-beat singing style in all his songs. That's what made him so unique. His words and things—when you think he should come in—he don't come in there. He comes in a little later."

Perhaps it was the slight delay in Ace's delivery, the extent to which he stayed a step behind the pulse of the music, that served to intensify the sadness and vulnerability communicated by his voice. "He was always singing sad lines," St. Clair says. "And he made a delay when he came in, and he kept people off balance. But he always sang it in a sad way." St. Clair is convinced that Johnny "knew what he was doing."[17]

Ace also knew what he was doing at the piano, but his ability there was more limited. Paul Monday, a member of the Ace road band known to be an excellent pianist, played piano when Willie Mae Thornton was on stage, and though Ace preferred to perform his set while playing his own piano, Monday may have played at Ace recording sessions when the material involved difficult chord changes or progressions. But according to Milton Hopkins, the band's guitarist, Johnny Ace did the piano work on all the blues numbers and on the "heart ballads" that made him famous:

> Ace was the type piano player who played his things. He couldn't go outside of his material. There was a certain style of piano that he played. He played on most of his sessions, but you could get over his head with chord changes and stuff like that. You hit most of the I–vi–ii–V stuff— that was him playing. But when you started playing up-beat chord changes and moving things around orchestra-wise, he wasn't into that, not at all. But he played blues piano and barrel-house piano.[18]

Ace's vocal style may have been unique and distinctive and his piano style competent if limited, but his music business experience as a black songwriter/performer was certainly prototypical. "It is indisputable that African Americans were exploited by the race record business in the years preceding World War II," historians Thomas Morgan and William Barlow contend. "They were paid lower wages than their white counterparts, they were cheated out of their copyright royalties, and they were forced to water down their music."[19] The same exploitation existed, of course, in the postwar period. As Nelson George points out, "the record-company owners knew better than to let on that things like song publishing or record royalties could produce long-term earnings. At first some owners didn't know it themselves."[20]

It was not just Don Robey who kept such important business matters secret. At Roulette Records in New York, Morris Levy is said to have told performers who came looking for royalty checks, "Royalty? You want royalty, go to England!"[21] Ben E. King, lead singer for the Drifters during the late 1950s, told Marc Eliot that he gave away half of everything he wrote ("There Goes My Baby," "Save the Last Dance for Me," "This Magic Moment") because he didn't know anything about publishing and just wanted to sing. "The only thing I have to say about Ahmet [Ertegun, founder of Atlantic Records] is that he saw me walking into a situation with the Drifters and never warned me about things like publishing, or how to look out for the sharks."[22]

White men were not the exclusive exploiters of black talent. Eliot reports that Stevie Wonder's publishing deal with Berry Gordy until 1971 was "down from the standard 50-50 split to 2 percent for Wonder, 98 percent for Motown."[23] Nelson George compares the relationship between the artists and record owners "as complicated as any love affair between a couple of different color and class":

> The artists, who could be characterized as naive country types or smart-ass city kids, saw in these embryonic record-makers a way to escape the "line syndrome" that confined black dreams: assembly line, picket line or unemployment line. There was no question in their minds that making records was the ticket to red Cadillacs, long, tall ladies (or lean, cool gents), and diamond pinky rings—the symbols of the ghetto hustler.
>
> Blacks who knew better were rarely involved in show business and certainly with nothing as rough and uncultivated as the bluesy shouters, street-corner singers, and chugging rhythm sections of R&B.[24]

Though Milton Hopkins saw dozens of people move in and out of Don Robey's Duke and Peacock Records operation who "didn't have any inkling about what was going on," Robey certainly did not invent the industry practices that were so exploitative. Ritchie Cordell, who wrote "It's Only Love" for Tommy James and the Shondells learned quickly what was expected of hit songwriters. "Morris [Levy]," he said, "gave me back the demo [record] bent in half and told me if his name wasn't on it, the song didn't come out."[25] "So far as the buying of the songs," Evelyn Johnson says, "all of the people on our side [R&B] of the business were doing it, but by the same token the big boys were doing it too. They were buying whole songs. This was just normal business."[26] Indeed it was. "The presence of [Elvis] Presley's name on songs like 'Don't Be Cruel' simply indicated business-as-usual in the music-publishing business," Gary Giddins says. "One remembers Irving Mills sharing the credit for Duke Ellington songs, Ed Kirkeby taking credit from Fats Waller, and Benny Goodman getting credit on several tunes he cheerfully admits he did not write."[27]

Charles Hamm finds that writers and composers of American popular music were deliberately giving up potential royalties even before the Civil War. In 1857, Stephen Foster, who seemed always in need of cash, sold all future rights to thirty-six of his most popular songs to his publisher for less than $2,000.[28] A few years later, in 1863, composer Walter Kittredge is known to have given the head of the Hutchinson Singing Family a share of "Tenting Tonight on the Old Camp Ground" in exchange for singing the song at concerts.[29] In Houston almost one hundred years later, things had changed little. "So-called songwriters," as Evelyn Johnson calls the people who "wrote poems and rhymes," were always hanging around the office, always on the scene: "Joe Medwick would come and sit in the waiting room, and he might write five. And then he would go in and sell them to [Robey] for maybe 5 dollars a piece. Then [Robey] had people like Joe Scott and different musicians to write scores, and they were either paid scale for the job or they were salaried people."[30] Galen Gart describes Medwick as a "broker" for other songwriters as well. He would accumulate song ideas, pitch them to Robey, and pay out a portion of the fee he received for acceptable tunes. Or, Gart says, he would work in the studio with a piano player on song ideas, humming melodies that would eventually get turned into whole songs. "For each song that he liked, Robey would pay Medwick $100, who turned over $25 to [the piano player]."[31]

"Don't you write nothin' bad about Don Robey," Joe Medwick told the *Houston Chronicle* in 1990. "If you came to him meaning business, he'd treat you like business. If you came to him wanting $30, he'd treat you like a $30 person. He got a bad name, but he was a man with a soft heart." Even so, Medwick acknowledges he would be "a rich man today" if he hadn't sold songs outright to Robey. "We didn't know no better," he explains.[32] It was Robey's "practice," Peter Guralnick says, to buy songs for a fee and put his own name on them.[33] Bobby Bland told him that a lot of writers came through Robey's office. "They always got what they asked for," Bland explained. "It's not [Robey's] fault that they didn't have time enough to wait."[34]

Of course, none of what Evelyn Johnson calls "this business of the songs" had anything to do with waiting; it had to do with power. Robey saw early in the game that song ownership brought rewards and that he was in a position to mandate ownership, or co-ownership, in any title he recorded. Despite the fact that he could not play an instrument (he could "only play the radio" Evelyn Johnson says), sing (he had a "tin ear"), read music or write it ("Are you kidding?"), at the end of twenty-five years Robey had writer credit on 1,200 songs, according to BMI "more songs than Holland-Dozier-Holland and Harlan Howard put together."[35] Robey's songwriter credit ranged from the sacred "Our Father" and "Love of Jesus" to the secular "Pledging My Love" and "Baby, What's Your Pants Doing Wet?"

Most of the copyrights were written under the pseudonym "Deadric Malone" (Robey's middle name plus the surname of his second wife) because early on he had provoked criticism by using his real name. As Robey explained to *Record World*, writers had said, "'Well, he wants to be all of it.

He wants to manufacture the records, maintain the artists and write the songs.' So I thought it was hurting a little bit and I stopped it; I wouldn't use Robey anymore."[36] Gatemouth Brown calls Deadric Malone the "fictitious name" Robey used to claim "authorship to things he didn't write. It was his way to get the royalties," he says.[37]

Though Alan Govenar suggests in *Meeting the Blues* that Robey's racial background may have included "Jewish ancestry,"[38] it is likely that he merely heard Robey referred to in the African American community as a "black Jew"—an epithet embodying what Lawrence Levine calls the "ambivalence" of black attitudes toward Jews and other minority groups. Historically, blacks held simultaneous "philo-Semitic and anti-Semitic" convictions, Levine says, and a "striking characteristic of black humor concerning Jews was how often it played on not merely the Jewish stereotypes but the Negro stereotypes as well."[39] One connotation of Robey as a black Jew had to do with his material success as a businessman, another for his ability as a manager or supervisor. "That goes back even farther other than the record business," Evelyn Johnson says, "because Jewish people are supposed to be people who make money and know how to manipulate folk in order to do so, and that's why there's that old cliché in the black race. There's always been, 'Oh, he's a black Jew.' It's really a black term."[40]

Given the standards and practices of the music business in the postwar era, the true extent of Ace's contribution as a songwriter will forever remain a mystery. He was, however, known both in Memphis and Houston to have been a prolific songwriter. David Mattis, of course, had written songs with him. "I think he composed with his piano," he says. "I mean it just came out of his soul somewhere. But he couldn't [notate] any music, and neither could I. But the main thing is, I'd write all the lyrics."[41] According to Jean Alexander, his widow, Ace composed music all the time. "Sometimes you would see him writing," she says. "I guess it was just coming in his head."[42] "Johnny did writing, yeah," says Milton Hopkins. "I don't know if he got credit for any of it, but you know how that was. That's where the money was. And wherever the money was, that's where Robey was."[43] Gatemouth Brown suffered a similar fate as a songwriter, though he will not admit that he deliberately gave up his rights in order to record. "No one has to do anything," he says, "but what can happen [is this]: the man was a businessman and we're young kids and this is a flying life for us, so therefore what do we know about writer royalties? Let's say [Robey] was a great businessman, okay?"[44]

In regard to song ownership, Robey's first inclination seems to have been to take all of the songwriting credit if he could get it, or half of the credit if he could not. Occasionally, he had to give up all claims to writer credit, but even then it was his practice to keep secret the fact that songs earned perpetual royalties for their writers. Robey let Dave Mattis and Johnny Ace share songwriting credit for "My Song" and "The Clock," for example, but he never filed the necessary BMI paperwork nor indicated to them that in order to receive performance rights money for the songs they had to register as affiliated writers with BMI. Mattis accidentally found out about BMI affiliation in 1968, when a friend told him how much radio airplay Aretha Franklin's remake of "My Song" was getting. "Hey, Dave," he said, "looks like you're really going to get rich."[45] At that point, sixteen years after Mattis had written the lyrics and Johnny Ace had composed the melody for a song that had been a number one R&B hit, Mattis registered himself as a songwriter with BMI and began receiving royalties for his half of the writing effort. Johnny Ace, who had been dead for almost fourteen years by this time, obviously never did find out how that side of the business worked.

In 1990, BMI records revealed that Johnny Ace's performance rights money for "My Song," "The Clock," and other copyrights was being sent to England, since the author was believed to be affiliated with the United Kingdom's Performing Rights Society. Ace's widow and heir to his musical properties had been receiving mechanical rights money for Ace's compositions from MCA Records, but she first heard of the existence of BMI from the author of this book. In June 1992 the attorneys for BMI agreed to change their records and affiliate posthumously the singer/songwriter as a BMI writer as soon as the necessary legal documents could be processed. The registration was finalized in March 1996 for "John Alexander, also known as Johnny Ace."

The stage name "Johnny Ace," St. Clair Alexander always believed, was an unlucky one for his brother. An "ace," he insists, represented in his time and place "a dead man's card, a dead man's hand in poker." But for other gamblers and jazz musicians of the period, an "ace" was also a dollar bill ("Can you lend me an ace?") and in the Negro community a person's best buddy or "bosom friend." To be "aced in" meant "to place yourself or a friend in the good graces of someone," usually helping someone get a job, for example, and "less frequently, an introduction to a woman."[46] To "be aces" meant to be the absolute best, and "to stand ace high" was a measure of a person's high esteem.[47]

"Ace-high" is a poker term used in two ways: it denotes a weak hand (no pairs but an ace as the high card) or a strong one (a ten, jack, queen, king, and ace), but more than one hundred years ago "ace-high" came to mean "successful, respected." An "ace" could also be an "agreeable, generous, kind male person," or a person "of proved and outstanding skill" in any field. In World War I it was a pilot who had shot down at least five enemy planes. When John Alexander told David James Mattis in 1952, "Well, just call me Ace, but don't let my momma know, because I'm the ace in the hole," he was employing a meaning from stud poker, representing the important card (or plan or argument) held in reserve "until needed to turn failure into success."

The term "ace of spades" has several levels of meaning. While it can denote excellence, proficiency, diligence, and skill, it also carries more offensive connotations: a very dark Negro could be "black as the ace of spades." Less common, and obscene, is the use of "ace of spades" to refer to the female pudendum ("the shape and color of the pubic hair"). In this regard an "ace lane" is a husband or male lover, figuratively "one who has the right to use the 'road' to a woman's ace of spades."[48]

At the time John Alexander became Johnny Ace, his local reputation, says Charles Sawyer, was that of "an affable, happy-go-lucky kid" who was "rowdy with boys and shy with girls, despite his evident sex appeal."[49] For friends in the male world he inhabited, Johnny's jokes and horseplay made him the proverbial hail-fellow-well-met, everybody's ace. The men who hung out on the corner of Mississippi and Walker knew him to be generous, always good for an ace. Johnny was, by all accounts, simply an ace of a fellow, whose ace in the hole proved to be his own latent talent for singing sentimental ballads. His proficiency and skill made him aces at this—he stood ace-high and was recognized as the ace of spades in this regard. But when he died from the dead man's hand he held, scores of women mourned their ace lane, and teenage girls and adult women who never met him wept openly for the one man in the field of rhythm and blues who most symbolized love and romance.

It was, however, the ace of a different suit that epitomized his career as the postwar rhythm and blues performer who crossed over to pop. Ace's "Pledging My Love" will forever be *the* transitional record between rhythm and blues and rock 'n' roll, and the singer/songwriter himself will always be associated with the card still featured prominently on the cover of his only LP: Johnny Ace was, after all, the ace of hearts.

Appendix A Interviews

Except where noted, the following were telephone interviews, conducted by the author. Locations indicate the places from which the interviewees spoke. All transcripts and notes are in the author's files.

Alexander, Lois Jean (Palmer). Memphis; 1 October 1991; personal interview
  (with Donna Salem) 10 June 1992; personal interview 27 September 1994.
Alexander, St. Clair. Memphis; personal interview 28 September 1994.
Badger, Rodney J. Falls Church, Va.; 12 October 1994.
Baird, Pat. New York; 25 July 1990; 10 December 1991.
Brown, Clarence "Gatemouth." Birmingham, Ala.; personal interview
  10 October 1990.
Cantor, Louis. Fort Wayne, Ind.; 15 July 1992.
Fields, Mattie. Buffalo, N.Y.; 5 February 1995.
Fults, Drayton M. "Doc." Houston; 31 July 1989.
Holford, Bill. Houston; personal interview 8 March 1991.
Hopkins, Milton. Houston; personal interview 8 March 1991.
Johnson, Evelyn. Houston; personal interview (with Donna Salem)
  6 October 1993; 9 November 1993; 19 November 1993; 16 December 1993;
  12 January 1994; 10 January 1995; 27 April 1995.
Mattis, David James. Wheeling, W.Va.; 3 November 1992.
Mitchell, Ernestine. Memphis; personal interview 18 October 1990.
Moody, Larry. Tuscaloosa, Ala.; 10 August 1989.
Otis, Johnny. Los Angeles; 7 November 1989.
Williams, Norma (Alexander). Memphis; 8 February 1991; personal interview
  (with Donna Salem) 9 June 1992; 15 September 1994; personal interview
  28 September 1994; 12 September 1995.
Withers, Ernest. Memphis; 23 February 1990; personal interview (with
  Donna Salem) 18 October 1990; 9 January 1997.

Appendix B Selected Discography

The annotated Johnny Ace section of this discography does not include sides in which Ace is merely the pianist in a backup group for Bobby Bland, Earl Forest, or any other featured performer. For the identification of musicians, citations rely heavily upon Leadbitter and Slaven; for locations on Bill Holford's ACA studio logbooks, see Gart and Ames, 205–23. I have also used relevant information from interviews with Bill Holford, Johnny Otis, Milton Hopkins, and David James Mattis where appropriate. For assistance with the musical analysis of Ace's Duke records I am indebted to my colleague Steve Sample, director of Jazz Ensembles and Professor of Music Emeritus, School of Music, the University of Alabama. For copyright registration number, status, and date I have used the appropriate *Catalog of Copyright Entries*, published annually in Washington, D.C., by the Library of Congress.

JOHNNY ACE

The Twenty-one Recorded Sides (Annotated)

1951, Memphis, Memphis YMCA. Johnny Ace, vocals and piano; Earl Forest, drums; Matt Murphy (?), guitar; James Walker (?), bass; Adolph "Billy" Duncan (?), sax; Onzie Horn (?), vibes.

1. (FL-133) "Midnight Hours Journey" (Flair 1015): A single side recorded with portable equipment by Jules and Joe Bihari at the Memphis YMCA before the Ace name was adopted. Smooth, cleanly arranged slow blues credited to "Josea." Not copyrighted. Released September 1953, after Ace was an established Duke Records star, as the "A" side of Flair 1015 (Earl Forest's "Trouble and Me" is the flip side). No chart action. For Ace record collectors, "Midnight Hours Journey" represents the most difficult single to acquire.

Spring 1952, Memphis, WDIA studios. Johnny Ace, vocals and piano; Earl Forest, drums; Adolph "Billy" Duncan, sax; unknown guitarist on "Follow the Rule."

2. (R-102-A) "My Song" (Duke 102): Recorded with the Beale Streeters by David James Mattis's Tri State Recording Co. An AABA ballad (I–vi–ii–V⁷) credited to "James" on the record label but copyrighted (unpublished) 11 July 1952 as a David James Mattis/John L. [*sic*] Alexander collaboration (Copyright Office catalog #EU280969). Released June 1952 by Tri State Recording Co. (first pressings specify Tri State Recording Co., Memphis, Tenn.). Subsequent pressings administered by Don D. Robey substitute, below the Duke logo, "PEACOCK RECORDS

AFFILIATE — Houston, Texas." Debuted on *Billboard*'s R&B charts 9 August 1952 — a number one song for nine weeks and the record that started Ace's career.

3. (R-102-B) "Follow the Rule" (Duke 102): Backup group is the Beale Streeters. A blues composition credited to "Ace." Not copyrighted. Released June 1952 as the "B" side of "My Song."

August or September 1952, Houston, Audio Company of America. Johnny Ace, vocals and piano (organ on "Cross My Heart"); Earl Forest, drums; George Joyner, bass; unknown tenor sax; unknown alto sax; unknown vibes player on "Cross My Heart" and "Burlie Cutie."

4. (ACA 2268) "Angel" (Duke 107): With the Beale Streeters. An AABA ballad with the plagal formula I–vi–IV–[iv]–I credited to David James Mattis and John Alexander, copyrighted (unpublished) 1 December 1952 (EU295783). Released December 1952 as the "B" side of "Cross My Heart." Robey insisted it was the second hit song of Duke 107, but it never appeared on the *Billboard* charts.

5. (ACA 2271) "Aces Wild" ["Ace's Wild"] (Duke 112): With the Beale Streeters. Instrumental blues credited to John Alexander. It features Ace's piano. Copyrighted by Lion Musical Pub. Co. (unpublished) as "Ace's Wild" 20 July 1953 (EU311271). Planned as the flip side of "Angel," it was actually released May 1953 as the "B" side of "The Clock."

6. (ACA 2285) "Cross My Heart" (Duke 107): With the Beale Streeters, featuring Ace playing a Hammond organ, which happened to be in the ACA studio for another project. An AABA ballad (I–vi–ii–V^7) credited to Don Deadric Robey and David James Mattis, copyrighted (unpublished) 25 September 1952 (EU289157). Released December 1952, debuting on *Billboard*'s R&B charts 31 January 1953 — Ace's second straight hit, peaking at number three.

7. (ACA 2288) "Burlie Cutie" (Duke 132): With the Beale Streeters but credited on the label to "Johnny Board and His Orchestra." An instrumental blues composed, according to the record label, by "John Alexander" but never copyrighted. Held for more than two years before being released October 1954 as the "B" side of "Never Let Me Go."

13 January 1953, Houston, Audio Company of America. Johnny Ace, vocals and piano; Earl Forest, drums; Fats Theus (?) or Bill Fort (?) sax; George Joyner, bass; unknown guitarist; Johnny Otis, percussion.

8. (ACA 2463) "The Clock" (Duke 112): Accompaniment wrongly credited on the label to the Beale Streeters. Only one song recorded at this session. An AABA ballad (I–I–V^7–I verse with IV–I–V of V–V bridge) with the remarkably slow tempo of 47

beats a minute. BMI lists David James Mattis and John Alexander as writers; copyrighted (unpublished) by Lion Musical Pub. Co. 4 September 1953 with only Mattis credited as writer (EU311272). Released May 1953, debuting on *Billboard*'s R&B charts 4 July 1953—Ace's third straight hit and a number one song for five weeks.

28 August 1953, Los Angeles, Radio Recorders. Johnny Ace, vocals and piano (organ on "Please Forgive Me"); Don Johnson, trumpet; George Washington, trombone; James Von Street, tenor sax; Fred Ford, baritone sax; Pete Lewis, guitar; Albert Winston, bass; Leard Bell, drums; Johnny Otis, vibes; Willie Mae Thornton, vocals on "Yes Baby."

9. (RR-109-11) "Please Forgive Me" (Duke 128): With the Johnny Otis Orchestra. An AABA ballad (I–V^7 of IV–[iv]–I–vi–ii–V^7) credited to Joseph August and Don Deadric Robey, copyrighted (unpublished) by Lion Pub. Co. 2 November 1953 (EU336479). Released April 1954, debuting on *Billboard*'s R&B charts 19 June 1954, peaking at number six. Ace's fifth consecutive hit.

10. (RR-110-1) "Saving My Love For You" (Duke 118): An arrangement featuring Otis on vibes. An AABA ballad (I–iii–IV–[iv]–I–vi–ii–V^7) credited to Sherman "Blues" Johnson on the label and copyrighted (unpublished) 15 October 1951 (EU253097) with words and music by Sherman Johnson as an employee for hire of Diamond Record Co., Inc. Additionally copyrighted (unpublished) by Lion Pub. Co. with words and music by Don Deadric Robey 2 November 1953 (EU336478). Released December 1953, debuting on *Billboard*'s R&B charts 26 December 1953, climbing to number two and representing Ace's fourth consecutive hit.

11. (RR-111-1) "Yes Baby" (Duke 118): An uptempo blues duet with Willie Mae "Big Mama" Thornton. Arrangement features tenor sax solo and guitar solo. Credited on the label to "J. Ace" but copyrighted (unpublished) by Lion Pub. Co. 2 November 1953 with words and music by Don Deadric Robey (EU336477). Released December 1953 as the "B" side of "Saving My Love for You." Robey claimed it was a hit single on its own. "Yes Baby" was the last song ever sung by Johnny Ace.

12. (ACA 3336; RR matrix unknown) "Still Love You So" (Duke 154): Not mastered until April 1956 at the Audio Company of America studio in Houston. ACA owner Bill Holford's logbooks indicate the song was "an outside tape." An AABA ballad (V^7 of IV–[iv]–I–vi–ii–V) credited to Sherman Johnson and copyrighted (unpublished) by Lion Pub. Co. 2 November 1953 (EU336476.) Released June 1956 with no chart action.

17 January 1954, Houston, Audio Company of America. Johnny Ace, vocals and piano; James Von Streeter, sax; Pete Lewis, guitar; Albert Winston, bass; Leard

Bell, drums; Johnny Otis, vibes; George Washington (?), trombone on "You've Been Gone So Long."

13. (ACA 2798) "Anymore" (Duke 144): Accompaniment wrongly credited on the label to the Johnny Board Orchestra. Arrangement features Otis's vibes and a tenor sax solo. An AABA ballad (I–vi–ii–V), credited on the record label to "D. Robey-Fats Washington" and copyrighted (unpublished) by Lion Pub. Co. twice—on 7 June 1954 with Robey as sole author (EU360289) and on 18 February 1955 as a collaboration between Don Deadric Robey and Ferdinand Washington (EU387067). Released June 1955, entering the *Billboard* R&B charts 6 August 1955 and reaching number eight (the only Ace hit released posthumously). Note: the original release of this side was backed with the Ace blues composition "How Can You Be So Mean?" Three-and-a-half years later, "Anymore" was remastered with a vocal track by the Jordanaires, becoming the "B" side of a remastered version of "Pledging My Love," and released December 1958 as Duke 136 (originally Duke 136 was "Pledging My Love" b/w "No Money").

14. (ACA 2799) "So Lonely" (Duke 148): Accompaniment wrongly credited on the label to the Johnny Board Orchestra. Ace's vocal is mournful and vulnerable—his Charles Brown side. A blues composition credited to "John Alexander" and copyrighted (unpublished) by Lion Pub. Co. 15 March 1954 (EU351078). Released January 1956 as the "B" side of "I'm Crazy, Baby."

15. (ACA 2800) "You've Been Gone (So Long)" (Duke 128): A tightly arranged shuffle blues. Composition credited to "Johnny Ace" on the label and copyrighted (unpublished) by Lion Pub. Co. 15 March 1954 with words and music by John Alexander (EU351079). Wrongly credited at BMI to "Johnny Acea." Released April 1954 as the "B" side of "Please Forgive Me."

16. (ACA 2801) "Pledging My Love" (Duke 136): Accompaniment wrongly credited on the label to the Johnny Board Orchestra—the vibe work in the arrangement clearly belongs to Johnny Otis. An AABA ballad (I–ii⁷–V⁷–ii⁷–V⁷–I), credited to "Washington-Robey" on the label and representing a complicated copyright history. The song was copyrighted twice (unpublished) by Lion Pub. Co. with Don Deadric Robey as sole author (15 March 1954, EU351083 and 26 January 1955, EU384205). On 27 January 1955 it was copyrighted (published) by "Wemar Music Corp. & Lion Musical Pub. Co." with words and music by Don D. Robey and F. Washington (Ferdinand "Fats" Washington, the author of "Anymore")—this for the purpose of securing pop cover versions (EP86776). On 9 February 1955 Lion Pub. Co. copyrighted the song (published) as a Robey/Washington composition for purposes of sheet music sales, crediting the arrangement to Stanley Applebaum (EP88950). Released December 1954, the side debuted on

Billboard's R&B charts 22 January 1955, becoming a number one record for ten weeks and winning *Billboard*'s R&B Triple Crown award (first in sales, radio airplay, and juke box play). It entered the white pop charts 19 February 1955 (highest position: number seventeen) and made the prestigious "Honor Roll of Hits" list a week later. A BMI Millionaire Song, logging over a million performances, *Billboard*'s Most Played R&B Record of 1955, and the first Duke or Peacock record to sell initially more 45 rpm units than 78s. Note: the original release of this side was backed with the Ace blues composition "No Money." Four years later it was remastered with a vocal track by the Jordanaires, recoupled with a remastered "Anymore," and released all over again as Duke 136.

22 July 1954, Houston, Audio Company of America. Johnny Ace, vocals and piano; Paul Monday, piano on "Never Let Me Go" and "I'm Crazy, Baby" (?); Johnny Board, tenor and alto sax; Milton Bradford, baritone and tenor sax; Joe Scott, trumpet; Milton Hopkins, guitar; Curtis Tillman, bass; C.C. Pinkston, drums and vibes.

17. (ACA 2934) "Never Let Me Go" (Duke 132): With the Johnny Board Band. Ace's vocal is soft and relaxed. An AABA ballad (I–vi–ii–V), but employing more extended contemporary harmonies: major 7ths, 9ths, and 13ths. Slow tempo of 56 beats a minute. Credited to Joe Scott as sole author and copyrighted (unpublished) 9 August 1954 by Lion Pub. Co. (EU367000). Released October 1954, debuting on *Billboard*'s R&B charts 23 October 1954 (highest position number nine on the juke box play chart). Ace's sixth straight hit but the most marginal.

18. (ACA 2935) "Don't You Know" (Duke 154): Backed by the Johnny Board Band. Big band shuffle blues, Tommy Dorsey style, featuring Ace's piano, complete with a gospel turnaround, and vocals as close to blues shouting as Ace ever gets. Composition credited to him and copyrighted (unpublished) by Lion Pub. Co. 9 August 1954 (EU367004). Released June 1956 as the last Ace record. No chart action.

19. (ACA 2936) "No Money" (Duke 136): Backed by the Johnny Board Band. Big band blues (Nick Tosches thinks this is Ace's best), featuring excellent tenor sax work. Composition credited to "John Alexander" and copyrighted (unpublished) by Lion Pub. Co. 9 August 1954 (EU367003). Wrongly credited at BMI to "James Alexander." Released December 1954 as the "B" side of "Pledging My Love."

20. (ACA 2937) "How Can You Be So Mean?" (Duke 144): Backed by the Johnny Board Band. Big band blues composition credited to "John Alexander" and copyrighted (unpublished) by Lion Pub. Co. 9 August 1954 (EU367002). Released June 1955 as the "B" side of "Anymore."

21. (ACA 2938) "I'm Crazy, Baby" (Duke 148): The last Ace side recorded in Houston at the last Ace session, backed by the Johnny Board Band. Ace is a big band crooner here, for the first time employing his lower register and angular, Sammy Davis Jr. phrasing. Showcases Ace's tinkling piano, which is high in the mix. The arrangement is in the style of Count Basie, the most musically sophisticated of any of Ace's sides. An AABA ballad in A♭ (most of Ace's music is in the key of C) with the following progression: A♭–A⁷–A♭–D⁷–D♭–D°–A♭/E♭–F⁷–B♭⁷–E♭⁷–A♭ with a I–vi–ii–V turnaround. Credited to Christopher Columbus Pinkston and copyrighted (unpublished) by Lion Pub. Co. 3 September 1954 (EU369673). Released January 1956. No chart action.

The Albums

Memorial Album: Johnny Ace. Duke EP 80, 1955. (Includes the following sides, listed by number above: 4, 9, 10, 16)

A Tribute to Johnny Ace. Duke EP 81, 1955. (Includes sides 2, 6, 8, 17)

Memorial Album for Johnny Ace. Duke LP-70, 1955. (Includes sides 2, 4, 6, 8, 9, 10, 16, 17)

Memorial Album for Johnny Ace (Number II). Duke DLP-71, 1957. (Includes sides 2, 6, 8, 10, 12, 13, 14, 16, 17, 18, 20, 21)

Memorial Album for Johnny Ace (Number II) for stereo juke boxes. Duke LP-71, 1962–65. (Includes sides 8, 6, 10, 14, 16, 17)

Memorial Album: Johnny Ace (Number II). MCA-27014, 1973. (Same as Duke DLP-71.) Reissued as MCAD-31183 in compact disc format.

OTHER ARTISTS

Ace, Buddy. "Back Home." Duke 155, 1956.

———. "Hold On." Duke 414, 1967.

———. "Nothing in the World Can Hurt Me." Duke 397, 1966.

———. "What Can I Do." Duke 155, 1956.

Ace, St. Clair. "Radiation Flu." Toma [number unknown], 1986.

Adams, Marie. "In Memory." Peacock 1649, 1955.

Armstrong, Louis. "Pledging My Love." Decca 29421, 1955.

August, Joseph "Google Eyes." "Oh What a Fool." Duke 117, 1953.

———. "Play the Game." Duke 117, 1953.

Baker, LaVern. "Tweedlee Dee." Atlantic 1047, 1955.

Ballard, Hank and the Midnighters. "Annie Had a Baby." Federal 12195, 1954.

———. "Sexy Ways." Federal 12185, 1954.

———. "Work With Me, Annie." Federal 12169, 1954.

Bland, Bobby "Blue." "Ain't Nothing You Can Do." Duke 375, 1964.

———. "Farther Up the Road." Duke 170, 1957.

Brewer, Teresa. "Pledging My Love." Coral 61362, 1955.

Brooks, Hadda. "My Song." Okeh 6910, 1952.

Brown, Charles. "Drifting Blues." Aladdin 112, 1945.

Brown, Clarence "Gatemouth." "Atomic Energy." Peacock 1500, 1949.

———. "Didn't Reach My Goal." Peacock 1500, 1949.

———. "Ditch Diggin' Daddy." Peacock 1501, 1949.

———. "Mary Is Fine." Peacock 1504, 1950.

———. "Mercy On Me." Peacock 1500 and 1501, 1949.

———. "My Time Is Expensive." Peacock 1504, 1950.

Brown, Ruth. "So Long." Atlantic 879, 1949.

Carr, Leroy. "How Long, How Long Blues." Vocalion 1191, 1928.

———. "In the Evening (When the Sun Goes Down)." Aladdin 45-3030, 1949.

Chords. "Sh-Boom." Cat 104, 1954.

Clovers. "Lovey Dovey." Atlantic 1022, 1954.

Coasters. "Yakety Yak." Atco 6116, 1958.

Clapton, Eric. "Willie and the Hand Jive." RSO 503, 1974.

Como, Perry. "Two Loves Have I." RCA Victor 2545, 1948.

Crewcuts. "Sh-Boom." Mercury 70404X45, 1954.

Diamonds. "Two Loves Have I." Atlantic 1003, 1953.

Dillard, Varetta. "Johnny Has Gone." Savoy 1153, 1955.

———. "I Miss You, Jimmy." Groove 167, 1956.

Dixon, Floyd. "Sad Journey Blues." Peacock 1544, 1950.

Domino, Fats. "Ain't That a Shame." Imperial 5348, 1955.

Drifters. "Honey Love." Atlantic 1029, 1954.

Five Blind Boys of Mississippi. "Jesus Is a Rock in a Weary Land." Peacock 1723, 1954.

———. "Our Father." Peacock 1550, 1950.

Five Wings. "Johnny Has Gone." King 4778, 1955

———. "Johnny's Still Singing." King 4778, 1955.

Forest, Earl. "Baby, Baby." Duke 103, 1952.

———. "Last Night's Dream." Duke 113, 1953.

———. "Rock the Bottle." Duke 103, 1952.

———. "Trouble and Me." Flair 1015, 1953.

Four Lads. "Pledging My Love." Columbia 40436, 1955.

Four Tunes. "I Understand Just How You Feel." Jubilee 5132, 1954.

Franklin, Aretha. "My Song." Atlantic 2574, 1968.

Fuller, Johnny. "Johnny Ace's Last Letter." Aladdin, 3278, 1955.

Gant, Cecil. "I Wonder." Gilt Edge 500, 1944.

——. "In the Evening (When the Sun Goes Down)." Gilt Edge 526, 1945–46.

Gibbs, Georgia. "Dance With Me Henry." Mercury 70572, 1955.

——. "Tweedlee Dee." Mercury 70517, 1955.

Gordon, Rosco. "Gotta Find My Baby." RPM 360, 1952.

——. "Hey, Fat Girl." Duke R-101, 1952.

——. "No More Doggin'." RPM 350, 1952.

——. "Tell Daddy." Duke R-101, 1952.

Gospel Travelers. "God's Chariot." Duke G-1, 1952.

Haley, Bill, & the Comets. "Rock Around the Clock." Decca 29124, 1955.

——. "Shake, Rattle & Roll." Decca 29204, 1954.

Head, Roy. "Treat Her Right." Back Beat 546, 1965.

James, Etta. "Wallflower" ("Roll with Me Henry"). Modern 947, 1955.

James, Tommy, and the Shondells. "It's Only Love." Roulette 4710, 1966.

Jordan, Louis. "Ain't Nobody Here But Us Chickens." Decca 23741, 1946.

——. "Barnyard Boogie." Decca 24300, 1948.

——. "Beans and Cornbread." Decca 24673, 1949.

——. "G.I. Jive." Decca 8659, 1944.

——. "I'm Gonna Leave You at the Outskirts of Town." Decca 8638, 1942.

——. "Is You Is Or Is You Ain't (My Baby)." Decca 8659, 1944.

——. "Ration Blues." Decca 8654, 1943.

——. "Saturday Night Fish Fry." Decca 24725, 1949.

King, B. B. "Gotta Find My Baby." RPM 360, 1952.

——. "My Own Fault Darlin'." RPM 355, 1952.

——. "That Ain't the Way to Do It." RPM 339, 1952.

——. "Three O'Clock Blues." RPM 339, 1952.

——. "The Thrill Is Gone." Blues Way 61032, 1970.

King, Ben E. "Stand By Me." Atco 6194, 1961.

Knight, Evelyn. "A Little Bird Told Me." Decca 24514, 1948.

Laine, Frankie. "Two Loves Have I." Mercury 5064, 1947.

Lee, Peggy. "Is That All There Is." Capitol 2602, 1969.

McGuire Sisters. "Goodnight, Sweetheart, Goodnight." Coral, 9-61187, 1954.

Mighty Dukes. "No Other Love." Duke 104, 1952.

——. "Why Can't I Have You." Duke 104, 1952.

Moore, Johnny, and the Three Blazers, vocal credit: Frankie Erwin. "Johnny Ace's Last Letter." Hollywood 1031, 1955.

————, vocal credit: Linda Hayes. "Why, Johnny, Why." Hollywood 1031, 1955.

Original Memphis Blues Brothers. Ace CHAD 265, 1989.

Orioles. "Crying in the Chapel." Jubilee 5122, 1953.

Otis, Johnny. "Rock Me Baby." Peacock 1625, 1953.

————. "Rockin' Blues." Savoy 766, 1950.

————. "Willie and the Hand Jive." Capitol 3966, 1958.

Parker, Little Junior. "Next Time You See Me." Duke 164, 1957.

Penguins. "Earth Angel." Dootone 348, 1954.

Presley, Elvis. "Baby Let's Play House." Sun 217, 1955.

————. "Don't Be Cruel." RCA 47-6604, 1956.

————. "Hound Dog." RCA 47-6604, 1956.

————. "Jailhouse Rock." RCA 47-7035.

————. "Loving You." RCA 47-7000.

————. "Mystery Train." Sun 223, 1955.

————. "Pledging My Love." RCA PB-10998, 1977.

————. "That's All Right Mama." Sun 209, 1954.

————. "Way Down." RCA PB-10998, 1977.

Ray, Johnnie. "Cry." Okeh 6840, 1951.

————. "The Little White Cloud That Cried." Okeh 6840, 1951.

Rovers. "Salute to Johnny Ace." Music City [number unknown], 1955.

Shake, Rattle & Roll: Rock 'n' Roll in the 1950s. New World Records NW 249, 1978.

Simon, Paul. "The Late Great Johnny Ace." *Hearts and Bones,* WBR CD 2-23942, 1983.

Spaniels. "Goodnight, Sweetheart, Goodnight." Vee Jay 107, 1954.

Thornton, Willie Mae "Big Mama." "Everytime I Think of You." Peacock 1603, 1952.

————. "Hound Dog." Peacock 1612, 1953.

————. "I Smell a Rat." Peacock 1632, 1954.

————. "I'm All Fed Up." Peacock 1567, 1951.

————. "Mischievous Boogie." Peacock 1603, 1952.

————. "Night Mare." Peacock 1612, 1953.

————. "Partnership Blues." Peacock 1567, 1951.

————. "Rock A Bye Baby." Peacock 1612, 1953.

Turner, Joe. "Shake, Rattle & Roll." Atlantic 1026, 1954.

Washington, Dinah. "My Song." Mercury 8294, 1952.

Watson, Paula. "A Little Bird Told Me." Supreme 1507, 1948.

Williams, Billy, Quartet. "Sh-Boom." Coral 61212, 1954.

Notes

Prologue

1. Guralnick, *Last Train to Memphis*, 46.
2. George, *Death of Rhythm & Blues*, 62.
3. Ernest Withers, 23 February 1990 interview.
4. Elvis had already cut two two-sided vanity acetates at Memphis Recording Service, a business also owned by Sam Phillips at 706 Union Avenue, but this was his first experience in a professional recording studio.
5. Guralnick, *Last Train to Memphis*, 101.

Chapter 1: Memphis

1. Norma (Alexander) Williams, sister of Johnny Ace, 15 September 1994 interview.
2. Capers, 149.
3. Sigafoos, 45–46.
4. Capers, 188.
5. Ibid.
6. Ibid., 198–99.
7. Booth, 87.
8. Capers, 198.
9. Lee, *Beale Street: Where the Blues Began*, 23–24. In 1939, Yale Ph.D. Gerald M. Capers Jr. used Lee's *Beale Street* in writing his own book on Memphis. Capers reveals his attitude on race when he says of Lee's work, "Definitely spectacular, but written by a Memphis Negro" (276).
10. Barlow, 50.
11. Sigafoos, 50.
12. Giddings, 17–20.
13. Sigafoos, 97–98.
14. Ibid., 137.
15. Barlow, 204.
16. McKee and Chisenhall, 52.
17. Handy, 97.
18. Norma Williams, 15 September 1994 interview.
19. Sigafoos, 104.
20. Norma Williams, 15 September 1994 interview.

21. Ibid.

22. St. Clair Alexander, brother of Johnny Ace, 28 September 1994 interview. Information and quotations attributed to St. Clair Alexander are from this interview.

23. Lois Jean (Palmer) Alexander, widow of Johnny Ace, 27 September 1994 interview.

24. Norma Williams, 28 September 1994 interview.

25. Sigafoos, 182.

26. Ernest Withers, 23 February 1990 interview. For additional information on Withers's career see Salem, "Ernest C. Withers."

27. Norma Williams, 15 September 1994 interview.

28. Ernest Withers, 18 October 1990 interview. According to Withers, neither B.B. King nor Bobby "Blue" Bland could read or write at the beginning of their careers. When King first went on the road he took an elementary teacher named Wilson with him. "I don't know who taught Bobby Bland," Withers says, "but [he] had to learn to read and had to do it quick, because there was a great big void that had to be filled when Ace died."

29. Norma Williams, 9 June 1992 interview.

30. Cantor, 12. For additional information on Nat D. Williams see McKee and Chisenhall.

31. Norma Williams, 9 June 1992 interview.

32. Norma Williams, 28 September 1994 interview.

33. Rodney J. Badger, 12 October 1994 interview.

34. Virtually all encyclopedias and dictionaries make John Alexander a WW II vet, including Hitchcock and Sadie (*New Grove Dictionary of American Music*) and Piccarella, Pareles, and Romanowski (*Rolling Stone Encyclopedia of Rock & Roll*).

35. St. Clair Alexander, 28 September 1994 interview.

36. Ibid.

37. Westbrooks Jr., 2.

38. Cantor, 70.

39. Williams, 21.

40. Lois Jean Alexander, 10 June 1992 interview.

41. No one has ever suggested that the Ace Theater may have been the inspiration for Johnny's stage name (the founder of Duke Records is supposed to have given him his name), but it is certainly possible.

42. Lois Jean Alexander, 27 September 1994 interview.

43. Norma Williams, 28 September 1994 interview.

44. Lois Jean Alexander, 27 September 1994 interview.

45. Lois Jean Alexander, 10 June 1992 interview.

46. Lois Jean Alexander, 27 September 1994 interview.

47. Norma Williams, 28 September 1994 interview.

48. Lois Jean Alexander, 10 June 1992 interview.

49. Ernest Withers, 23 February 1990 interview.

50. Quoted in Guralnick, *Sweet Soul Music*, 5.

51. Norma Williams, 9 June 1992 interview.

Chapter 2: Beale Street

1. Lee, *Beale Street*, 13–14.

2. Barlow, 205.

3. McKee and Chisenhall, 17.

4. Ibid., 15.

5. Lee, *Beale Street*, 62–63.

6. Ibid., 119.

7. Barlow, 208.

8. Quoted in Barlow, 209.

9. Ibid., 228.

10. McKee and Chisenhall, 81–82.

11. Lee, *Beale Street*, 103.

12. Sigafoos, 216.

13. Cantor, 8.

14. Lee, *Beale Street*, 62.

15. Cantor, 8.

16. *All Day and All Night*, video cassette.

17. Ibid.

18. Ibid.

19. Ibid.

20. Cantor, 37–38.

21. Lee, *Beale Street Sundown*, 9. Martin was Amusements Editor and Columnist for the *Memphis Commercial Appeal*.

22. *All Day and All Night*.

23. Keil, 66.

24. Ibid., 218–19.

25. Booth, 108.

26. Cantor, 2–4.

27. Ibid., 43.

28. Ibid., 25.

29. Ibid., 1.

30. Ibid., 170.

31. *All Day and All Night.*

32. Sawyer, 55–63. Sawyer names Richard Sanders (sax), Earl Forest and Solomon Hardy (drums), "Junior" Lockwood (guitar), and Ford Nelson and John Alexander (piano) as the first generation of bandmembers. Encyclopedias sometimes include Junior Parker in the list of musicians, and sax player Willie Nix.

33. Roberts, 10.

34. Sawyer, 63.

35. Shaw, *Honkers and Shouters,* 225.

36. King, 135.

37. Sawyer, 63. It is also likely that family, friends, other gigs, and party opportunities explained this.

38. Tosches, 133.

39. Ernestine Mitchell, 18 October 1990 interview.

40. Grendysa, 28.

41. Keil, 66.

42. Quoted in McKee and Chisenhall, 248.

43. *All Day and All Night.*

44. Ibid.

45. *Beale Street Collection,* 7.

46. *All Day and All Night.*

47. Ibid.

48. Gart and Ames, 16.

49. Sawyer, 71.

50. King, 138.

51. *All Day and All Night.*

52. "Bilbo Belt Heads Back to Banjo Bands and Blackface," 32.

53. *All Day and All Night.*

54. Lee, *Beale Street Sundown,* 8.

55. *All Day and All Night.*

56. Tosches, 133.

57. Cantor, 205.

58. "WDIA Holds Third Annual Goodwill Revue," 1–2.

59. "Moohah" [A. C. Williams], 10. Quotation is presented in its original spelling and punctuation.

60. Giddins, *Riding On a Blue Note,* 41–42.

Chapter 3: Signing Your Mama Away

1. Govenar, *Meeting the Blues*, 75.
2. Escott, *Good Rockin' Tonight*, 13–24.
3. Ibid., 4.
4. Ibid., 21–24.
5. Ibid., 23
6. Ibid., 26–27.
7. Gart and Ames, 66.
8. Quoted in Shaw, *Honkers and Shouters*, 204; Topping, liner notes.
9. Leadbitter and Slaven credit John Alexander as the piano player on Bland's "Drifting from Town to Town" and "Love My Baby" (106), and on King's "Gotta Find My Baby," "My Own Fault Darlin'," and "That Ain't the Way to Do It" (772).
10. Sawyer, 66.
11. Ibid., 68–69.
12. Ibid., 67.
13. Moonoogian and Meeden, 20–21. While virtually all accounts of the early Duke years rely on this 1984 interview, Mattis's memory of events some thirty years before may be flawed and certainly is influenced by the unsatisfactory conclusion to the struggle with Don Robey over the ownership of Duke Records.
14. Palmer, 230.
15. Tosches, 134.
16. Cantor, 178–79.
17. Moonoogian and Meeden, 18.
18. Cantor, 180–81.
19. Ibid., 182.
20. Ibid., 182–83.
21. Gillett, 93.
22. Escott, *Good Rockin' Tonight*, 32.
23. *That Rhythm . . . Those Blues*, video cassette.
24. Ibid.
25. Moonoogian and Meeden, 33.
26. Ibid., 19.
27. Moonoogian and Meeden, 19.
28. Gart and Ames, 27.
29. David James Mattis, 3 November 1992 interview. Unless otherwise noted, quotations attributed to Mattis are from this interview.

30. Ibid.

31. Gart and Ames, 32.

32. Shaw, *Rockin' '50s*, 93.

33. Moonoogian and Meeden, 31.

34. Ernest Withers, 23 February 1990 interview. Invariably, the black community believes that white recording company owners automatically make fortunes on black talent, but it is not always true. Mattis, in particular, was the fairest and most generous operator Ace would ever meet in the music business.

35. David James Mattis, 3 November 1992 interview.

36. Pat Baird, 25 July 1990 interview. Ms. Baird is senior director, national publicity, for BMI.

37. *That Rhythm . . . Those Blues.*

38. Gart and Ames, 3.

39. Moonoogian and Meeden, 19.

Chapter 4: Las Vegas in Houston

1. Shelton, 71.

2. McComb, 61.

3. Wintz, 15–16.

4. Haynes, 35.

5. Shelton, 71.

6. Wintz, 27.

7. Haynes, 28.

8. McComb, 108.

9. Haynes, 27.

10. McComb, 110.

11. Haynes, 32.

12. Ibid., 47–52.

13. Ibid., 41.

14. Ibid., 44.

15. Ibid., 63–64.

16. Ibid., 19–30.

17. Ibid., 92–98.

18. Ibid., 157. McComb suggests that an additional rumor circulating at the camp involved the impending arrival of a white mob (111).

19. Ibid., 7.

20. Ibid., 296–302.

21. Shelton, 73.

22. Wintz, 32.

23. Ibid., 25.

24. Barlow, 235.

25. Govenar, *Living Texas Blues*, 54.

26. McComb, 114.

27. Ibid., 84–85.

28. Wintz, 20.

29. McComb, 152; Wintz, 21.

30. Wintz, 23–25.

31. McComb, 131.

32. Govenar, *Early Years of Rhythm & Blues*, 3.

33. Quoted in Govenar, *Living Texas Blues*, 52.

34. Govenar, *Early Years of Rhythm & Blues*, 15.

35. Govenar, *Meeting the Blues*, 75.

36. George, *Death of Rhythm & Blues*, 27.

37. Evelyn Johnson, business partner to Don Robey from 1946 until his death, and Robey's wife from 1953 to 1960, 10 January 1995 interview.

38. Gart and Ames, 5.

39. Fisher, 3.

40. Ibid.

41. Evelyn Johnson, 9 November 1993 interview.

42. "Don Robey, Prominent Local Businessman, Dies," 1.

43. Evelyn Johnson, 19 November 1993 interview.

44. Evelyn Johnson, 12 January 1994 interview.

45. Gart and Ames, 7.

46. Evelyn Johnson, 6 October 1993 interview.

47. Govenar, *Meeting the Blues*, 75.

48. Shelton, 71–73.

49. "Don Robey, Prominent Local Businessman, Dies," 1.

50. Evelyn Johnson, 19 November 1993 interview.

51. See Govenar, *Early Years of Rhythm & Blues*, 5.

52. Clarence "Gatemouth" Brown, 10 October 1990 interview. Information and quotations attributed to Gatemouth Brown not otherwise documented are taken from this interview.

53. Johnson, "Women in the Music Industry," audiotape.

54. Evelyn Johnson, 6 October 1993 interview.

55. Evelyn Johnson, 19 November 1993 interview.

56. See Gart and Ames, 9, and the "Peacock Singles Discography," 134–61.

57. Fisher, 3.

58. Govenar, *Meeting the Blues*, 103.

59. Evelyn Johnson, 19 November 1993 interview.

60. Johnson, "Women in the Music Industry."

61. Evelyn Johnson, 6 October 1993 interview.

62. Maultsby, "Women in the Music Industry," audiotape.

63. Johnson, "Women in the Music Industry."

64. Evelyn Johnson, 6 October 1993 interview.

65. Johnson, "Women in the Music Industry."

66. Evelyn Johnson, 9 November 1993 interview.

67. Gart and Ames, 18.

68. Evelyn Johnson, 6 October 1993 interview.

69. Eliot, 38.

70. Lhamon Jr., 12.

71. Gart and Ames, 3.

72. George, *Death of Rhythm & Blues*, 31.

73. Quoted in Govenar, *Meeting the Blues*, 100.

74. George, *Death of Rhythm & Blues*, 34.

75. George, "Why I Promote the Blues," 76. Clark once dressed up as the chauffeur of the owner of station WNEW to get a Jimmy Lunceford record played on Martin Block's "Make Believe Ballroom" show (75). His "Swing Row Is My Beat" column dates from 1934. According to Clark, his obituary of King Oliver represented the first time Oliver's name appeared in print (76).

76. Evelyn Johnson, 9 November 1993 interview.

77. Evelyn Johnson, 12 January 1994 interview.

78. "Record Reviews," *Billboard*, 18 February 1950, 118.

79. Shaw, *Honkers and Shouters*, 67.

80. Ibid., 87.

81. George, *Death of Rhythm & Blues*, 19.

82. Chilton, 95.

83. "Sad Journey Blues" was number eight of the "Most-Played Juke Box Rhythm & Blues Records" for *Billboard* on 11 November 1950 (26). Also see Gart and Ames, 14–15.

84. Evelyn Johnson, 12 January 1994 interview.

85. Fisher, 3.

86. Gart and Ames, 49.

87. Evelyn Johnson, 12 January 1994 interview.

88. Gart and Ames, 16.

89. *Billboard* began its R&B column in the 22 April 1950 issue, called "R.&B. Blue Notes," which may have been written by Jerry Wexler.

90. Bill Holford, 8 March 1991 interview. Information and quotations attributed to Bill Holford are from this interview.

91. Evelyn Johnson, 19 November 1993 interview, and Fisher, 3.

92. For these entries see Library of Congress, *Catalog of Copyright Entries, Third Series*, vol. 4, part 5B, number 2, *Unpublished Music*, July–December 1950, p. 412; and vol. 5, part 5B, number 1, January–June 1951, p. 153.

93. "Houston Pressery Bought by Peacock," 20.

94. James Oden (St. Louis Jimmy) and Country Jim Bledsoe were said to be signed by Peacock (Gart and Ames, 22), but neither appears in the ACA logbooks for recording sessions nor in Peacock releases during this period. Peacock had, however, recorded or released singles by the following artists, listed alphabetically: Marie Adams, Bells of Joy, Edgar Blanchard, Skippy Brooks, Clarence "Gatemouth" Brown, Ollie Brown, Walter Brown, Carl Campbell, Christland Singers, Silver Cooks, Dixie Hummingbirds, Floyd Dixon, Norman Dunlap, Lavada Durst (Dr. Hep Cat), Joe "Papoose" Fitz, Five Blind Boys, Valli Ford, Golden Echoes, Golden Harp Singers, Rev. I. H. Gordon, Gospel Tone Singers, Clarence Green, Al Grey Orchestra, Bill Heyman, Willie Holiday, Bea Johnson, Harry "Slick" Johnson, Mildred Jones, Willie "Doc" Jones, Papa Lightfoot, Smiling Smokey Lynn, Joe Lutcher, Jimmy McCracklin, Paul Monday, Nightingales, Elmore Nixon, Sonny Parker, Jesse Mae Renfro, J. Riggins Jr., Memphis Slim ("L. C. Frazier" in the ACA logbook), Fat Man Smith, Southern Wonders, Stars of Hope, R. B. Thibadeaux, Willie Mae "Big Mama" Thornton, Andrew Tibbs, Iona Wade, Betty Jean Washington, and Wilson and Watson.

95. Evelyn Johnson, 12 January 1994 interview.

96. Quoted in Govenar, *Living Texas Blues*, 57.

97. Evelyn Johnson, 6 October 1993 interview.

98. Ibid.

99. David James Mattis, 3 November 1992 interview.

100. Evelyn Johnson, 6 October 1993 interview.

Chapter 5: Heart Ballads

1. See Cantor, 183. Cantor cites gospel historian Kip Lornell's estimate that in the 1950s Robey's Peacock label and Buffalo Booking Agency recorded and booked fifty-two of the ninety Memphis gospel groups.

2. Pavlow, 38.

3. Moonoogian and Meeden, 22.

4. Johnny Otis, 7 November 1989 interview. Unless otherwise noted, quotations attributed to Johnny Otis are from this interview.

5. *Billboard*, 2 August 1952, 105. Mattis had been given a tour of the Houston operation in the summer of 1952, though he had not met Robey personally, and probably signed partnership papers in July. Mattis remembers signing the papers in the fall, when he met Robey at a New York convention (Moonoogian and Meeden, 19), but Robey was clearly running the show well before then.

6. Weekly chart positions in this book have been taken from rhythm and blues charts of dated issues of *Billboard* as noted. For summaries of the various race and rhythm and blues charts as published by *Billboard*, beginning with the World War II "Harlem Hit Parade," see Whitburn, *Top R&B Singles 1942–1988*.

7. "Gun Game Fatal to 'Wax' Star," 5.

8. Moonoogian and Meeden, 19.

9. Ibid., 25. The ten Duke sides recorded in Memphis are cataloged as follows: Gospel Travelers, "God's Chariot Part 1" b/w "Part 2" (G-1); Rosco Gordon, "Hey Fat Girl" b/w "Tell Daddy" (R-101); Johnny Ace with the Beale Streeters, "My Song" b/w "Follow the Rule" (102); Earl Forest with the Beale Streeters, "Baby, Baby" b/w "Rock the Bottle" (103); and the Mighty Dukes, "No Other Love" b/w "Why Can't I Have You" (104).

10. Moonoogian and Meeden, 22.

11. David James Mattis, 3 November 1992 interview.

12. Evelyn Johnson, 6 October 1993 interview.

13. Gatemouth Brown, 10 October 1990 interview.

14. Quoted in Guralnick, *Sweet Soul Music*, 283. Also see Gart and Ames, 93.

15. White, 37–38.

16. Evelyn Johnson, 6 October 1993 interview.

17. Fisher, 49. Robey and Don Carter began Don Music as a joint venture in the late 1960s, but Robey, as he had with Mattis, "bought his interest out."

18. Evelyn Johnson, 9 November 1993 interview.

19. "Strange Case of Johnny Ace," 65.

20. Gart and Ames, 3.

21. George, *Death of Rhythm & Blues*, 34.

22. Shaw, *Honkers and Shouters*, 92. Leroy Carr was born in Nashville and raised in Indianapolis. His death in 1935 is "shrouded in mystery" (7).

23. Ibid., 6.

24. Ibid., 89–91. Other black artists in this tradition, contemporary with Ace, in-

clude Lowell Fulson, Percy Mayfield, Amos Milburn, Jesse Belvin, Ivory Joe Hunter, and pre-gospel Ray Charles. In an earlier work (*The World of Soul*), Shaw called such black crooners "the Oreo singers." "Although it is doubtless a pejorative term," he explained, "I am using it merely as a descriptive one" (105). Arnold Shaw was involved with postwar R&B from 1945, when as director of publicity for Leeds Music Corporation (MCA) he promoted Cecil Gant's "I Wonder," through the period of the 1950s when R&B became rock 'n' roll. As the general professional manager for Hill & Range Songs in the spring of 1954, for example, he arranged for his mainstream publishing powerhouse to buy half of "Sh-Boom," the song that started the frantic activity of white acts covering black artists in the season of 1954–55.

25. Gillett, 56.

26. Tosches, 26.

27. Gillett, 143. Brown's first hit was "Drifting Blues" (Aladdin, 1945), a song performed "tear-stained with self-pity" (Shaw, *Honkers and Shouters*, 230).

28. "Talent Corner," 34.

29. Rolontz, "Rhythm & Blues Notes," 23 August 1952, 35. Contemporary cover versions of "My Song" were released by Dinah Washington (Mercury), Hadda Brooks (Okeh), and Marie Adams (Peacock), in which Don Robey was in effect covering his own song. In *Duke/Peacock Records*, Gart quotes from a *Cash Box* item that Irving Marcus was seeing "that the lid he nailed on the 'My Song' bootleggers" stayed shut (32), an additional, though illegal, indicator of popularity. Seven weeks after breaking into the Top 10 in retail sales, "My Song" listed number five on juke box plays (20 September 1952). For the entire year it placed number six (retail) and number seven (juke box) according to *Billboard* (27 December 1952, 19).

30. "Rhythm & Blues," *Down Beat*, 8 October 1952, 11.

31. Evelyn Johnson, "Women in the Music Industry," audiotape.

32. Rolontz, "Rhythm & Blues Notes," 8 November 1952, 48.

33. "Notes from the R.&B. Beat," reproduced without attribution but believed to be a *Cash Box* item, January 1953, reprinted in Gart, *First Pressings*, vol. 3, 1953, 7. Gart's *First Pressings* series reprints valuable material from contemporary issues of *Cash Box* not readily available in their original form.

34. The copyright for "Cross My Heart" (EU289157) was registered as an unpublished song by Robey's Lion Publishing Company on 15 September 1952, with words and music by Don Deadric Robey and David James Mattis.

35. David James Mattis, 3 November 1992 interview.

36. See Gart and Ames, 32–33.

37. Bill Holford, 8 March 1991 interview. It is generally believed that these sides by Ace, Bland, Forest, and Gordon were recorded in Memphis at the WDIA studio. The standard discography in the postwar blues field (Leadbitter and Slaven, *Blues Records*) lists Memphis as the recording location, and indeed, David James Mattis specifically remembers cutting "Cross My Heart" and "Angel." Bill Holford, however, kept meticulous studio logbooks of not only songs that he recorded but "outside material" that he mastered for pressing. I have seen these logbooks in their original form, and I believe the evidence suggests that the only Ace songs *recorded and released* from Memphis were "Midnight Hours Journey," "My Song," and "Follow the Rule." The ACA log numbers for the Ace sides are 2268 ("Angel"), 2271 ("Aces Wild"), 2285 ("Cross My Heart"), and 2288 ("Burlie Cutie"). See Gart and Ames for a reproduction of the ACA logs (205–23).

38. Bill Holford, 8 March 1991 interview.

39. Grendysa, 28.

40. *Billboard*, 3 January 1953, 29; 10 January 1953, 24; 17 January 1953, 42, 44, 52; 24 January 1953, 28.

41. "Rhythm & Blues," *Down Beat*, 11 February 1953, 15–S.

42. "Odd But True! Hit Disc May Lose Money," 9. Robey told this story in connection with Duke 118 ("Saving My Love for You" b/w "Yes, Baby"), a second record he claimed was a two-sided hit.

43. Evelyn Johnson, 6 October 1993 interview.

44. Moonoogian and Meeden, 22. Mattis came up with his notion of a fair artist royalty rate, he says, when he was told that Nat Cole received five cents a record.

45. "Strange Case of Johnny Ace," 67.

46. LaIsac, liner notes.

47. Sawyer, 72–73.

48. Quoted in Govenar, *Meeting the Blues*, 100.

49. "1952's Top R & B Records," 19.

50. Evelyn Johnson, 6 October 1993 interview.

51. Travis, 205–17.

52. Milton Hopkins, 8 March 1991 interview. Hopkins, a guitar player and the cousin of legendary blues guitarist Lightnin' Hopkins, joined the Johnny Ace band in late 1952.

53. Mattie Fields, 5 February 1995 interview. Mattie Fields and Willie Mae Thornton had the same father but grew up in separate households. Though they did not meet until Mattie was thirteen years old (Willie Mae was nineteen), it is Mattie who knew Willie Mae best and who lived with her and cared for her

at the end of her life. Additional information and quotations attributed to Mattie Fields are from this interview.

54. Gart and Ames, 17–18.
55. Quoted in Gart and Ames, 17.
56. See Shaw, *Honkers & Shouters*, 482–84.
57. Evelyn Johnson, 9 November 1993 interview.
58. Display ad, *Billboard*, 27 January 1951, 35. The ad was repeated in the next issue (3 February 1951, 28).
59. Webman, "Rhythm and Blues Notes," 24 February 1951, 31, and 17 November 1951, 35.
60. "Rhythm & Blues Record Reviews," 29 December 1951, 23.
61. "'Big Mama' Thornton Is Johnny Otis' New Find," 22.
62. Quoted in Gart and Ames, 51.
63. Quoted in Shaw, *World of Soul*, 125.
64. The record, incorrectly titled "My Nights Are Long and Sleepless," derived from the second half of the title line of the lyrics: "Everytime I Think of You (My Nights Are Long and Sleepless)." See *Billboard*, "New Records to Watch," 4 October 1952, 41.
65. Display ad, *Billboard*, 11 October 1952, 44.
66. Evelyn Johnson, 6 October 1993 interview.
67. Gart and Ames, 54.
68. Windham, 38.
69. Ibid.
70. Display ad, *Billboard*, 7 March 1953, 49.
71. "New Records to Watch," 14 March 1953, 32.
72. *Cash Box* column reprinted in Moonoogian, 6.
73. Ibid., 5.
74. "'Down Beat' Best Bets: Rhythm and Blues," 13–S.
75. Moonoogian, 5.
76. Fisher, 24.
77. For a full discussion of the Sun Records answer to Thornton's hit see Moonoogian, 7.
78. Rolontz, "Rhythm & Blues Notes," 28 March 1953, 42.
79. "Answer to the 'Answers,'" 18, 45.
80. See dated issues of *Billboard*. A display ad in 11 April 1953 (p. 40) warns against "Hound Dog" imitations. "Bear Cat" makes the national R&B charts on 18 April 1953 (p. 46). The Sun Record becomes more popular than the original in New Orleans on 2 May 1953 and in St. Louis on 30 May 1953.

81. Moonoogian, 8.
82. "New Howl Goes Up Over 'Hound Dog' Infringement," 28.
83. "This Week's New Records," 26 September 1953, 34.
84. For an account of Thornton's career after the blues revival of the 1960s created a new demand for her performances, see Salem, "Willie Mae Thornton."

Chapter 6: Potent Wax

1. Rolontz, "Rhythm & Blues Notes," 18 April 1953, 48.
2. Evelyn Johnson, "Women in the Music Industry," audiotape.
3. Quoted in Travis, 214, 216.
4. Evelyn Johnson, 16 December 1993 interview.
5. David James Mattis, 3 November 1992 interview. "Two Loves Have I," a song written in the early 1930s, was a hit in 1947 for Frankie Laine and in 1948 for Perry Como. The Diamonds R&B version was released in late 1953.
6. Johnny Otis, 7 November 1989 interview.
7. Moonoogian and Meeden, 22. The exact date of the dissolution of the partnership has been established in a letter discovered by Galen Gart. The letter, written by Earl F. Walborg, a Houston certified public accountant, is dated 14 August 1953 but sets 15 April 1953 as the date "Mr. Don Robey purchased the [Duke Records] partnership interest of Mr. David J. Mattis" (Gart and Ames, 35.)
8. The title of this song is spelled both with and without the apostrophe. The title as filed with the copyright office, "Ace's Wild," does, however seem to state accurately an important aspect of the artist's personality.
9. Display ad, *Billboard*, 20 June 1953, 52.
10. Display ad, *Billboard*, 4 July 1953, 46.
11. "New Records to Watch," 20 June 1953, 36.
12. "This Week's Best Buys," 27 June 1953, 28.
13. "This Week's New Records," 27 June 1953, 26. The "B" side of a record, which didn't get played often on the radio and didn't sell records, could still be successful as a juke box selection — especially an instrumental side that provided good background music. Patterns of juke box play are considerably different from patterns of airplay.
14. "Down Beat Record Reviews," 15–S.
15. Display ad, reprinted in Gart, *First Pressings*, vol.3, 1953, 51.
16. Display ad, *Billboard*, 29 August 1953, 61.
17. Gart and Ames, 56.

18. Rolontz, "Rhythm & Blues Notes," 12 September 1953, 41.

19. "Robey Cuts 3 Wax Stars," 22.

20. "Peacock, Duke to Houston," 22.

21. Gart and Ames, 58–60. One of Robey's new artists, singer/songwriter Joseph "Google Eyes" August, recorded two songs at this Radio Recorders session with the Johnny Otis band (released as Duke 117) and furnished Ace with one of his future hits, "Please Forgive Me," the writer credit of which August would have to split with Robey. It is clear that Little Richard was too wild for Robey's taste, and his records were not successful until Bumps Blackwell produced him in New Orleans for Art Rupe's Specialty label (see Charles White's *Life and Times of Little Richard*).

22. "Rhythm & Blues Records Reviews," 19 September 1953, 39.

23. Display ad, *Tri-State Defender*, 23 August 1952, 10.

24. "Scribo's Sports Spot Shots," 8.

25. Ernestine Mitchell, 18 October 1990 interview.

26. Lois Jean Alexander, 10 June 1992 interview.

27. Norma Williams, 28 September 1994 interview.

28. St. Clair Alexander, 28 September 1994 interview.

29. Review of Johnny Ace, 55.

30. Evelyn Johnson, 6 October 1993 interview.

31. St. Clair Alexander, 28 September 1994 interview.

32. Evelyn Johnson, 6 October 1993 interview.

33. Rolontz, "Rhythm & Blues Notes," 5 December 1953, 38.

34. Giddins, liner notes. Both verse and bridge of this AABA song are four measures long, making a 16-bar song (half the amount of the traditional American popular song). Twenty eight measures is, in fact, the length of the complete recording of "The Clock."

35. Shaw, *Honkers and Shouters*, 448.

36. Wexler, 15–S.

37. Quoted in Cage, 17.

38. "New Records to Watch," 12 December 1953, 32.

39. "This Week's New Records," 19 December 1953, 38, and "This Week's Best Buys," 19 December 1953, 40.

40. Evelyn Johnson, "Women in the Music Industry."

41. Gillett, 41.

42. Broven, "A Rap with Johnny Otis," 11.

43. "1953's Top R&B Records," 29.

44. Evelyn Johnson, 19 November 1993 interview.

45. "4 Records—6 Hits" Robey declared in a display ad for "Saving My Love for You," *Billboard*, 2 January 1959, 30.

46. See "Broadcasting Has Good '53; Worry Is Color," 1, 2.

47. See "Theater, Club Foldings Hurt Live-Act Mart," 1, 10.

48. See "Continuing Flux Forecast in All Areas of Music," 1, 11, 13.

49. Ross and Hill, 18. Income for male wage and salary Negroes in America averaged 54 percent of white income in 1947, 55 percent in 1962, but 62 percent in 1951.

50. Rolontz, "Rhythm & Blues Notes, 16 January 1954, 42.

51. Ibid., 20 February 1954, 43.

52. "Johnny Ace Discs Hits [*sic*]," 9.

53. Leadbitter and Slaven, 12.

54. Shaw, *Honkers and Shouters*, 158.

55. Broven, "Rap with Johnny Otis," 1.

56. Shaw, *Honkers and Shouters*, 162–64.

57. Gillett, 212.

58. Ibid., 60.

59. Lipsitz, 273.

60. Otis, 12.

61. George, *Death of Rhythm & Blues*, 29.

62. Rolontz, "Rhythm & Blues Notes," 27 March 1954, 35.

63. Evelyn Johnson, 12 January 1994 interview.

64. "Station Demonstrates Its Listening Power," reprinted without attribution in Gart, *First Pressings*, vol. 4, 1954, 25.

65. "Notes from the R.&B. Beat," March 1954, 29; April 1954, 40–41, 43. Also see Rolontz, "Rhythm & Blues Notes," 30 January 1954, 47; 20 March 1954, 43; and 3 April 1954, 32.

66. "Blues 'Royalty' on Apollo Stage," 6.

67. Review of Johnny Ace and Willie Mae Thornton, 53. Presented in its original spelling and punctuation.

68. Rolontz and Friedman, 1, 18, 24.

69. "Bursting Old Barriers," 13.

70. "Enterprise of Placing R&B Talent Turns Stars in Pop Field Green," 20.

71. Rolontz, "Rhythm & Blues Notes," 24 April 1954, 23.

72. Display ad, *Billboard*, 24 April 1954, 16.

73. George, *Death of Rhythm & Blues*, 36.

74. "Review Spotlight on . . . Willie Mae (Big Mama) Thornton," 8 May 1954, 33.

75. Display ad, *Billboard*, 22 May 1954, 59.

76. "Review Spotlight on . . . Johnny Ace," 22 May 1954, 59.

77. Rolontz, "Rhythm & Blues Notes," 5 June 1954, 44.

78. "This Week's Best Buys," 5 June 1954, 44.

79. Tosches, 136.

80. Grendysa, 28.

81. Johnny Otis, 7 November 1989 interview.

82. On the Ace recordings, orchestral credits for the Ace aggregation ("We were all working for Johnny Ace," Milton Hopkins says) are attributed to "The Johnny Board Band," "The Johnny Board Orchestra," or "Johnny Board & His Orchestra," sometimes naming this group erroneously.

83. "Notes from the R.&B. Beat," June 1954, 61; July 1954, 72.

84. Evelyn Johnson, 19 November 1993 interview.

Chapter 7: Dirty Talk and One-Night Stands

1. Bobby Williamson had the C&W version of "Sh-Boom." "Honey Love," (Drifters), "I Understand Just How You Feel," (Four Tunes), and "Lovey Dovey" (Clovers) were the other R&B tunes with pop covers. For a more complete account of pop cover versions in 1954 see Salem, "Johnny Ace: A Case Study in the Diffusion and Transformation of Minority Culture," 213–19.

2. Rolontz, "Rhythm & Blues Notes," 17 July 1954, 63.

3. "The Winner—Nobody!" 14.

4. "Pubs in Middle of DJ-45 Battle," 18.

5. "Shell out for Shellac," 19.

6. Holford, ACA Master Book, Entry #2934, pp. 32–33, dated 27 July 1954. This information is reprinted in Gart and Ames, *Duke/Peacock Records*, 220.

7. Barret E. Hansen (Dr. Demento), letter to the author, 6 October 1989.

8. Grendysa, 28.

9. Escott, "Johnny Ace: The First Rock 'n' Roll Casualty," 16.

10. "Review Spotlight on . . . Johny [sic] Ace," 18 September 1954, 38.

11. Rolontz, "Rhythm & Blues Notes," 18 September 1954, 38.

12. Martin, "11 Labels Have Best-Selling Pops," 19.

13. Rolontz, "Rhythm & Blues Notes," 4 September 1954, 32.

14. "Blames A.&R. Men for Poor Music Tastes," 19.

15. "Trend in R&B: Syndicated Deejay Shows Expanding," 11. These syndicated programs were taped segments from live shows with the local ads removed, then played outside of the original market by independent stations. WNJR in Newark, New Jersey, for example, programmed shows Freed had made in New

York (previously it ran his Cleveland shows), Hunter had made in Los Angeles, and Sears in Atlanta on a daily basis.

16. "Major Firms Must Keep Alert to Maintain 'Coverage' in R&B Field," 11.
17. "Control the Dim-Wits!" 33.
18. "Finger Points at You!" 19.
19. "Trade Views Off-Color Disk Situation With Mixed Feeling," 19, 86.
20. Shaw, *Honkers and Shouters*, 243–44.
21. For chart positions see "1954's Top R&B Records," 17.
22. Broven, 14.
23. Brown, "Billy Rowe's Notebook," 16. Brown's attack began on 16 October 1948.
24. Brown, "Sponsors Leery of Smutty Disc Jocks," 18.
25. Brown, "OK Deejays Rap Smutty Wax," 23.
26. Brown, "Campaign against Smutty Wax on Air Gains Support," 31.
27. Brown, "FCC Urged to Monitor Smutty Records on Radio," 22.
28. Brown, "Readers Praise Courier's Smutty Record Drive," 29.
29. Brown, "Blues Singers Share Blame for Bad Wax," 19.
30. McMillan, "Protest (Moondog) Freed Coming to WINS," 17.
31. McMillan, "New York Is My Beat," 17.
32. "Alan Freed to Emcee Rythm [*sic*] and Blues Show," 5B. Also see display ad on p. 6B.
33. "Record Crowd of 9000 Fans Attend Public Hall Rythm [*sic*] and Blues Show," 7B.
34. "Izzy Rowe's Notebook," 18.
35. Murrain, 17. Interestingly, Murrain alludes to the issue of payola. "Another reason (not given)," he says, "is financial 'favors' given these disk spinners by the record companies."
36. Brown, "No Cover Charge," 18.
37. Jackson, 71.
38. Brown, "Music Publisher Defends Moondog Show," 18.
39. "R&B Hassle Envelopes Alan Freed," 16.
40. "Courier Anti-Smutty Disc Drive Praised," 19.
41. Brown, "Teen-agers Want to Know," 18.
42. Richardson, 1-D, 2-D.
43. Douglas, 19.
44. Rolontz, "Rhythm & Blues Notes," 9 October 1954, 20.
45. Ibid., 16 October 1954, 22.
46. Ibid., 23 October 1954, 18.
47. "50% of U.S. Homes Own Phonos," 13.

48. "WDIA's Got a Broom," 16.

49. "Indie Diskers Back WDIA's R&B Bans," 16.

50. See Ewen, "The ASCAP and BMI Story," in *All the Years of American Popular Music*, 300–304. For a fuller account of the ASCAP-BMI competition see Sanjek, *American Popular Music and Its Business*, vol. 3.

51. "BMI, SPA in Fight Vs. Off-Color Disks," 22, 24.

52. Ackerman, "ASCAP Stand Due on BMI Collaboration," 12.

53. "This Week's Best Buys," 2 October 1954, 44.

54. "Reviews of New R&B Records," 2 October 1954, 44.

55. Tosches, 136.

56. Rolontz, "1-Nighter Packages Find Road's Rocky," 16.

57. "New 'Top Ten R&B' Show to Do 60 One-Nighters," 14. The ten acts consisted of the Clovers, Faye Adams, Fats Domino, Joe Turner, the Moonglows, Amos Milburn, Charlie and Ray, the Paul Williams orchestra, the Bill Doggett Trio, and the Spence Twins.

58. Sawyer, 73.

59. Evelyn Johnson, 27 April 1995 interview.

60. Sawyer, 73.

61. Broven, *Rhythm & Blues in New Orleans*, 100.

62. Evelyn Johnson, 16 December 1993 interview.

63. See Woodward, 118.

64. Sawyer, 73.

65. Pomerance, 119.

66. Davis and Boyar, 44.

67. Ibid., 52.

68. Pomerance, 124–25.

69. Davis and Boyar, 50.

70. Ibid., 62.

71. Sawyer, 74.

72. Ibid., 139.

73. Ibid., 76–77.

74. Evelyn Johnson, 27 April 1995 interview.

75. Evelyn Johnson, 12 January 1994 interview.

76. Mitchell, 6. Also see Barlow, 240.

77. Evelyn Johnson, 12 January 1994 interview.

78. Sanjek, *American Popular Music and Its Business*, vol. 3, 217.

79. Evelyn Johnson, "Women in the Music Industry," audiotape.

80. Evelyn Johnson, 6 October 1993 interview.

81. Evelyn Johnson, 9 November 1993 interview.
82. Quoted in Govenar, *Early Years of Rhythm & Blues*, 7.
83. "Booking Queen," 18.
84. Gatemouth Brown, 10 October 1990 interview.
85. Evelyn Johnson, 27 April 1995 interview.
86. Evelyn Johnson, 9 November 1993 interview.
87. Ibid.

Chapter 8: Silent Night, Deadly Night

1. Rolontz, "Diskers Aim Guns on Christmas Wax," 13, and "In a Tavern Hot Gun Play," 1.
2. Larry Moody, 10 August 1989 interview.
3. The technical description of the H&R Model 6 is: "Solid frame. Caliber: 22 Long Rifle. 7-shot cylinder. Barrel lengths: 2½-, 4½-, and 6-inch. Weight: about 10 oz. Fixed sights. Blued or nickel finish. Hard rubber stocks." See Wahl, 64.
4. Sawyer, 136.
5. Quoted in Travis, 216.
6. Milton Hopkins, 8 March 1991 interview.
7. Quoted in Sawyer, 135.
8. Johnny Otis, 7 November 1989 interview.
9. Gart and Ames, 71–72.
10. Sawyer, 138.
11. Gart and Ames, 71.
12. Sawyer, 137.
13. Gatemouth Brown, 10 October 1990 interview.
14. Sawyer, 139.
15. Gibbs, Deposition.
16. "Strange Case of Johnny Ace," 67.
17. Display ad, *Billboard*, 25 December 1954, 38.
18. Evelyn Johnson, 6 October 1993 interview.
19. Thornton, Deposition. The correct name of the man referred to as Joe Hamilton is Joe Hammond.
20. Gibbs, Deposition.
21. Carter, Deposition.
22. Tosches, 136.
23. Johnny Otis, 7 November 1989 interview.
24. Evelyn Johnson, 6 October 1993 interview.

25. Quoted in Govenar, *Meeting the Blues*, 99.
26. Sawyer, 137.
27. Evelyn Johnson, 19 November 1993 interview.
28. Inquest Proceedings: John Alexander known as Johnnie [*sic*] Ace. It was appropriate for a Justice of the Peace to rule on the cause of death in Texas before the state's Medical Examiner Law was established in 1958.
29. Drayton M. "Doc" Fults, 31 July 1989 interview.
30. Johnny Otis, 7 November 1989 interview.
31. Ernest Withers, 9 January 1997 interview.
32. Rohan, 244.
33. Lermontov, 182–86.
34. Parry, 22.
35. Marchand, *Byron's Letters and Journals*, vol. 8, 25.
36. Marchand, *Byron: A Biography*, vol. 1, 126.
37. Litman et al., 494–95.
38. Matthews, 1–D, 3–D.
39. Johnny Otis, 7 November 1989 interview.
40. Quoted in Travis, 216.
41. King, 147.
42. "Strange Case of Johnny Ace," 63.

Chapter 9: Life after Death

1. Gillett, 7 14. Out of 163 million-selling records during this period, the majors accounted for 158.
2. George, *Death of Rhythm & Blues*, 60.
3. Hecht and MacArthur, 61.
4. Bradlee, 125.
5. "Bandleader Killed in 'Roulette,'" 21.
6. "Singer Johnny Ace Will Be Buried Sunday," 2.
7. "Juke Star Johnny Ace Kills Self," 1.
8. Matthews, 1–D. This is also the most complete newspaper account of Ace's career, though it does erroneously report that the singer was brought up in Birmingham—probably a corruption of a section of Memphis called Binghampton.
9. "Body of Johnny Ace Will Be Shipped to Memphis," 1, 8.
10. Ernest Withers, 23 February 1990 interview.
11. Withers, typed manuscript titled "FINAL NOTE" and handwritten draft of a

letter to "Mr. Robey"; Robey, letter to Withers. In another handwritten page, the newspapers serviced are listed: *Miami Times, San Antonio Register, Dallas Star-Post, Houston Informer, St. Louis Argus, Oklahoma Eagle, Florida Star, The Carolina, Cleveland Call and Post, Pittsburgh Courier, Afro-American,* and the *Defender* chain.

12. "5,000 Jam the Last Rites of 'Johnny Ace,'" 1.

13. Westbrooks, 1.

14. "Famous Blues Singer of 'My Song' and 'The Clock' Buried," 1.

15. "Johnny Ace Is Buried," 1.

16. For additional newspaper coverage of Ace's funeral, see "Famous Blues Singer of 'My Song' and 'The Clock' Buried," 1; "Final Note," 5; "Final Notes Sound for Johnny Ace," 1; "Johnny Ace Rites Attended by Famous Show Business Notables: Famous Blues Singer of 'My Song' and 'The Clock' Buried," 1; and "Singer Johnny Ace Will Be Buried Sunday," 2.

17. Cantor, 68.

18. Louis Cantor, 15 July 1992 interview.

19. Norma Williams, 12 September 1995 interview.

20. Levine, 285–86.

21. "Death Spun the Cylinder for Johnny Ace," 14.

22. "Johnny Ace Story," 1, 5.

23. Gibbs, "Says Death of 'Johnny Ace' Wasn't Suicide," 1.

24. Matthews, 3–D.

25. Murray, 45.

26. Ibid., 50.

27. "Johnny Ace Story," 1, 5.

28. "Death Spun the Cylinder," 14.

29. Matthews, 1–D.

30. Quoted in Sawyer, 222.

31. Moonoogian and Meeden, 21.

Chapter 10: "Pledging My Love"

1. Rolontz, "Rhythm & Blues Notes," 1 January 1955, 32.

2. "Johnny Ace Is Victim of Russ Roulette," 14.

3. Martin, "Music-Record Year Ends Up With Bang," 1.

4. Rolontz, "Rhythm & Blues Notes," 15 January 1955, 36.

5. Ackerman and Martin, 1, 32.

6. "Majors Really Jump with the R&B Beat," 33, 38.

7. "This Week's Best Buys," 15 January 1955, 60.

8. Gart and Ames, 77.

9. Evelyn Johnson, 12 January 1994 interview.

10. Rolontz, "Rhythm & Blues Notes," 22 January 1955, 16.

11. "Reviews of New R&B Records," 22 January 1955, 43.

12. Display ad, *Billboard*, 22 January 1955, 43.

13. Friedman, 65.

14. Rolontz, "R&B Packages' Big-Time Hit," 58.

15. "Groups Drown Out Singles," 56.

16. Bundy, "R&B Disks Sock Pop Market," 56.

17. "Buyer's Always Right," 56.

18. Jarvis, 58, 69.

19. Rolontz, "Rhythm & Blues Notes," 29 January 1955, 22.

20. "Talent Corner," 34.

21. Gart and Ames, 75.

22. Rolontz, "Rhythm & Blues Notes," 5 February 1955, 18.

23. "Review Spotlight on . . . ," 5 February 1955, 46.

24. Display ad, *Billboard*, 5 February 1955, 46.

25. Bundy, "DJ Surveys," 14.

26. "Kids Prefer Radio's DJ for Entertainment," 15, 18.

27. "Reviews of New Pop Records," 46.

28. Quoted in George, "Why I Promote the Blues," 76.

29. "Chart Comments," 38.

30. "This Week's Best Buys," 26 February 1955, 46.

31. Horowitz, "45 Disks Gain Edge," 27.

32. "Private" Cecil Gant's "I Wonder" (Gilt-Edge 500), an R&B release from 1944, entered the pop charts during the last year of World War II (number twenty for the week of 17 March 1945 only), setting the crossover precedent for a ballad by a solo black male performer signed to an independent label. After Ace's "Pledging My Love," Fats Domino's "Ain't That a Shame" (Imperial 5348) would crossover on 16 July 1955, eventually reaching the number ten position in pop music.

33. Pavlow, 51. The Penguins' ballad had entered the pop charts in December 1954.

34. Malone, 243.

35. "Reviews of New R&B Records," 12 February 1955, 57.

36. Ibid., 26 February 1955, 57.

37. "This Week's Best Buys," 19 February 1955, 53.

38. Rolontz, "Rhythm & Blues Notes," 12 February 1955, 30.

39. Shaw, *Honkers and Shouters*, 254, 358.

40. "This Week's Best Buys," 12 March 1955, 46.

41. *Billboard*, 26 March 1955, 139.

42. "Notes from the R.&B. Beat," March 1955, 38.

43. Ackerman, "R&B Tunes' Boom," 18.

44. "8th Annual Juke Box Operators Poll," 78.

45. "Morris Grabs 'Pledging' Tune," 26.

46. Sanjek, *From Print to Plastic*, 8–12. Sanjek marvels at just how extraordinary the compulsory license decision was in a free market economy: "For the first time in American history," he says, "the peacetime bargaining process between a supplier and a user was regulated by the federal government, and the price for use of private property fixed by national law" (9).

47. McNeil, 796.

48. Pavlow, 51–52.

49. Hughes, 10. For additional information, see Toll, *Blacking Up*, and Lott, *Love and Theft*.

50. "TV Ain't the Real Thing," 9.

51. Shaw, *Rockin' '50s*, 125–26.

52. "LaVern Baker Smiles," 6. Actually, there were six covers in all, including a country version by Pee Wee King, but Vicki Young (Capitol) was the only other singer Baker mentioned.

53. "Evelyn Knight Decca Sensash," 14.

54. "Supreme Loses Case for 400G against Decca," 12.

55. "No Copyright on Arrangement," 35.

56. "When Is a 'Copy' Not a Steal?" 35.

57. Sanjek, *American Popular Music and Its Business*, vol. 3, 43–44.

58. "Lavern Baker Seeks Bill to Halt Arrangement 'Thefts,'" 13.

59. Atlas, 14. The Diggs bill was identical to a House bill filed in January by Rep. Frank J. Thompson Jr., a New Jersey Democrat. *Billboard* labeled the Congressional activity a "new flurry of interest in copyright fact-finding," with Diggs providing "a boost on the House side" to favorable treatment by the House Judiciary Committee.

60. "R.&B. Disks Dropped for Miss Gibbs," 22.

61. Whitburn lists Gibbs's "Dance With Me Henry (Wallflower)" as a number one pop song (*Billboard Book of Top 40 Hits*, 123), but his summary calculations credit the highest position achieved on any of the charts, in this case "Most Played in Juke Boxes" (28 May 1955).

62. "Coast Girl Asks $10,000," 18.

63. "Ban on 'Copy' Records Enacted by Station WINS," reprinted in Gart, *First Pressings: 1955*, 91.

64. "Victor Quits 'Coverage,'" 13, 16.

65. Gillett, 38.

66. Gart and Ames, 75.

67. Horowitz, "New Horizons," 55. Besides "Pledging My Love," other R&B songs mentioned include "Maybellene," "Sincerely," "Seventeen," "Tweedlee Dee," "Earth Angel," "Ain't That a Shame," "I Hear You Knockin'," and "Dance With Me Henry."

68. It is a British notion that Ace was the "coloured James Dean" (Leadbitter, *Nothing But the Blues*, 183); Grendysa, 28; Tosches, 133; and Escott, "Johnny Ace," 16.

Chapter 11: Imitations of Love

1. LaIsac, liner notes. Quotations are presented in their original spelling. "He was quite a brilliant person, a very learned man, a college man, and a writer," Evelyn Johnson says of LaIsac. "His [real] last name was Harper, and he worked for Peacock as a writer and may have done some of the accounts. He had the pseudonym when he came to work there." LaIsac's liner notes first appeared with Duke LP-70, a ten-inch album, and have been reprinted as part of every version of the *Memorial Album*, including Duke DLP-71, a twelve-inch LP, originally released in 1957 and sometimes called "*Memorial Album Number II*" to distinguish it from the shorter version. MCA acquired the Johnny Ace catalog from ABC/Dunhill, which purchased Duke/Peacock from Don Robey. MCA-27014 is a reissue of DLP-71.

2. EP 80 consisted of "Pledging My Love," "Saving My Love for You," "Angel," and "Please Forgive Me." EP 81 was made up of "The Clock," "Never Let Me Go," "Cross My Heart," and "My Song." The ten-inch LP-70 contained the eight songs that made up EP 80 and EP 81. In their discography of Duke albums, Gart and Ames include a third extended play album, EP 71, described as a six song selection ("Pledging My Love," "Never Let Me Go," "Saving My Love for You," "The Clock," "Cross My Heart," and "So Lonely") designed for jukeboxes (201). This record does not exist in a 45 rpm configuration, however. Rather, these songs were released as a seven-inch, 33⅓ rpm LP in the early 1960s to be played on stereo juke boxes. Like other juke box LPs of the time, the back cover is blank. Robey gave this record the catalog number LP-71; he called its full counterpart (twelve songs) DLP-71.

3. "Notes from the R.&B. Beat," April 1955, 48.

4. Paul Simon, "The Late Great Johnny Ace," *Hearts and Bones*, WBR CD 2-23942, 1983.

5. Five cuts were recorded at this Houston session, on or about 22 July 1954, with ACA log numbers 2934 through 2938. ACA 2934, "Never Let Me Go," had been released in October 1954 as the "A" side of Duke 132; ACA 2936, "No Money," had been the "B" side of "Pledging My Love" (Duke 136). Bill Holford's records identify "How Can You Be So Mean?" as number 2937.

6. "Strange Case of Johnny Ace," 68. The magazine erroneously referred to this song as "No More."

7. "Singer Johnny Ace Killed Playing Russian Roulette," 59.

8. See Walter White, "The Strange Case of Paul Robeson."

9. "Strange Case of Johnny Ace," 67.

10. Ibid., 63–68. While essays in *Ebony* are not scholarly, they do have high informational value, photographs, and "contemporaneous documentation of aspects of American social history" (Vann, v).

11. "Review Spotlight on . . . ," 16 July 1955, 45.

12. "This Week's Best Buys," 23 July 1955, 89.

13. *Billboard*, 23 July 1955, 92. This display ad was also published in *Cash Box*. It is reprinted in Salem, "Death and the Rhythm-and-Bluesman: The Life and Recordings of Johnny Ace," 346.

14. *Billboard*, 27 August 1955, 61.

15. *Billboard*, 8 October 1955, 53.

16. *Billboard*, 7 January 1956, 47. In addition, the ad promised that Duke had yet another Ace release "in our record library."

17. "Review Spotlight on . . . ," 21 January 1956, 52.

18. *Billboard*, 4 February 1956, 60.

19. Simon, "Term R&B Hardly Covers Multi-Material," 55.

20. Horowitz, "New Horizons for R&B Exploitation," 55.

21. Rolontz, "Rhythm & Blues Notes," 19 February 1955, 28.

22. Simon, "Rhythm & Blues Notes," 28 April 1956, 61; display ad, *Billboard*, 28 July 1956, 78. Quotations are presented in their original spelling and usage.

23. Simon, "Rhythm & Blues Notes," 4 August 1956, 79.

24. "Johnny Ace Is Buried," 8.

25. "Reviews of New R&B Records," 18 August 1956, 70. The Johnny Ace sides were rated 71 and 70 respectively. Both sides of the "Buddy Ace Band" were rated 72.

26. McKee and Chisenhall, 249.

27. St. Clair Alexander, 28 September 1994 interview.

28. St. Clair Ace recorded his song "Radiation Flu" in 1986 on the Toma label.

29. Gart and Ames, 83. Jimmie Lee Land, from Jasper, Texas, was a "competent but somewhat second-string" singer whom Robey used to open shows for Joe Hinton and Little Junior Parker (20). Using the professional name "Buddy Ace," he released eleven Duke singles before two charted in the late sixties : "Nothing in the World Can Hurt Me" (1966) and "Hold On" (1967). Though the authors insist that St. Clair Alexander sang the vocals on Duke 155, St. Clair himself declares the voice is not his. Indeed, according to many encyclopedias and music reference books, Jimmy Lee Land began his career as "Buddy Ace" with Duke 155.

30. "I'm Crazy, Baby" (July 1954) was logged in as ACA 2938. "Still Love You So," two years later, is ACA 3336.

31. Kramer, "Rhythm-Blues Notes," 55.

32. Quoted in Kramer, "On the Beat," 20.

33. "On the Beat," 103.

34. Grevati, 54. (On 23 February 1957 Billboard merged rock 'n' roll with R&B in its notes column. In the issue dated 24 June 1957 the magazine discontinued listing the Top 10 most played R&B records in juke boxes and on 20 October 1958 discontinued all "multiple charts," since R&B was now clearly mainstream pop music.)

35. The album programs songs in this order: "Pledging My Love," "Don't You Know," "Never Let Me Go," "So Lonely," "I'm Crazy, Baby," "My Song," "Saving My Love for You," "The Clock," "How Can You Be So Mean?" "Still Love You So," "Cross My Heart," and "Anymore."

36. Billboard, 1 December 1958, 10. The original spelling of "exhuberant," is the work of Duke copywriter Dzondria LaIsac, who wrote the liner notes for the Memorial Album.

37. Johnny Otis, 7 November 1989 interview.

38. "Rhythm & Blues," Billboard, 1 December 1958, 48. The reissued Duke 136 is rare and hard to find today, mostly because demand for the records was so slight that few records were actually pressed.

39. Shaw, Honkers and Shouters, 482.

40. Gart and Ames, 116.

41. The R&B and pop charts were so similar that Billboard suspended publication of a separate R&B chart between 30 November 1963 and 23 January 1965.

42. Evelyn Johnson, 19 November 1993 interview.

43. Gart and Ames, 126–27.

44. Paul, 5.

45. Patoski, 22.

46. Evelyn Johnson, 6 October 1993 interview.

47. "Body of Johnny Ace Will Be Shipped to Memphis," 8.

48. *Alexander v. ABC Records*, C75–213, Western District of Tennessee, U.S. District Court (1976).

49. Kirsch, 52. Kirsch believed the album was titled *Again . . . Johnny Sings*, since that phrase, in large, bold type, is the heading on the back cover.

50. Johnny Otis, 7 November 1989 interview.

51. Quoted in Govenar, *Meeting the Blues*, 99.

52. Shaw, *World of Soul*, 127.

53. Sawyer, 135.

54. Quoted in DeCurtis and Henke, 91.

Chapter 12: Ace of Hearts

1. Harris, 50, 407. *Blues Who's Who* is only one of many other histories and reference books that ignores Ace.

2. Halberstam, 456.

3. Goldman, 2–3.

4. Ibid., 700–701.

5. Marcus, 47.

6. Pugh, 10.

7. Marcus, iv.

8. Ward, 98–99. Perhaps the most outrageous allegation by Ward is that Robey was "less than meticulous when it came to contracts," since Robey sued his competitors vigorously and quickly over any infringement of his artists' contracts.

9. Escott, "Johnny Ace," 16.

10. Tosches, 136.

11. Duncan, 13–15.

12. Tudor, 79.

13. Escott, "Johnny Ace," 17.

14. Topping, liner notes. For purposes of this album, the "Memphis Blues Brothers" are said to be Little Junior Parker, Earl Forest, Bobby "Blue" Bland, and Johnny Ace. The phony telegram is dated to correspond with Topping's understanding that Ace shot himself on Christmas Eve.

15. Evelyn Johnson, 6 October 1993 interview.

16. Hoekstra, 30.

17. St. Clair Alexander, 28 September 1994 interview.
18. Milton Hopkins, 8 March 1991 interview.
19. Morgan and Barlow, 127.
20. George, *Death of Rhythm & Blues*, 31.
21. Eliot, 48.
22. Ibid., 97.
23. Ibid., 165–66.
24. George, *Death of Rhythm & Blues*, 31.
25. Dannen, 48–49.
26. Evelyn Johnson, 9 November 1993 interview.
27. Giddins, *Riding on a Blue Note*, 35–36.
28. Hamm, 226.
29. Eliot, 70.
30. Evelyn Johnson, 9 November 1993 interview.
31. Gart and Ames, 107.
32. Mitchell, 10.
33. Guralnick, *Sweet Soul Music*, 286.
34. Guralnick, *Lost Highway*, 80.
35. Pat Baird, 25 July 1990 interview.
36. Quoted in Fisher, 24.
37. Govenar, *Meeting the Blues*, 106.
38. Ibid., 75.
39. Levine, 304–6.
40. Evelyn Johnson, 6 October 1993 interview.
41. David James Mattis, 3 November 1992 interview.
42. Lois Jean Alexander, 1 October 1991 interview.
43. Milton Hopkins, Texas, 8 March 1991 interview.
44. Gatemouth Brown, 10 October 1990 interview
45. Moonoogian and Meeden, 24.
46. Gold, 1–2.
47. Flexner, 290.
48. Wentworth and Flexner, 1–2.
49. Sawyer, 134.

Works Cited

Ackerman, Paul. "ASCAP Stand Due on BMI Collaboration." *Billboard*, 18 December 1954, 12.

——. "R&B Tunes' Boom Relegates Pop Field to Cover Activity." *Billboard*, 26 March 1955, 18, 22.

——, and Joe Martin. "New Income Studies Face Publishers as Sheet Music Drops." *Billboard*, 15 January 1955, 1, 32.

"Alan Freed to Emcee Rythm [*sic*] and Blues Show." *Cleveland Call & Post*, 7 August 1954, 5B.

Alexander v. ABC Records. C75–213, Western District of Tennessee, U.S. District Court, 1976.

All Day and All Night: Memories from Beale Street Musicians. Documentary film produced by Judy Peiser. 30 min. Southern Folklore Center, Inc., 1990. Video cassette.

"Answer to the 'Answers': Pubbers Train Legal Guns on Tail-Riding Indie Labels." *Billboard*, 4 April 1953, 18, 45.

Atlas, Ben. "Diggs Intros Copyright Fact-Finding Measure." *Billboard*, 9 April 1955, 14, 136.

"Bandleader Killed in 'Roulette.'" *New York Times*, 27 December 1954, 21.

Barlow, William. *"Looking Up at Down": The Emergence of Blues Culture*. Philadelphia: Temple University Press, 1989.

The Beale Street Collection. Memphis: Memphis/Shelby County Library & Information Center, n.d.

"'Big Mama' Thornton Is Johnny Otis' New Find." *Chicago Defender*, 2 August 1952, 22.

"Bilbo Belt Heads Back to Banjo Bands and Blackface; Beat Bandsmen With Bats." *Billboard*, 30 November 1946, 15, 32.

"Blames A.&R. Men for Poor Music Tastes." *Billboard*, 11 September 1954, 19.

"Blues 'Royalty' on Apollo Stage." *New York Age Defender*, 24 April 1954, 6.

"BMI, SPA in Fight Vs. Off-Color Disks." *Billboard*, 6 November 1954, 22, 24.

"Body of Johnny Ace Will Be Shipped to Memphis." *Houston Informer*, 1 January 1955, 1, 8.

"Booking Queen." *Pittsburgh Courier*, 24 July 1954, 18.

Booth, Stanley. "A Rainy Night in Memphis." In *Memphis 1948–1958*, ed. J. Richard Gruber, 86–91. Memphis: Memphis Brooks Museum of Art, 1986.

Bradlee, Ben. *A Good Life: Newspapering and Other Adventures.* New York: Simon and Schuster, 1995.

"Broadcasting Has Good '53; Worry Is Color." *Billboard,* 2 January 1954, 1, 2.

Broven, John. "A Rap with Johnny Otis." *Blues Unlimited,* April 1973, 11–18.

——. *Rhythm & Blues in New Orleans.* Gretna, La.: Pelican Publishing Co., 1988.

Brown, George F. "Billy Rowe's Notebook." *Pittsburgh Courier,* 24 February 1951, 16.

——. "Blues Singers Share Blame for Bad Wax: Hit Disc Jockeys for Playing Dirty Records on Airwaves." *Pittsburgh Courier,* 1 August 1953, 19.

——. "Campaign against Smutty Wax on Air Gains Support." *Pittsburgh Courier,* 6 June 1953, 31.

——. "FCC Urged to Monitor Smutty Records on Radio." *Pittsburgh Courier,* 13 June 1953, 22.

——. "Music Publisher Defends Moondog Show." *Pittsburgh Courier,* 16 October 1954, 18.

——. "No Cover Charge." *Pittsburgh Courier,* 2 October 1954, 18.

——. "OK Deejays Rap Smutty Wax." *Pittsburgh Courier,* 30 May 1953, 23.

——. "Readers Praise Courier's Smutty Record Drive." *Pittsburgh Courier,* 20 June 1953, 29.

——. "Sponsors Leery of Smutty Disc Jocks." *Pittsburgh Courier,* 23 May 1953, 18.

——. "Teen-agers Want to Know: 'What Is a Smutty Record?'" *Pittsburgh Courier,* 4 December 1954, 18.

Bundy, June. "DJ Surveys Show Top Jocks May Not Be Best Pluggers." *Billboard,* 5 February 1955, 14, 18.

——. "R&B Disks Sock Pop Market; Major Firms Jump into Ring." *Billboard,* 29 January 1955, 56.

"Bursting Old Barriers." *Billboard,* 24 April 1954, 13.

"Buyer's Always Right." *Billboard,* 29 January 1955, 56.

Cage, Ruth. "Rhythm & Blues Notes." *Down Beat,* 1 December 1954, 17.

Cantor, Louis. *Wheelin' on Beale.* New York: Pharos Books, 1992.

Capers, Gerald M., Jr. *The Biography of a River Town: Memphis: Its Heroic Age.* Chapel Hill: University of North Carolina Press, 1939.

Carter, Mary. Deposition. State of Texas, County of Harris, 26 December 1954.

"Chart Comments." *Billboard,* 19 February 1955, 38.

Chilton, John. *Let the Good Times Roll: The Story of Louis Jordan and His Music.* London: Quartet Books, 1992.

"Coast Girl Asks $10,000: Thinks Tune Was Born of Her Hit The 'Wallflower.'"
   Chicago Defender, 4 June 1955, 18.
"Continuing Flux Forecast in All Areas of Music." *Billboard*, 2 January 1954, 1, 11,
   13.
"Control the Dim-Wits!" *Billboard*, 25 September 1954, 33.
"Courier Anti-Smutty Disc Drive Praised." *Pittsburgh Courier*, 13 November
   1954, 19.
Dannen, Fredric. *Hit Men: Power Brokers and Fast Money Inside the Music
   Business.* New York: Times Books, 1990.
Davis, Sammy, Jr., and Jane and Burt Boyar. *Why Me?: The Sammy Davis, Jr.
   Story.* New York: Farrar, Straus and Giroux, 1989.
"Death Spun the Cylinder for Johnny Ace—But for What Reason." *Tri-State
   Defender*, 5 March 1955, 14 (reprinted from the *Louisville Defender*).
DeCurtis, Anthony, James Henke, with Holly George-Warren, eds.; original
   editor, Jim Miller. New ed. *The Rolling Stone Illustrated History of Rock &
   Roll.* New York: Random House, 1992.
Display ads. *Billboard*, 2 August 1952, 105; 20 June 1953, 52; 4 July 1953, 46; 29
   August 1953, 61; 24 April 1954, 16; 22 May 1954, 59; 25 December 1954, 38; 22
   January 1955, 43; 5 February 1955, 46; 23 July 1955, 92; 27 August 1955, 61; 8
   October 1955, 53; 7 January 1956, 47; 4 February 1956, 60; 28 July 1956, 78; 1
   December 1958, 10; 2 January 1959, 30; Cart, *First Pressings*, 1953, 51; *Tri-State
   Defender*, 23 August 1952, 10.
"Don Robey, Prominent Local Businessman, Dies." *Informer and Texas Freeman*,
   21 June 1975, 1.
Douglas, Larry. "Douglas Lauds 'Moondog' Freed." *New York Age Defender*, 23
   December 1954, 19.
"'Down Beat' Best Bets: Rhythm and Blues." *Down Beat*, 6 May 1953, 13–S.
"Down Beat Record Reviews." *Down Beat*, 15 July 1953, 15–S.
Duncan, Robert. *Only the Good Die Young.* New York: Harmony Books, 1986.
"8th Annual Juke Box Operators Poll." *Billboard*, 26 March 1955, 78.
Eliot, Marc. *Rockonomics: The Money Behind the Music.* New York: Franklin
   Watts, 1989.
"Enterprise of Placing R&B Talent Turns Stars in Pop Field Green." *Billboard*,
   24 April 1954, 20.
Escott, Colin. "Johnny Ace: The First Rock 'n' Roll Casualty." *Goldmine*, 21
   November 1986, 16–17.
———, with Martin Hawkins. *Good Rockin' Tonight: Sun Records and the Birth
   of Rock 'n' Roll.* New York: St. Martin's Press, 1991.

"Evelyn Knight Decca Sensash." *Variety*, 8 January 1949, 14.

Ewen, David. *All the Years of American Popular Music*. Englewood Cliffs, N.J.: Prentice-Hall, 1977.

"Famous Blues Singer of 'My Song' and 'The Clock' Buried." *Birmingham World*, 7 January 1955, 1.

"50% of U.S. Homes Own Phonos; ⅛ Buy Disks." *Billboard*, 23 October 1954, 13.

"Final Note." *Chicago Defender*, 15 January 1955, nat. ed., 5.

"Final Notes Sound for Johnny Ace." *Memphis World*, 7 January 1955, 1, 2.

"Finger Points at You!" *Billboard*, 2 October 1954, 19.

Fisher, Craig. "Don Robey—A Lifetime of Music." *Record World*, 24 March 1973, 3, 24, 49.

"5,000 Jam the Last Rites of 'Johnny Ace.'" *Houston Informer*, 8 January 1955, 1.

Flexner, Stuart Berg. *Listening to America: An Illustrated History of Words and Phrases from Our Lively and Splendid Past*. New York: Simon and Schuster, 1982.

Friedman, Joel. "Coast Lends Spark to Giant $25,000.000 R&B Year." *Billboard*, 29 January 1955, 65, 69.

Gart, Galen, ed. *First Pressings: The History of Rhythm & Blues*, vol. 3, 1953; vol. 4, 1954; vol. 5, 1955. Milford, N.H.: Big Nickel Publications, 1989, 1990.

———, and Roy C. Ames. *Duke/Peacock Records: An Illustrated History with Discography*. Milford, N.H.: Big Nickel Publications, 1990.

George, Nelson. *The Death of Rhythm & Blues*. New York: Penguin Books, 1988; rpt., Plume, 1988.

———. "Why I Promote the Blues: Dave Clark Was a Promotion Man Before the Term's Creation. To Him, James Brown is a Kid." *Village Voice*, 26 August 1986, 74–77.

Gibbs, Olivia. Deposition. State of Texas, County of Harris, 26 December 1954.

———. "Says Death of 'Johnny Ace' Wasn't Suicide." *Houston Informer*, 5 February 1955, 1.

Giddins, Gary. Liner notes to *Shake, Rattle & Roll: Rock 'n' Roll in the 1950s*. New World Records, NW 249, 1978.

———. *Riding On a Blue Note: Jazz and American Pop*. New York: Oxford University Press, 1981.

Giddings, Paula. *When and Where I Enter: The Impact of Black Women on Race and Sex in America*. New York: Bantam, 1984.

Gillett, Charlie. *The Sound of the City: The Rise of Rock and Roll*. Revised and expanded ed. New York: Pantheon, 1983.

Gold, Robert S. *Jazz Talk*. New York: Bobbs-Merrill Co., 1975.

Goldman, Albert. *Elvis*. New York: Avon Books, 1981.

Govenar, Alan. *The Early Years of Rhythm & Blues: Focus on Houston*. Houston: Rice University Press, 1990.

———. *Living Texas Blues*. Dallas: Dallas Museum of Art, 1985.

———. *Meeting the Blues*. Dallas: Taylor Publishing Co., 1988.

Grendysa, Peter. "Johnny Ace, The 'Ace' of Duke." *Goldmine* 25 September 1987, 28, 91.

Grevati, Ren. "On the Beat: Rhythm & Blues—Rock & Roll." *Billboard*, 22 July 1957, 54.

"Groups Drown Out Singles, Orks When It Comes to Success." *Billboard*, 29 January 1955, 56, 68.

"Gun Game Fatal to 'Wax' Star." *Pittsburgh Courier*, 1 January 1955, 1, 4.

Guralnick, Peter. *Last Train to Memphis: The Rise of Elvis Presley*. Boston: Little, Brown and Co., 1994.

———. *Lost Highway: Journeys & Arrivals of American Musicians*. Boston: David R. Godine, Pub., 1979.

———. *Sweet Soul Music: Rhythm and Blues and the Southern Dream of Freedom*. New York: Harper & Row, 1986.

Halberstam, David. *The Fifties*. New York: Villard Books, 1993.

Hamm, Charles. *Yesterdays: Popular Song in America*. New York: W. W. Norton & Co., 1979.

Handy, W. C. *Father of the Blues*. New York: Macmillan, 1941; rpt., Collier Books, 1970.

Harris, Sheldon. *Blues Who's Who*. New Rochelle, N.Y.: Arlington House, 1979.

Haynes, Robert V. *A Night of Violence: The Houston Riot of 1917*. Baton Rouge: Louisiana State University Press, 1976.

Hecht, Ben, and Charles MacArthur. *The Front Page*. In *Sixteen Famous American Plays*, ed. Bennett A. Cerf and Van H. Cartmell, 55–140. New York: Modern Library, 1941.

Hitchcock, H. Wiley, and Stanley Sadie, eds. *The New Grove Dictionary of American Music*. New York: Macmillan, 1986. S.v. "Ace, Johnny."

Hoekstra, Dave. "Brother Sings Hits of the Late Johnny Ace." *Chicago Sun-Times*, 24 December 1986, 30, 42.

Holford, Bill. ACA Master Book, 27 January 1953 to 28 May 1956. Business records of William C. Holford, Houston, Texas.

Horowitz, Is. "45 Disks Gain Edge Over 78 Pop Singles." *Billboard*, 26 February 1955, 27, 36.

———. "New Horizons for R&B Exploitation Upset Old Guard." *Billboard*, 4 February 1956, 55.

"Houston Pressery Bought by Peacock." *Billboard*, 19 January 1952, 20.

Hughes, Langston. "Highway Robbery Across the Color Line in Rhythm and Blues." *New York Age Defender*, 2 July 1955, 10.

"In a Tavern Hot Gun Play." *Billboard*, 20 November 1954, 1.

"Indie Diskers Back WDIA's R&B Bans." *Billboard*, 30 October 1954, 16.

Inquest Proceedings: John Alexander known as Johnnie [*sic*] Ace. State of Texas, County of Harris, 26 December 1954.

"Izzy Rowe's Notebook." *Pittsburgh Courier*, 18 September 1954, 18.

Jackson, John A. *Big Beat Heat: Alan Freed and the Early Years of Rock & Roll*. New York: Macmillan, 1991.

Jarvis, Al. "If They Want R&B, Play It, Says Jarvis." *Billboard*, 29 January 1955, 58, 69.

"Johnny Ace Discs Hits [*sic*]." *New York Age Defender*, 13 February 1954, 9.

"'Johnny Ace' Is Buried." *Pittsburgh Courier*, 15 January 1955, 1, 4.

"Johnny Ace Is Victim of Russ Roulette." *Billboard*, 8 January 1955, 14.

"Johnny Ace Rites Attended by Famous Show Business Notables: Famous Blues Singer of 'My Song' and 'The Clock' Buried." *Memphis World*, 4 January 1955, 1.

"The Johnny Ace Story." *Pittsburgh Courier*, 5 February 1955, 1, 5.

Johnson, Evelyn. "Women in the Music Industry: Yesterday. Today and Tomorrow." Audiotape of Ramsey Series Lecture, Indiana University, Bloomington, Indiana, 12 February 1990.

"Juke Star Johnny Ace Kills Self." *Chicago Defender*, 8 January 1955, nat. ed., 1.

Keil, Charles. *Urban Blues*. Chicago, University of Chicago Press, 1966.

"Kids Prefer Radio's DJ for Entertainment." *Billboard*, 5 February 1955, 15, 18.

King, B.B., with David Ritz. *Blues All Around Me: The Autobiography of B.B. King*. New York: Avon Books, 1996.

Kirsch, Bob. Review of [*Memorial Album: Johnny Ace*], (Duke LP-71). *Rolling Stone*, 19 March 1970, 52.

Kramer, Gary. "On the Beat." *Billboard*, 16 March 1957, 20.

———. "Rhythm-Blues Notes." *Billboard*, 8 September 1956, 55.

LaIsac, Dzondria. Liner notes to *Johnny Ace: Memorial Album*, MCA-27014, 1973.

"Lavern Baker Seeks Bill to Halt Arrangement 'Thefts.'" *Billboard*, 5 March 1955, 13, 18.

"LaVern Baker Smiles Over Tune's Success While Defying 'Lifts.'" *Chicago Defender*, 19 February 1955, 6.

Leadbitter, Mike, ed. *Nothing But the Blues*. London: Hanover Books, 1971.

———, and Neil Slaven. *Blues Records, 1943–1987: A Selective Discography*. London: Record Information Services, 1987.

Lee, George W. *Beale Street Sundown*. New York: House of Field, 1942.

———. *Beale Street: Where the Blues Began*. New York: Robert O. Ballou, 1934.

Lermontov, Mikhail. *A Hero of Our Time*. Translated by Vladimir Nabokov in collaboration with Dmitri Nabokov. Ann Arbor: Ardis Publishers, 1988.

Levine, Lawrence W. *Black Culture and Black Consciousness: Afro-American Folk Thought from Slavery to Freedom*. New York: Oxford University Press, 1977; rpt., 1978.

Lhamon, W. T., Jr. *Deliberate Speed: The Origins of a Cultural Style in the American 1950s*. Washington, D.C.: Smithsonian Institution Press, 1990.

Library of Congress. *Catalog of Copyright Entries, Third Series: Published Music*. Vols. 6–10, 1952–56. Washington, D.C.: U.S. Government Printing Office, 1953–57.

———. *Catalog of Copyright Entries, Third Series: Unpublished Music*. Vols. 4–11, 1950–57. Washington, D.C.: U.S. Government Printing Office, 1951–58.

Lipsitz, George. "Land of a Thousand Dances: Youth, Minorities, and the Rise of Rock and Roll." In *Recasting America: Culture and Politics in the Age of Cold War*, ed. Lary May, 267–84. Chicago: University of Chicago Press, 1989.

Litman, Robert E., Theodore Curphey, Edwin S. Shneidman, Norman L. Farberow, and Norman Tabachnick. "The Psychological Autopsy of Equivocal Deaths." *Journal of the American Medical Association* 184 (1963): 924–29. Rpt. in *The Psychology of Suicide*, ed. Edwin S. Schneidman, Norman L. Farberow, and Robert E. Litman. New York: Science House, 1970. 486–96.

Lott, Eric. *Love and Theft: Blackface Minstrelsy and the American Working Class*. New York: Oxford University Press, 1993.

McComb, David G. *Houston: A History*. Austin: University of Texas Press, 1981.

McKee, Margaret, and Fred Chisenhall. *Beale Black & Blue*. Baton Rouge: Louisiana State University Press, 1981.

McMillan, Allan. "New York Is My Beat." *New York Age Defender*, 21 August 1954, 17.

———. "Protest (Moondog) Freed Coming to WINS: 'Apes Negro' Record Fans Say of 'Ofay.'" *New York Age Defender*, 17 July 1954, 17.

McNeil, Alex. *Total Television: A Comprehensive Guide to Programming from 1948 to 1980*. New York: Penguin Books, 1980.

"Major Firms Must Keep Alert to Maintain 'Coverage' in R&B Field." *Billboard*, 18 September 1954, 11.

"Majors Really Jump with the R&B Beat." *Billboard*, 15 January 1955, 33, 38.

Malone, Bill C. *Country Music U.S.A.* Revised ed. Austin: University of Texas Press, 1985.

Marchand, Leslie A. *Byron: A Biography*. Vol. 1. New York: Alfred A. Knopf, 1957.

———, ed. *Byron's Letters and Journals*. Vol. 8, *1821*. Cambridge: Harvard University Press, 1978.

Marcus, Greil. *Dead Elvis*. New York: Doubleday, 1991.

Martin, Joe. "11 Labels Have Best-Selling Pops, But Diskers Just Getting Started." *Billboard*, 21 August 1954, 19.

———. "Music-Record Year Ends Up With Bang." *Billboard*, 8 January 1955, 1, 13.

Matthews, Ralph. "He Gambled with Death and Lost: Johnny Ace Lived on Borrowed Time." *Cleveland Call and Post*, 15 January 1955, city ed., D-1, D-3.

Maultsby, Portia K. "Women in the Music Industry: Yesterday. Today and Tomorrow." Audiotape of introduction to Evelyn Johnson, Ramsey Series Lecture, Indiana University, Bloomington, Indiana, 12 February 1990.

Mitchell, Rick. "Houston's Musical Soul." *Texas: Houston Chronicle Magazine*, 17 June 1990, 6–8, 10–11, 17.

"Moohah" [A. C. Williams]. "What's Happening in the Big 'M.'" *Tri-State Defender*, 24 November 1951, 10.

Moonoogian, George A. "Ain't Nothin' But a Hound Dog." *Whiskey, Women, and . . .*, June 1984, 4–10.

———, and Roger Meeden. "Duke Records—the Early Years: An Interview with David J. Mattis." *Whiskey, Women, and . . .*, June 1984, 18–25.

Morgan, Thomas L., and William Barlow. *From Cakewalks to Concert Halls: An Illustrated History of African American Popular Music from 1895 to 1930*. Washington, D.C.: Elliott & Clark Publishing, 1992.

"Morris Grabs 'Pledging' Tune." *Billboard*, 12 February 1955, 26.

Murrain, Edward (Sonny). "Front and Center." *New York Age Defender*, 18 September 1954, 17.

Murray, Albert. *Stomping the Blues*. New York: McGraw-Hill, 1976; rpt., Vintage Books, 1982.

"New Howl Goes Up Over 'Hound Dog' Infringement." *Pittsburgh Courier*, 8 August 1953, 28.

"New Records to Watch." *Billboard,* 4 October 1952, 41; 3 January 1953, 29; 10
    January 1953, 24; 17 January 1953, 24, 42; 24 January 1953, 28; 14 March 1953,
    32; 20 June 1953, 36; 12 December 1953, 32.

"New 'Top Ten R&B' Show to Do 60 One-Nighters." *Billboard,* 27 November
    1954, 14.

"1952's Top R&B Records." *Billboard,* 27 December 1952, 19.

"1953's Top R&B Records." *Billboard,* 19 December 1953, 29.

"1954's Top R&B Records." *Billboard,* 25 December 1954, 17.

"No Copyright on Arrangement." *Variety,* 10 May 1950, 35.

"Notes from the R.&B. Beat." *Cash Box,* March, April, June, July 1954; March,
    April 1955. In Gart, *First Pressings,* vol. 4, 1954, 26–29; 40–41, 43, 46; 59–63, 66;
    70–73, 75; vol. 5, 1955, 31–35, 38; 43–48, 51.

"Odd But True! Hit Disc May Lose Money." *New York Age Defender,* 12 June
    1954, 9.

"On the Beat." *Billboard,* 26 August 1957, 103.

Otis, Johnny. *Listen to the Lambs.* New York: W. W. Norton, 1968.

Palmer, Robert. *Deep Blues.* New York: Viking Press, 1981; rpt., Penguin Books,
    1988.

Parry, Albert. "Origin of Russian Roulette." Letter to the Editor, *New York Times,*
    23 August 1949, 22.

Patoski, Joe Nick. "Don D. Robey, R&B Pioneer, Dead at 71." *Rolling Stone,* 31
    July 1975, 22.

Paul, Mike. "Don Robey." *Living Blues,* September–October 1975, 5.

Pavlow, Big Al. *The R & B Book.* Providence: Music House Publishing, 1983.

"Peacock, Duke to Houston." *Billboard,* 30 January 1954, 22.

Piccarella, John, Jon Pareles, and Patricia Romanowski, eds. *The Rolling Stone
    Encyclopedia of Rock & Roll.* New York: Rolling Stone Press, 1983. S.v.
    "Johnny Ace."

Pomerance, Alan. *Repeal of the Blues.* Secaucus, N.J.: Citadel, 1988.

"Pubs in Middle of DJ-45 Battle; They Have Songs to Be Played!" *Billboard,* 21
    August 1954, 18.

Pugh, Clifford. "Eternally Elvis." *Texas: Houston Chronicle Magazine,* 17
    September 1995, 6–10, 14.

"R.&B. Disks Dropped for Miss Gibbs." *Billboard,* 12 March 1955, 22.

"R&B Hassle Envelopes [*sic*] Alan Freed." *Billboard,* 9 October 1954, 16.

"Record Crowd of 9000 Fans Attend Public Hall Rythm [*sic*] and Blues Show."
    Cleveland Call & Post, 14 August 1954, B-7.

"Record Reviews." *Billboard,* 18 February 1950, 118.

Review of Johnny Ace. Apollo Theater, New York. *Variety,* 28 October 1953, 55.

Review of Johnny Ace and Willie Mae Thornton. Apollo Theater, New York. *Variety,* 28 April 1954, 53.

"Review Spotlight on. . . ." *Billboard,* 8 May 1954, 33; 22 May 1954, 59; 18 September 1954, 38; 5 February 1955, 46; 16 July 1955, 45; 21 January 1956, 52.

"Reviews of New Pop Records." *Billboard,* 12 February 1955, 46.

"Reviews of New R&B Records." *Billboard,* 2 October 1954, 44; 12 February 1955, 57; 26 February 1955, 57; 22 January 1955, 43; 18 August 1956, 70.

"Rhythm & Blues." *Down Beat,* 8 October 1952, 11; 11 February 1953, 15–S; *Billboard,* 1 December 1958, 48.

"Rhythm & Blues Record Reviews." *Billboard,* 29 December 1951, 23; 19 September 1953, 39.

Richardson, Marty. "Dirty Dics [*sic*] Pollute the Air Waves." *Cleveland Call & Post,* 11 December 1954, 1–D, 2–D.

Roberts, Jim. "From Itta Bena to Fame: B.B. King: Hit Tune Brings National Fame to Disc Jockey." *Tri-State Defender,* 29 March 1952, 10.

"Robey Cuts 3 Wax Stars." *Pittsburgh Courier,* 12 September 1953, 22.

Robey, Don D. Letter to Mr. Ernest C. Withers, photographer, 17 January 1955. Business records of Ernest Withers, Memphis, Tennessee.

Rohan, Jack. *Yankee Arms Maker: The Incredible Career of Samuel Colt.* New York: Harper & Brothers, 1935.

Rolontz, Bob. "Diskers Aim Guns on Christmas Wax." *Billboard,* 20 November 1954, 13, 18.

———. "1-Nighter Packages Find Road's Rocky." *Billboard,* 13 November 1954, 16.

———. "R&B Packages' Big-Time Hit Peaks All Around Solid Year." *Billboard,* 29 January 1955, 58, 68.

———. "Rhythm & Blues Notes." *Billboard,* 23 August 1952, 35; 8 November 1952, 48; 28 March 1953, 42; 18 April 1953, 48; 12 September 1953, 41; 5 December 1953, 38; 16 January 1954, 42–43; 30 January 1954, 47; 20 February 1954, 43; 20 March 1954, 43; 27 March 1954, 35–36; 3 April 1954, 32; 24 April 1954, 23; 5 June 1954, 44; 17 July 1954, 63; 4 September 1954, 32; 18 September 1954, 38; 9 October 1954, 20, 64; 16 October 1954, 22; 23 October 1954, 18; 1 January 1955, 32; 15 January 1955, 36; 22 January 1955, 16; 29 January 1955, 22, 54; 5 February 1955, 18; 12 February 1955, 30, 57; 19 February 1955, 28.

———, and Joel Friedman. "Teen-Agers Demand Music with a Beat, Spur Rhythm-Blues." *Billboard,* 24 April 1954, 1, 18, 24.

Ross, Arthur M., and Herbert Hill, eds. *Employment, Race, and Poverty.* New York: Harcourt, Brace & World, 1967.

Salem, James M. "Death and the Rhythm-and-Bluesman: The Life and Recordings of Johnny Ace." *American Music* (Fall 1993): 316–67.

———. "Ernest C. Withers." In Salzman, 2868–69.

———. "Johnny Ace: A Case Study in the Diffusion and Transformation of Minority Culture." *Prospects: An Annual of American Cultural Studies* 17 (1992): 211–41.

———. "Willie Mae Thornton." In Salzman, 2656.

Salzman, Jack, David Lionel Smith, and Cornel West, eds. *Encyclopedia of African-American Culture and History.* New York: Simon & Schuster Macmillan, 1996.

Sanjek, Russell. *American Popular Music and Its Business.* Vol. 3, *From 1900 to 1984.* New York: Oxford University Press, 1988.

———. *From Print to Plastic: Publishing and Promoting America's Popular Music (1900–1980).* Brooklyn: Institute for Studies in American Music, 1983.

Sawyer, Charles. *The Arrival of B.B. King: The Authorized Biography.* New York: Doubleday, 1980.

"Scribo's Sports Spot Shots." *Tri-State Defender,* 30 August 1952, 8.

Shaw, Arnold. *Honkers and Shouters: The Golden Years of Rhythm and Blues.* New York: Macmillan, 1978.

———. *The Rockin' '50s.* New York: Hawthorn Books, 1974.

———. *The World of Soul.* New York: Paperback Library, 1971.

"Shell out for Shellac: 45-Less DJ's Prove Costly to Publishers." *Billboard,* 2 October 1954, 19.

Shelton, Beth Ann, Nestor P. Rodriguez, Joe R. Feagin, Robert D. Ballard, and Robert D. Thomas. *Houston: Growth and Decline in a Sunbelt Boomtown.* Philadelphia: Temple University Press, 1989.

Sigafoos, Robert A. *Cotton Row to Beale Street: A Business History of Memphis.* Memphis: Memphis State University Press, 1979.

Simon, Bill. "Rhythm & Blues Notes." *Billboard,* 28 April 1956, 61; 4 August 1956, 79.

———. "Term R&B Hardly Covers Multi-Material So Grouped." *Billboard,* 4 February 1956, 55.

"Singer Johnny Ace Killed Playing Russian Roulette." *Jet,* 6 January, 1955, 59.

"Singer Johnny Ace Will Be Buried Sunday." *Los Angeles Sentinel,* 30 December 1954, 2.

"Station Demonstrates Its Listening Power." In Gart, *First Pressings,* vol.4, 1954, 25.

"Strange Case of Johnny Ace." *Ebony,* July 1955, 63–68.

"Supreme Loses Case for 400G against Decca," *Billboard*, 13 May 1950, 12.

"Talent Corner." *Billboard*, 29 January 1955, 34.

That Rhythm . . . Those Blues. Documentary film produced and directed by
   George T. Nierenberg. 60 min. Broadcast on *The American Experience*, 1988.
   Video cassette.

"Theater, Club Foldings Hurt Live-Act Mart." *Billboard*, 2 January 1954, 1, 10.

"This Week's Best Buys." *Billboard*, 27 June 1953, 28; 19 December 1953, 40; 5
   June 1954, 44; 2 October 1954, 44; 15 January 1955, 60; 19 February 1955, 53; 26
   February 1955, 46; 12 March 1955, 46; 23 July 1955, 89.

"This Week's New Records." *Billboard*, 27 June 1953, 26; 26 September 1953, 34;
   19 December 1953, 38.

Thornton, Willie Mae. Deposition. State of Texas, County of Harris, 26
   December 1954.

Toll, Robert C. *Blacking Up: The Minstrel Show in Nineteenth-Century America.*
   New York: Oxford University Press, 1974.

Topping, Ray. Liner notes to *The Original Memphis Blues Brothers*, Ace-CHAD
   265, 1989.

Tosches, Nick. *Unsung Heroes of Rock 'n' Roll.* New York: Charles Scribner's
   Sons, 1984.

"Trade Views Off-Color Disk Situation with Mixed Feeling." *Billboard*, 2
   October 1954, 19, 86.

Travis, Dempsey J. *An Autobiography of Black Jazz.* Chicago: Urban Research
   Institute, 1983.

"Trend in R&B: Syndicated Deejay Shows Expanding." *Billboard*, 18 September
   1954, 11.

Tudor, Dean. *Popular Music: An Annotated Guide to Recordings.* Littleton,
   Colo.: Libraries Unlimited, 1983.

"TV Ain't the Real Thing." *Chicago Defender*, 19 March 1955, 9.

Vann, Kimberly R. *Black Music in Ebony: An Annotated Guide to the Articles on
   Music in Ebony Magazine, 1945–1985.* Chicago: Columbia College Chicago
   Center for Black Music Research, 1990.

"Victor Quits 'Coverage': Pop Policy to Stress Originals & Exclusives." *Billboard*,
   2 April 1955, 13, 16.

"WDIA Holds Third Annual Goodwill Revue Wednesday Night, Nov. 21." *Tri-
   State Defender*, 17 November 1951, 1–2.

"WDIA's Got a Broom." *Billboard*, 30 October 1954, 16.

Wahl, Paul. *Gun Trader's Guide.* 13th ed. South Hackensack, N.J.: Stoeger, 1987.

Ward, Ed, Geoffrey Stokes, and Ken Tucker. *Rock of Ages: The Rolling Stone History of Rock & Roll*. New York: Summit Books, 1986.

Webman, Hal. "Rhythm and Blues Notes." *Billboard*, 24 February 1951, 31; 17 November 1951, 35.

Wentworth, Harold, and Stuart Berg Flexner, comp. and ed. *Dictionary of American Slang*. 2d supplemented ed. New York: Thomas Y. Crowell, 1975.

Westbrooks, Al, Jr. "Bury Johnny Ace, Suicide Victim." *Tri-State Defender*, 8 January 1955, 1–2.

Wexler, Jerry. "Mainstream of Jazz Is R And B: Wexler." *Down Beat*, 15 July 1953, 15–S.

"When Is a 'Copy' Not a Steal? When It's a 'Cover' of a Disk." *Variety*, 21 December 1955, 35.

Whitburn, Joel. *The Billboard Book of Top 40 Hits: 1955 to Present*. New York: Billboard Publications, 1983.

———. *Joel Whitburn's Top R&B Singles 1942–1988*. Menomonee Falls, Wis.: Record Research, 1988.

White, Charles. *The Life and Times of Little Richard*. New York: Harmony Books, 1984.

White, Walter. "The Strange Case of Paul Robeson." *Ebony*, February 1951, 78–84.

Williams, Nat D. "Down On Beale." *Pittsburgh Courier*, 21 January 1950, 21.

Windham, Ben. "Big Mama Thornton." *Alabama Heritage*, Fall 1987, 30–43.

"The Winner—Nobody!" *Billboard*, 14 August 1954, 14.

Wintz, Cary D. "Blacks." In *The Ethnic Groups of Houston*, ed. Fred R. von der Mehden, 9–40. Houston: Rice University Studies, 1984.

Withers, Ernest. Manuscript titled "FINAL NOTE" and letter requesting payment to Mr. Robey, n.d.

Woodward, C. Vann. *The Strange Career of Jim Crow*. 3d rev. ed. New York: Oxford University Press, 1974.

Index

Afro-American (newspaper), 232n11
"Ain't Nobody Here But Us Chickens,"
 62
"Ain't Nothing You Can Do," 34
"Ain't That a Shame," 173, 235n67
Aladdin Records, 55, 60, 104, 221n27
Alexander, Glenn (son), 20, 187
Alexander, Janet (daughter), 21, 187
Alexander, John Marshall, Jr., 29, 30, 33,
 34, 89, 143–45, 182, 200, 214n32, 215n9;
 as Beale Streeter, 37; becomes BMI
 writer (1996), 199; born, 11; inherits
 Beale Streeter's band, 39; "Midnight
 Hours Journey," 37–38; Mitchell
 Hotel as residence, 31; "My Song,"
 42–43; name changed, 43; named in
 wife's lawsuit, 187. See also Ace,
 Johnny
Alexander, Leslie Newsome (mother),
 21, 39, 193–94; arranges son's funeral,
 147–48, 149; attitude toward son, 22;
 described, 12; early life, 7–8; as
 mother, 13–17; on school, 11, 20; seeks
 payment for son's widow and
 children, 186; stops WDIA from
 playing son's records, 147
Alexander, Lois Jean (wife), 21, 93, 147;
 files suit against Robey and associated
 businesses, 187; on husband as
 composer, 198; marriage and
 children, 20–21; meets John
 Alexander, 19; moves into Alexander
 household, 20; sees husband at Club
 Handy, 92
Alexander, Mamie (sister), 92
Alexander, Norma Williams (sister), 18,
 21; on brother's navy experience, 16–
 17; on brother's youth, 15–16; as family
 historian, 11–12; on meeting Robey,
 Johnson, and Gibbs, 147, 149; on
 parents, 13–16; parents' attitude
 toward their son, 21–22; stops brother's
 van in Memphis, 92; travels to
 Houston seeking payment for

brother's widow and children, 186–
 87; on wildness of Alexander males,
 22
Alexander, Rev. John Marshall, Sr.
 (father), 11, 16, 17, 18, 39;
 arrangements for son's funeral, 148;
 described, 12; early life, 7–8; as father,
 13–17; on God's plan for son, 22;
 marriage to Leslie Newsome, 11; as
 rural pastor, 12–13, 15
Alexander, St. Clair (brother), 30, 93,
 237n28; beginning of brother's
 musical career, 19; on brother's arrest
 in Mississippi, 18; on brother's
 penchant for horseplay, 15; on
 brother's shyness, 94; on brother's
 vocal timing, 88; on family, 14–15; on
 father's ministry, 13; meaning of
 "Ace," 39, 199; on meeting Evelyn
 Johnson and Olivia Gibbs, 149; sings
 brother's songs professionally, 194;
 tryout with Robey's Duke Records,
 181
Alexander II (czar), 135–36
Alexander v. ABC Records, 187
Alger, Horatio, 54
Al Grey Orchestra, 82, 219n94
Amateur Night at the Palace Theater
 (stage show), 4, 19, 27
American Federation of Musicians, 58,
 125
American Society of Composers,
 Authors, and Publishers (ASCAP),
 117–20
"Amos and Andy" (radio show), 114
Andrews, Lee. See Lee Andrews and the
 Hearts
Andrus, Walter, 186
"Angel," 74, 75–76, 87, 177
"Annie Had a Baby," 112
"Annie" songs, 117
Answer songs, 83–85, 104–5
Antilynching campaign, 10
"Anymore," 175, 176, 177, 178, 184

"Biggest Show of 1954" (stage show), 120–21

Big Maybelle, 114

Bihari Brothers (Jules, Joe, Saul, and Lester), 36–38, 41, 44, 60, 91, 125; feud with Sam Phillips, 41; first to record Ace, 37–38

Billboard (magazine), 3, 38, 63, 64, 65, 71, 73, 75, 76, 78, 80, 81, 82, 90, 94, 101, 124, 128, 159, 166, 174; on Ace tribute records, 162–64; ad introducing Duke Records, 68; ad promoting remastered "Pledging My Love," 184; adds R&B radio airplay chart, 157; on Alan Freed controversy, 115; on answer record controversy ("Hound Dog"/"Bear Cat"), 84–85; on ASCAP/BMI feud, 119–20; on Buddy Ace, 180; on consumer demand for R&B, 158; on cover version of "My Song," 72; on DJ-45 Battle, 109; Elvis as eighth most promising hillbilly talent, 5; on entertainment business (1954), 97–98; first review of Peacock artists, 61–62; on hardships of Negro bands touring the South, 32; on James Dean tributes, 182; on "A Little Bird Told Me," 169; mourns loss of Ace, 154–55; on off-color R&B lyrics, 116–18; "Pledging My Love" advertised (Dec. 25, 1954), 131; "Pledging My Love" creating excitement, 160; "Pledging My Love" on Honor Roll of Hits, 162; rare to have two women on the R&B charts, 86; R&B a powerful influence on pop, 108–9; on R&B bookings, 104; on R&B business (early 1954), 102; on R&B lyrics as cause for alarm, 111–12; on R&B material (early 1956), 179; on R&B popularity, 98–99; on R&B publishing, 104–5; Robey is "hot as $1 pistol," 183; seven of top ten tunes in 1955 are BMI-licensed, 161; special section on R&B, 103–4; "Spotlight on

Rhythm & Blues," 157–59; story on Baker vs. Gibbs, 170–71; strength of R&B material in the pop field, 165; on syndicated R&B shows, 111; top R&B records (1953), 97; tribute to Ace, 158–59. *See also* Rolontz, Bob

—reviews of: "Anymore," 177; "Burlie Cutie," 120; "Clock," 89; "Don't You Know," 180; "Hound Dog," 83; "I'm Crazy, Baby," 178; "Midnight Hours Journey," 91; "Never Let Me Go," 110; "Please Forgive Me," 106; "Pledging My Love" (remastered), 184; "Saving My Love for You," 96

Bill Doggett Trio, 229n57

Bill Haley and the Comets, 34, 108, 155, 179, 188

Bill Harvey Band, 27, 31, 32

Billy Berg's 5-4 Ballroom (Los Angeles, Calif.), 3, 91

Billy Williams Quartet, 108

Black Culture and Black Consciousness: Afro-American Folk Thought from Slavery to Freedom (Levine), 148

Black Patti, 57

Black Swan, 57

Blackwell, Bumps, 225n21

Blackwell, Scrapper, 34

Blanchard, Edgar, 61, 219n94

Bland, Robert Calvin "Bobby Blue," 28, 33, 34, 44, 68, 81, 87, 186, 190, 212n28, 215n9, 238n14; as Beale Streeter, 37; on "Farther Up the Road," 183; records for Robey, 74; on Robey's frugality, 181; Robey's practice with writers, 197; Rosco Gordon's chauffeur, 30; second phase of Memphis synthesis, 27; supposed to record first Duke secular song, 42; too uptown for white blues fans, 185

Bledsoe, Country Jim, 219n94

Block, Martin, 218n75

Blue Flames, 91. *See also* Parker, Little Junior

Blues Who's Who (Harris), 190

Ku Klux Klan, 8, 50
KWEM (West Memphis, Ark.), 29
KYJK (Forest City, Ark.), 40
KYOK (Houston, Tex.), 51

Laine, Frankie, 224n5
LaIsac, Dzondria, 174–75, 235n1, 237n36
Land, Jimmie Lee, 181, 237n29
Lansky Brothers (Memphis, Tenn.), 4
Lanson, Snooky, 167
Larkin, Milt, 53
LaRose Grammar School (Memphis, Tenn.), 15
"Last Night's Dream," 89
"The Late Great Johnny Ace," 175
Lauderdale Courts (Memphis, Tenn.), 5
Laury, Booker T., 32
Leadbitter, Mike, 173
Lee, George W., 9, 23–27, 33
Lee, Peggy, 82, 120
Lee Andrews and the Hearts, 90
Leeds Music Corporation (MCA), 221n24
Leiber, Jerry, 82
Leonard's Barbeque (Memphis, Tenn.), 4
Lermontov, Mikhail, 136–38
"Let Your Tears Fall," 80, 103
Levine, Lawrence W., 148–49, 198
Levy, Morris, 195, 196
Lewis, Boss, 128
Lewis, Jerry Lee, 188
Lewis, Pete, 99–100, 106, 107
Lhamon, W. T., Jr., 59
Library of Congress, 6, 57, 64
Life and Times of Little Richard (White), 225n21
Liggins, Joe, 79
Lightfoot, Papa, 219n94
Lincoln Theater (Houston, Tex.), 50
Lindbergh, Charles, 135
Lion Music, 84–85, 124, 161. *See also* Lion Publishing Co.
Lion Publishing Co., 64, 70, 126, 166, 172, 176; copyright history of

"Pledging My Love," 165–66; sued by Ace estate, 187; sues Sun Records, 84–85. *See also* Lion Music
Lipsitz, George, 100
"A Little Bird Told Me," 169
Little Esther, 1, 81, 100
Little Richard, 70, 91, 105, 225n21; and the Tempo Toppers, 105
"Little Things Mean a Lot," 155
"The Little White Cloud That Cried," 95
Little Willie John, 100
Living Blues (magazine), 186
Lockwood, "Junior," 214n32
Long, Edward Noel, 137–38
Lord Calvert Hotel (Miami, Fla.), 123
Lornell, Kip, 219n1
Los Angeles Sentinel (newspaper), 143
Louis, Joe, 54, 113
Louis, Joe Hill, 18–19, 33, 36
Louisville Defender (newspaper), 152
"Love My Baby," 215n9
"Love of Jesus," 197
"Lovey Dovey," 227n1
"Loving You," 82
Lubinsky, Herman, 60
Lutcher, Joe, 219n94
Lynching, 50
Lynn, Smiling Smokey, 219n94

MacArthur, Charles, 142
Macedonia Baptist Church (Lansing, Ark.), 13
Macy's (label), 35, 53
Majestic Hotel (Cleveland, Ohio), 121
"Make Believe Ballroom" (radio show), 158, 192, 218n75
Malone, Deadric. *See* Robey, Don Deadric
"(Mama) He Treats Your Daughter Mean," 86
Mara, Tommy, 159, 166, 172
Marcus, Greil, 191
Marcus, Irving, 64, 65, 80, 155, 165,

Petrillo, James C., 125
Phillips, Dewey, 35–36
Phillips, Little Esther. *See* Little Esther
Phillips, Sam, 35–37, 40, 211n4; feud with
    Modern/RPM, 41; feud with Robey,
    83–85. *See also* Memphis Recording
    Service
Phillips Records, 36
Pinkston, Christopher Columbus
    (C.C.), 78, 107, 178; C.C. Pinkston
    Orchestra, 102, 107
Pittman, Jane, 126
Pittsburgh Courier (newspaper), 15, 85,
    91, 114, 180, 232n11; on Ace's death,
    143; on Ace's funeral, 146; on Evelyn
    Johnson, 126; "Johnny Ace Story,"
    151–52; on Olivia Gibbs, 150; smutty
    record drive, 113–15
Plantation Inn (West Memphis, Ark.), 135
Platters, 188
"Please Forgive Me," 3, 105–7, 109, 177,
    183
"Pledging My Love" (Ace), 1, 3, 6, 34,
    101, 141, 150, 163, 164, 165, 175, 176,
    177, 178, 197, 235n67; associated with
    personality of Johnny Ace, 172–73;
    benchmark for Duke/Peacock hits,
    183; as *Billboard*'s R&B Triple Crown
    and "Honor Roll of Hits," 162;
    copyright history, 165–66; demand
    for, 159; first advertised (Dec. 25,
    1954), 131; on first *Billboard* R&B
    airplay chart, 157; first Duke record to
    sell more 45s than 78s, 160; heavy
    radio airplay, 173; last Ace session,
    99–100; no. 1 on all R&B charts, 174;
    and payola, 161; performance, 155–56;
    pop covers, 166; refined ballads
    favored in early 1956, 179; reissued in
    remastered form, 183–84; transitional
    record between R&B and rock 'n'
    roll, 171–72, 200
"Pledging My Love" (Brewer), 161, 162,
    165, 166, 172, 174

"Pledging My Love" (Four Lads), 161,
    166, 172
"Pledging My Love" (Mara), 159, 166,
    172
"Pledging My Love" (Presley), 6
Plough Chemical Co. (Memphis,
    Tenn.), 10, 11
Pomerance, Alan, 122
Potter, Peter, 111
Powell, Robert, 50
Presley, Elvis, 52, 82, 83, 120, 182, 196;
    and Ace, 3–6; example of "cross
    cultural collision," 4; posthumous
    success of, 190–91
Presley, Priscilla, 191
Progressive Jazz (label), 91
Progressive Music Corporation, 111
Pruitt and Pruitt Funeral Home
    (Houston, Tex.), 144

Queen Records, 42
Quinn, Bill, 52

Race riots, 8, 48–50
"Radiation Flu," 237n28
Radio Recorders studio, 82, 90–91, 182
Rainey, Ma, 83
"Ration Blues," 62
"Ravenna Journal," 137
Rawls, Lou, 189
Ray, Johnnie, 39, 94–95
RCA Records, 6, 142, 171
Reagan, Walter, 134
Record labels, 35–41; postwar
    independents, 59–60. *See also
    individual companies*
Record World (magazine), 197
"Red, Hot, and Blue" (radio show), 36
Reinhardt, Django, 34
"Remember I Love You," 193
Renfro, Sr. Jesse Mae, 82, 219n94
Rhythm & Blues Caravan. *See* Otis,
    Johnny
Rhythm and blues labels, 60, 72–73, 157

JAMES M. SALEM is professor and chair of the

Department of American Studies at the University of Alabama.

He has published numerous plays, songs, articles, and essays and

is the author of eighteen books, including several reference

books on drama in America. His research focus is postwar

America, particularly the 1950s.

Typeset in 10.5/14.5 Electra

with Futura display

Designed by Rich Hendel

Composed by Barbara Evans

at the University of Illinois Press

Manufactured by Cushing-Malloy, Inc.